THE
UNHEAVENLY
CITY

Books by Edward C. Banfield

GOVERNMENT PROJECT

THE MORAL BASIS OF A BACKWARD SOCIETY

URBAN GOVERNMENT: A READER

POLITICAL INFLUENCE

BIG CITY POLITICS

POLITICS, PLANNING, AND THE PUBLIC INTEREST
(*with Martin Meyerson*)

GOVERNMENT AND HOUSING IN METROPOLITAN AREAS
(*with Morton Grodzins*)

CITY POLITICS
(*with James Q. Wilson*)

BOSTON: THE JOB AHEAD
(*with Martin Meyerson*)

THE UNHEAVENLY CITY: THE NATURE AND
FUTURE OF OUR URBAN CRISIS

THE
UNHEAVENLY
CITY *The Nature and*

Future of Our Urban Crisis

by EDWARD C. BANFIELD

LITTLE, BROWN AND COMPANY · BOSTON · TORONTO

LIBRARY OF CONGRESS CATALOG CARD NO.: 77–105564

SEVENTH PRINTING

Chapter 9, "Rioting Mainly for Fun and Profit," appeared originally in somewhat different form in *The Metropolitan Enigma,* published by Harvard University Press, 1968.

Part of Chapter 11, "Why Government Cannot Solve the Urban
Problem," appeared originally in different form in *Daedalus,* Fall,
1968, and is reprinted by permission of the American Academy of
Arts and Sciences. Copyright © 1968 by the American Academy
of Arts and Sciences.

Published simultaneously in Canada
by Little, Brown & Company (Canada) Limited

PRINTED IN THE UNITED STATES OF AMERICA

Come hither, and I will show you, an admirable Spectacle! 'Tis an Heavenly CITY. . . . A CITY to be inhabited by an Innumerable Company of Angels, and by the Spirits of Just Men . . .

Put on thy beautiful Garments,
O America, the Holy City!

— Cotton Mather, *Theopolis Americana: An Essay on the Golden Street of the Holy City* (1710)

Preface

THIS book will probably strike many readers as the work of an ill-tempered and mean-spirited fellow. I would not mind that especially if I did not think that it might prevent them from taking its argument as seriously as they should. I should like therefore to assure the reader that I am as well-meaning — probably even as soft-hearted — as he. But facts are facts, however unpleasant, and they have to be faced unblinkingly by anyone who really wants to improve matters in the cities.

It is, of course, impossible to be an expert on urban affairs — the range of subject matter is far too great. One can, however, learn enough of several disciplines to make useful applications of some of their major ideas and findings. This is what I have tried to do. Although I draw on work in economics, sociology, political science, psychology, history, planning, and other fields, this book is not really a work of social science. Rather, it is an attempt by a social scientist to think about the problems of the cities in the light of scholarly findings. If the attempt is thought presumptuous, I offer two defenses. First, the alternative — to discuss the problems of the city in the light of a single discipline — is clearly worse; better to be presumptuous than wrong. Second, one need not have a profound knowledge of any discipline in order to make the use of it that I am making, provided that one receives criticism from those who are specialists.

Fortunately, I have had a great deal of such criticism. Much came from Harvard students, undergraduates as well as graduates, some of whom had detailed and often firsthand knowledge of matters about which I knew little. In addition, I have to thank the following for reading particular chapters: Gary Becker, James S. Coleman, M. Kimbrough Marshall, Christopher De Muth, John F. Kain, Bruce Kovner, Garth Mangum, Gary T. Marx, Thomas A. Reppetto, David Riesman, Martin Shefter, and Lester C. Thurow. The entire, or almost entire, manuscript was read by Martin Meyerson, Margy Ellin Meyerson, Milton Friedman, Frances Fox Piven, and James Q. Wilson. Margaret Locke and Mark Petri provided research assistance in the early stages of the work. Lawrence D. Brown, who prepared the manuscript for the press, called attention to and helped eliminate numerous confusions of thought; if it were not for him the book would be in many respects poorer. Mrs. Karla Kirmani was a painstaking typist. I am very grateful to them all. I am grateful also to the Joint Center for Urban Studies of the Massachusetts Institute of Technology and Harvard University, which supported the undertaking generously over a considerable period.

Although written for this book, Chapter Nine appeared first in James Q. Wilson, ed., *The Metropolitan Enigma* (Cambridge, Mass., Harvard University Press, 1968). Chapter Eleven is a much-revised version of an article that appeared in the Fall, 1968, issue of *Daedalus*.

E.C.B.

Contents

THE
UNHEAVENLY
CITY

CHAPTER ONE

Introduction

. . . the clock is ticking, time is moving . . . , we must ask ourselves every night when we go home, are we doing all that we should do in our nation's capital, in all the other big cities of the country.
> — President Johnson, after the Watts Riot, August 1965

THAT we face an urban crisis of utmost seriousness has in recent years come to be part of the conventional wisdom. We are told on all sides that the cities are uninhabitable, that they must be torn down and rebuilt or new ones must be built from the ground up, that something drastic must be done — and soon — or else.

On the face of it this "crisis" view has a certain plausibility. One need not walk more than a few blocks in any city to see much that is wrong and in crying need of improvement. It is anomalous that in a society as technologically advanced and as affluent as ours there should be many square miles of slums and even more miles of dreary blight and chaotic sprawl. And when one considers that as many as 60 million more people may live in metropolitan areas in 1980 than lived there in 1960, it seems clear that unless something drastic is done things are bound to get worse.

There is, however, another side to the matter. The plain fact is that the overwhelming majority of city dwellers live more comfortably and conveniently than ever before. They have more and better housing, more and better schools, more and better transportation, and so on. By any conceivable measure of material welfare the present generation of urban Americans is, on the whole, better off than any other large group of people has ever been anywhere. What is more, there is every reason to expect that the general level of comfort and convenience will continue to rise at an even more rapid rate through the foreseeable future.

It is true that many people do not share, or do not share fully, this general prosperity, some because they are the victims of racial prejudice and others for other reasons that are equally beyond their control. If the chorus of complaint about the city arose mainly from these disadvantaged people or on behalf of them, it would be entirely understandable, especially if their numbers were increasing and their plight were getting worse. But the fact is that until very recently most of the talk about the urban crisis has had to do with the comfort, convenience, and business advantage of the well-off white majority and not with the more serious problems of the poor, the Negro, and others who stand outside the charmed circle. And the fact also is that the number of those standing outside the circle is decreasing, as is the relative disadvantage that they suffer. There is still much poverty and much racial discrimination. But there is less of both than ever before.

The question arises, therefore, not of whether we are faced with an urban crisis, but rather, *in what sense* we are faced with one. Whose interest and what interests are involved? How deeply? What should be done? Given the political and other realities of the situation, what *can* be done?

The first need is to clear away some semantic confusions. Consider the statement, so frequently used to alarm luncheon groups, that 70 percent of the population now lives in urban places and that this number may increase to 80 percent in the next two decades if present trends continue. Such figures give the impression of standing room only in the city, but what exactly do they mean?

When we are told that the population of the United States is rapidly becoming overwhelmingly urban, we probably suppose this to mean that most people are coming to live in the big cities. This is true in one sense but false in another. It is true that most people live closer physically and psychologically to a big city than ever before; rural occupations and a rural style of life are no longer widespread.

On the other hand, the percentage of the population living in cities of 250,000 or more (there are only fifty-one of them) is about the same now as it was in 1920. In Census terminology an "urban place" is any settlement having a population of 2,500 or more; obviously places of 2,500 are not what we have in mind when we use words like "urban" and "city."[1] It is somewhat misleading to say that the country is becoming more urban, when what is meant is that more people are living in places like White River Junction, Vermont (pop. 2,546), and fewer in places like Boston, Massachusetts (pop. 697,197). But it is not altogether misleading, for most of the small urban places are now close to large cities and part of a metropolitan complex. White River Junction, for example, is now close enough to Boston to be very much influenced by it.

A great many so-called urban problems are really conditions that we either cannot change or do not want to incur the disadvantages of changing. Consider the "problem of congestion." The presence of a great many people in one place is a cause of inconvenience, to say the least. But the advantages of having so many people in one place far outweigh these inconveniences, and we cannot possibly have the advantages without the disadvantages. To "eliminate congestion" in the city must mean eliminating the city's reason for being. Congestion in the city is a "problem" only in the sense that congestion in Times Square on New Year's Eve is one; in fact, of course, people come to the city, just as they do to Times Square, precisely *because* it is congested. If it were not congested, it would not be worth coming to.

Strictly speaking, a problem exists only as we should want something different from what we do want or as by better management we could get a larger total of what we want. If we think it a good thing that many people have the satisfaction of driving their cars in and out of the city, and if we see no way of arranging the situation to get them in and out more conveniently that does not entail more than offsetting disadvantages for them or others, then we ought not to speak of a "traffic congestion problem." By the same token, urban sprawl is a "problem," as opposed to an "unpleasant condition," only if (1) fewer people should have the satisfaction of living in the low-density fringe of the city, or (2) we

might, by better planning, build homes in the fringe without destroying so much landscape and without incurring costs (for example,
higher per-unit construction costs) or foregoing benefits (for example, a larger number of low-income families who can have the
satisfaction of living in the low-density area) of greater value than
the saving in landscape.

Few problems, in this strict sense, are anywhere near as big as
they seem. The amount of urban sprawl that could be eliminated
simply by better planning — that is, without the sacrifice of other
ends that are also wanted, such as giving the satisfaction of owning
a house and yard to many low-income people — is probably trivial
as compared to the total urban sprawl (that is, to the "problem"
defined simplemindedly as "a condition that is unpleasant").

Most so-called urban problems are more characteristic of rural
and small-town places than of cities. We have been conditioned to
associate "slums" with "cities," but in 1960 74 percent of all
deteriorating and 81 percent of all dilapidated housing was *outside*
cities of 100,000 or more population, and about 60 percent of all
families in substandard housing lived outside metropolitan areas.
The situation is similar in other matters. "Low verbal ability," Sloan
R. Wayland of Columbia Teachers College has written, "is described as though it could only happen in an urban slum."[2] Actually, he points out, all but a very small fraction of mankind has
always been "culturally deprived," and the task of formal education
has always been to attack such conditions.

Most of the "problems" that are generally supposed to constitute
"the urban crisis" could not conceivably lead to disaster. They
are — some of them — important in the sense that a bad cold is
important, but they are not serious in the sense that a cancer is
serious. They have to do with comfort, convenience, amenity, and
business advantage, all of which are important, but they do not
affect either the essential welfare of individuals or what may be
called the good health of the society.

Consider, for example, an item that often appears near the top of
the list of complaints about the city — the journey to work. It takes
the average worker in a metropolitan area about half an hour to get

to work, and only about 15 percent of workers spend more than three-quarters of an hour getting there.[3] It would, of course, be very nice if the journey to work were much shorter. No one can suppose, however, that the essential welfare of many people would be much affected even if it were fifteen minutes longer. Certainly its being longer or shorter would not make the difference between a good society and a bad.

Another matter causing widespread alarm is the decline of the central business district, by which is meant the loss of patronage to downtown department stores, theaters, restaurants, museums, and so on, which has resulted from the movement of many well-off people to suburbs. Clearly, the movement of good customers from one place to another involves inconvenience and business loss to many people, especially to the owners of real estate that is no longer in so great demand. These losses, however, are essentially no different from those that occur from other causes — say, a shift of consumers' tastes that suddenly renders a once-valuable patent valueless. Moreover, though some lose by the change, others gain by it: the overall gain of wealth by building in the suburbs may more than offset the loss of it caused by letting the downtown deteriorate.

There are those who claim that cultural and intellectual activity flourishes only in big cities and that therefore the decline of the downtown business districts and the replacement of cities by suburbs threatens the very survival of civilization. This claim is far-fetched, to say the very least, if it means that we cannot have good music and good theater (not to mention philosophy, literature, and science) unless customers do their shopping in the downtown districts of Oakland, St. Louis, Nashville, Boston, and so on, rather than in the suburbs around them. Public efforts to preserve the downtown districts of these and other cities may perhaps be worth what they cost; the return, however, will be in terms of comfort, convenience, and business advantage — the comfort, convenience, and business advantage of the relatively well-off — and not in terms of anyone's essential welfare.

The same can be said about efforts to "beautify" the cities. That for the most part the cities are dreary and depressing if not offensively ugly may be granted: the desirability of improving their appearance, even if only a little, cannot be questioned. It is very doubtful, however, that people are dehumanized (to use a favorite word of those who complain about the cities) by the ugliness of the city or that they would be in any sense humanized by its being made beautiful. (If they were humanized, they would doubtless build beautiful cities, but that is an entirely different matter. One has only to read Machiavelli's history of Florence to see that living in a beautiful city is not in itself enough to bring out the best in one. So far as their humanity is concerned, the people of, say, Jersey City compare very favorably to the Florentines of the era of that city's greatest glory.) At worst, the American city's ugliness — or, more, its lack of splendor or charm — occasions loss of visual pleasure. This loss is an important one (it is surely much larger than most people realize), but it cannot lead to any kind of disaster either for the individual or for the society.

Air pollution comes closer than any of these problems to threatening essential welfare, as opposed to comfort, convenience, amenity, and business advantage. Some people die early because of it and many more suffer various degrees of bad health; there is also some possibility (no one knows how much) that a meteorological coincidence (an "air inversion") over a large city might suddenly kill thousands or even tens of thousands. Important as it is, however, the air pollution problem is rather minor as compared to other threats to health and welfare not generally regarded as "crises." According to the U.S. Public Health Service, the most polluted air is nowhere near as dangerous as cigarette smoke.

Many of the "problems" that are supposed to constitute the "crisis" could be quickly and easily solved, or much alleviated, by the application of well-known measures that lie right at hand. In some instances, the money cost of these measures would be very small. For example, the rush-hour traffic problem in the central cities (which, incidentally, is almost the whole of the traffic problem in these cities) could be much reduced and in some cases eliminated entirely just by staggering working hours in the largest offices and factories. Manhattan presents the hardest case of all, but even there, an elaborate study showed, rush-hour crowding could be reduced by 25 percent, enough to make the strap-hanger reasonably comfortable.[4] Another quick and easy way of improving urban transportation in most cities would be to eliminate a mass of archaic regulations on the granting of public transit and taxi franchises. At present, the cities are in effect going out of their way to place obstacles in the paths of those who might offer the public better transportation.[5]

The "price" of solving, or alleviating, some much-talked-about urban problems is largely political. The proposal to reduce transit jams in Manhattan by staggering work hours was quickly and quietly killed by the city administration because the business community preferred the traditional nine-to-five pattern.[6]

If the rush-hour traffic problem is basically political, so is the revenue problem. A great part of the wealth of our country is in the cities. When a mayor says that his city is on the verge of bankruptcy, he really means that when the time comes to run for reelection he wants to be able to claim credit for straightening out a mess that was left him by his predecessor. What a mayor means when he says that his city *must* have state or federal aid to finance some improvements is (1) the taxpayers of the city (or some important group of them) would rather go without the improvement than pay for it themselves; or (2) although they would pay for it themselves if they had to, they would much prefer to have some other taxpayers pay for it. Rarely if ever does a mayor who makes such a statement mean (1) that for the city to pay for the improvement would necessarily force some taxpayers into poverty; or (2) that the city could not raise the money even if it were willing to force some of its taxpayers into poverty. In short, the "revenue crisis" mainly reflects the fact that people hate to pay taxes and that they think that by crying poverty they can shift some of the bill to someone else.

To some extent, also, the revenue problem of the cities arises from the way jurisdictional boundaries are drawn or, more precisely, from what are considered to be inequities resulting from the movement of taxable wealth from one side of a boundary line to another. When many large taxpayers move to the suburbs, the central city must tax those who remain at a higher rate if it is to maintain the same level of services. The "problem" in this case is not that the taxpayers who remain are absolutely unable to pay the increased taxes; rather, it is that they do not want to pay them and that they consider it unfair that they should have to pay more simply because other people have moved away. The simple and costless solution (in all but a political sense) would be to charge nonresidents for services that they receive from the city or, failing that, to redraw the boundary lines so that everyone in the metropolitan area would be taxed on the same basis.

That we have not yet been willing to pay the price of solving, or alleviating, such "problems" even when the price is a very small one suggests that they are not really as serious as they have been made out to be. Indeed, one might say that, by definition, a serious problem is one that people are willing to pay a considerable price to have solved.

With regard to these problems for which solutions are at hand, we will know that a real crisis impends when we see the solutions actually being applied. The solution, that is, will be applied when — and only when — the inconvenience or other disadvantage of allowing the problem to continue unabated is judged to have become greater than that of taking the necessary measures to abate it. In other words, a bad-but-not-quite-critical problem is one that it would almost-but-not-quite pay us to do something about.

If some real disaster impends in the city, it is not because parking spaces are hard to find, because architecture is bad, because department store sales are declining, or even because taxes are rising. If there is a genuine crisis, it has to do with the essential welfare of individuals or with the good health of the society, not merely with comfort, convenience, amenity, and business advantage, important as these are. It is not necessary here to try to define "essential welfare" rigorously: it is enough to say that whatever may cause people to die before their time, to suffer serious impairment of their health or of their powers, to waste their lives, to be deeply unhappy or happy in a way that is less than human affects their essential welfare. It is harder to indicate in a sentence or two what is meant by the "good health" of the society. The ability of the society to maintain itself as a going concern is certainly a primary consideration; so is its free and democratic character. In the last analysis, however, the quality of a society must be judged by its tendency to produce desirable human types; the healthy society, then, is one that not only stays alive but also moves in the direction of giving greater scope and expression to what is distinctively human. In general, of course, what serves the essential welfare of individuals also promotes the good health of the society; there are occasions, however, when the two goals conflict. In such cases, the essential welfare of individuals must be sacrificed for the good health of the society. This happens on a very large scale when there is a war, but it may happen at other times as well. The conditions about which we should be most concerned, therefore, are those that affect, or may affect, the good health of the society. If there is an urban crisis in any ultimate sense, it must be constituted of these conditions.

It is a good deal easier to say what matters are not serious (that is, do not affect either the essential welfare of individuals or the good health of the society) than it is to say what ones are. It is clear, however, that poverty, ignorance, and racial (and other) injustices are among the most important of the general conditions affecting the essential welfare of individuals. It is plausible, too, to suppose that these conditions have a very direct bearing upon the good health of the society, although in this connection other factors that are much harder to guess about — for example, the nature and strength of the consensual bonds that hold the society together — may be much more important. To begin with, anyway, it seems reasonable to look in these general directions for what may be called the serious problems of the cities.

It is clear at the outset that serious problems directly affect only a rather small minority of the whole urban population. In the relatively new residential suburbs and in the better residential neighborhoods in the outlying parts of the central cities and in the older, larger, suburbs, the overwhelming majority of people are safely above the poverty line, have at least a high school education, and do not suffer from racial discrimination. For something like two-thirds of all city dwellers, the urban problems that touch them directly have to do with comfort, convenience, amenity, and business advantage. In the terminology used here, these are "important" problems but not "serious" ones. In a great many cases, these problems cannot even fairly be called important; a considerable part of the urban population — those who reside in the "nicer" suburbs — lives under material conditions that will be hard to improve upon.

The serious problems are to be found in all large cities and in most small ones. But they affect only parts of these cities (and only a minority of the city populations). In the central cities and the larger, older suburbs the affected parts are usually adjacent to the central business district and spreading out from it. If these inner districts, which probably comprise somewhere between 10 and 20 percent of the total area classified as urban by the Census, were suddenly to disappear, along with the people who live in them, there would be no serious urban problems worth talking about. If what really matters is the essential welfare of individuals and the good health of the society as opposed to comfort, convenience, amenity, and business advantage, then what we have is not an "urban problem" but an "inner-central-city-and-larger-older-suburb" one.

The serious problems of these places, it should be stressed, are in most instances not caused by the conditions of urban life as such and are less characteristic of the city than of small-town and farm areas. Poverty, ignorance, and racial injustice are more widespread outside the cities than inside them.

One problem that is both serious and unique to the large cities is the existence of huge enclaves of people (many, but not all of them, Negro) of low skill, low income, and low status. In his book *Dark Ghetto,* Kenneth B. Clark presents Census data showing that eight cities — New York, Los Angeles, Baltimore, Washington, Cleveland, St. Louis, New Orleans, and Chicago — contain a total of sixteen areas, all of at least 15,000 population and five of more than 100,000, that are exclusively (more than 94 percent) Negro.[7] There are smaller Negro enclaves in many other cities, and there are large Puerto Rican and large Mexican ones in a few cities. Whether these places can properly be called ghettoes is open to some doubt, as will be explained later. However, there is no question but that they are largely cut off both physically and psychologically from the rest of the city. Whatever may be the effect of this separation on the essential welfare of the individual (and it is arguable that it is trivial), it is clear that the existence of huge enclaves of people who are in some degree alienated from it constitutes a kind of hazard not only to the present peace and safety but also to the long-run health of the society. The problems of individual welfare that these people present are no greater by virtue of the fact that they live together in huge enclaves rather than in isolation on farms, or in small neighborhoods in towns and cities (the problem of individual welfare *appears* greater when they live in huge enclaves, but that is because in this form it is too conspicuous to be ignored). The problem that they present to the good health of the society, on the other hand, is very different and vastly greater solely by virtue of the fact that they live in huge enclaves. Unlike those who live on farms and in small towns, disaffected people who live in huge enclaves may develop a collective consciousness and sense of identity. From many standpoints it is highly desirable that they do so. In the short run, however, they represent a threat to peace and order, and it must be admitted that even in the long run the accommodation that takes place may produce a politics that is less democratic, less mindful of individual rights, and less able to act effectively in the common interest than that which we have now.

This political danger in the presence of great concentrations of people who feel little attachment to the society has long been regarded by some as *the* serious problem of the cities — the one problem that might conceivably produce a disaster that would destroy the quality of the society. "The dark ghettoes," Dr. Clark has written, "now represent a nuclear stockpile which can annihilate the very foundations of America."[8] These words bring up-to-date apprehensions that were expressed by some of the Founding Fathers and that Tocqueville set forth in a famous passage of *Democracy in America:*

The United States has no metropolis, but it already contains several very large cities. Philadelphia reckoned 161,000 inhabitants, and New York 202,000, in the year 1830. The lower ranks which inhabit these cities constitute a rabble even more formidable than the populace of European towns. They consist of freed blacks, in the first place, who are condemned by the laws and by public opinion to a hereditary state of misery and degradation. They also contain a multitude of Europeans who have been driven to the shores of the New World by their misfortunes or their misconduct; and they bring to the United States all our greatest vices, without any of those interests which counteract their baneful influence. As inhabitants of a country where they have no civil rights, they are ready to turn all the passions which agitate the community to their own advantage; thus, within the last few months, serious riots have broken out in Philadelphia and New York. Disturbances of this kind are unknown in the rest of the country, which is not alarmed by them, because the population of the cities has hitherto exercised neither power nor influence over the rural districts.

Nevertheless, I look upon the size of certain American cities, and especially on the nature of their population, as a real danger which threatens the future security of the democratic republics of the New World; and I venture to predict that they will perish from this circumstance, unless the government succeeds in creating an armed force which, while it remains under the control of the majority of the nation, will be independent of the town population and able to repress its excesses.[9]

Strange as it may seem, the mammoth government programs to aid the cities are directed mainly toward the problems of comfort, convenience, amenity, and business advantage. Insofar as they have any effect on the serious problems, it is, on the whole, to aggravate them.

Two programs account for approximately 90 percent of federal government expenditure for the improvement of the cities (as opposed to the maintenance of more or less routine functions). Neither is intended to deal with the serious problems. Both make them worse.

The improvement of transportation is one program. The urban portions of the national expressway system are expected to cost about $18 billion. Their main effect will be to enable suburbanites to move about the metropolitan area more conveniently, to open up some areas for business and residential expansion, and to bring a few more customers from the suburbs downtown to shop. These are all worthy objects when considered by themselves; in context, however, their justification is doubtful, for their principal effect will be to encourage — in effect to subsidize — further movement of industry, commerce, and relatively well-off residents (mostly white) from the inner city. This, of course, will make matters worse for the poor by reducing the number of jobs for them and by making neighborhoods, schools, and other community facilities still more segregated. These injuries will be only partially offset by allowing a certain number of the inner-city poor to commute to jobs in the suburbs.

The huge expenditure being made for improvement of mass transit facilities (it may amount to $10 billion over a decade) may be justifiable for the contribution that it will make to comfort, convenience, and business advantage. It will not, however, make any contribution to the solution of the serious problems of the city. Even if every city had a subway as fancy as Moscow's, all these problems would remain.

The second great federal urban program concerns housing and renewal. Since the creation in 1934 of the Federal Housing Authority (FHA), the government has subsidized home building on a vast scale by insuring mortgages that are written on easy terms and, in the case of the Veterans Administration (VA), by guaranteeing mortgages. Most of the mortgages have been for the purchase of *new* homes. (This was partly because FHA wanted gilt-edged collateral behind the mortgages that it insured, but it was also because it shared the American predilection for newness.) It was cheaper to build on vacant land, but there was little such land left in the central cities and in their larger, older suburbs; therefore, most of the new homes were built in new suburbs. These were almost always zoned so as to exclude the relatively few Negroes and other "undesirables" who could afford to build new houses. In effect, then, the FHA and VA programs have subsidized the movement of the white middle class out of the central cities and older suburbs while at the same time penalizing investment in the rehabilitation of the run-down neighborhoods of these older cities. The poor — especially the Negro poor — have not received any direct benefit from these programs. (They have, however, received a very substantial unintended and indirect benefit, as will be explained later, because the departure of the white middle class has made more housing available to them.) After the appointment of Robert C. Weaver as head of the Housing and Home Finance Agency, FHA changed its regulations to encourage the rehabilitation of existing houses and neighborhoods. Very few such loans have been made, however.

Urban renewal has also turned out to be mainly for the advantage of the well-off — indeed, of the rich — and to do the poor more harm than good. The purpose of the federal housing program was declared by Congress to be "the realization as soon as feasible of the goal of a decent home and a suitable living environment for every American family." In practice, however, the principal objectives of the renewal program have been to attract the middle class back into the central city (as well as to slow its exodus out of the city) and to stabilize and restore the central business districts.[10] Unfortunately, these objectives can be served only at the expense of the poor. Hundreds of thousands of low-income people have been forced out of low-cost housing, by no means all of it substandard, in order to make way for luxury apartments, office buildings, hotels, civic centers, industrial parks, and the like. Insofar as renewal has involved the "conservation" or "rehabilitation" of residential areas, its effect has been to keep the poorest of the poor out of these neighborhoods — that is, to keep them in the highest-density slums. "At a cost of more than three billion dollars," sociologist Scott Greer wrote in 1965, "the Urban Renewal Agency (URA) has succeeded in materially reducing the supply of low-cost housing in American cities."[11]

The injury to the poor inflicted by renewal has not been offset by benefits to them in the form of public housing (that is, housing owned by public bodies and rented by them to families deemed eligible on income and other grounds). With the important exception of New York and the less important ones of some Southern cities, such housing is not a significant part of the total supply. Moreover, the poorest of the poor are usually, for one reason or another, ineligible for public housing.

Obviously, these government programs work at cross-purposes, one undoing (or trying to undo) what the other does (or tries to do). The expressway program and the FHA and VA mortgage insurance and guarantee programs in effect pay the middle-class white to leave the central city for the suburbs. At the same time, the urban renewal and mass transit programs pay him to stay in the central city or to move back to it.

In at least one respect, however, these government programs are consistent: they aim at problems of comfort, convenience, amenity, and business advantage, not at ones involving the essential welfare of individuals or the good health of the society. Indeed, on the contrary, they all sacrifice these latter, more important interests for the sake of the former, less important ones. In this the urban programs are no different from a great many other government programs. Price production programs in agriculture, Theodore Schultz has remarked, take up almost all the time of the Department of Agriculture, the agricultural committees of Congress, and the farm organizations, and exhaust the influence of farm people. But these programs, he says, "do not improve the schooling of farm children, they do not reduce the inequalities in personal distribution of wealth and income, they do not remove the causes of poverty in agriculture, nor do they alleviate it. On the contrary, they worsen the personal distribution of income within agriculture."[12]

It is widely supposed that the serious problems of the cities are unprecedented both in kind and in magnitude. Between 1950 and 1960 there occurred the greatest population increase in the nation's history. At the same time, a considerable part of the white middle class moved to the newer suburbs, and its place in the central cities and older suburbs was taken by Negroes (and in New York by Puerto Ricans as well). These and other events — especially the civil rights revolution — are widely supposed to have changed completely the character of "the urban problem."

If the present situation is indeed radically different from previous ones, then we have nothing to go on in judging what is likely to happen next. At the very least, we face a crisis of uncertainty.

In a real sense, of course, *every* situation is unique. Even in making statistical probability judgments, one must decide on more or less subjective grounds whether it is reasonable to treat certain events as if they were the "same." The National Safety Council, for example, must decide whether cars, highways, and drivers this year are enough like those of past years to justify predicting future experience from past. From a logical standpoint, it is no more possible to decide this question in a purely objective way than it is to decide, for example, whether the composition of the urban population is now so different from what it was that nothing can be inferred from the past about the future. Karl and Alma Taeuber are both right and wrong when they write that we do not know enough about immigrant and Negro assimilation patterns to be able to compare the two and that "such evidence as we could compile indicates that it is more likely to be misleading than instructive to make such comparisons."[13] They are certainly right in saying that one can only guess whether the pattern of Negro assimilation will resemble that of the immigrant. But they are wrong to imply that we can avoid making guesses and still compare things that are not known to be alike in all respects except one. (What, after all, would be the point of comparing immigrant and Negro assimilation patterns if we knew that the only difference between the two was, say, skin color?) They are also wrong in suggesting that the evidence indicates anything about what is likely to be instructive. If there were enough evidence to indicate that, there would be enough to indicate what is likely to happen; indeed, a judgment as to what is likely to be instructive is inseparable from one as to what is likely to happen. Strictly speaking, the Taeubers' statement expresses *their* guess as to what the evidence indicates.

The facts by no means compel one to take the view that the serious problems of the cities are unprecedented either in kind or in magnitude. That population growth in absolute numbers was greater in the decade 1950 to 1960 than ever before need not hold much significance from the present standpoint: American cities have frequently grown at fantastic rates (consider the growth of Chicago from a prairie village of 4,470 in 1840 to a metropolis of more than a million in fifty years). In any case, the population growth of the 1950's was not in the largest cities; most of them actually lost population in that decade. So far as numbers go, the migration of rural and small-town Negroes and Puerto Ricans to the large Northern cities in the 1950's was about equal to immigration from Italy in its peak decade. (In New York, Chicago, and many other cities in 1910, two out of every three schoolchildren were the sons and daughters of immigrants.) When one takes into account the vastly greater size and wealth of the cities now as compared to half a century or more ago, it is obvious that by the only relevant measure — namely, the number of immigrants relative to the capacity of the cities to provide for them and to absorb them — the movement in the 1950's from the South and from Puerto Rico was not large but small.

In many important respects, conditions in the large cities have been getting better. There is less poverty in the cities now than there has ever been. Housing, including that of the poor, is improving rapidly: one study predicts that substandard housing will have been eliminated by 1980.[14] In the last decade alone the improvement in housing has been marked. At the turn of the century only one child in fifteen went beyond elementary school; now most children finish high school. The treatment of racial and other minority groups is conspicuously better than it was. When, in 1964, a carefully drawn sample of Negroes was asked whether, in general, things were getting better or worse for Negroes in this country, approximately eight out of ten respondents said "better."[15]

If the situation is improving, why, it may be asked, is there so much talk of an urban crisis? The answer is that the improvements in performance, great as they have been, have not kept pace with rising expectations. In other words, although things have been getting better absolutely, they have been getting worse *relative to what we think they should be.* And this is because, as a people, we seem to act on the advice of the old jingle:

> *Good, better, best,*
> *Never let it rest*
> *Until your good is better*
> *And your better best.*

Consider the poverty problem, for example. Irving Kristol has pointed out that for nearly a century all studies, in all countries, have concluded that a third, a fourth, or a fifth of the nation in question is below the poverty line.[16] "Obviously," he remarks, "if one defines the poverty line as that which places one-fifth of the nation below it, then one-fifth of the nation will always be below the poverty line." The point is that even if everyone is better off there will be as much poverty as ever, provided that the line is redefined upward. Kristol notes that whereas in the depths of the Depression,

F.D.R. found only one-third of the nation "ill-housed, ill-clad, ill-nourished," Leon Keyserling, a former head of the Council of Economic Advisers, in 1962 published a book called *Poverty and Deprivation in the U.S. — the Plight of Two-Fifths of a Nation.*

Much the same thing has happened with respect to most urban problems. Police brutality, for example, would be a rather minor problem if we judged it by a fixed standard; it is a growing problem because we judge it by an ever more exacting standard. A generation ago the term meant hitting someone on the head with a nightstick. Now it often means something quite different:

> What the Negro community is presently complaining about when it cries "police brutality" is the more subtle attack on personal dignity that manifests itself in unexplainable questionings and searches, in hostile and insolent attitudes toward groups of young Negroes on the street, or in cars, and in the use of disrespectful and sometimes racist language . . . .[17]

Following Kristol, one can say that if the "police brutality line" is defined as that which places one-fifth of all police behavior below it, then one-fifth of all police behavior will always be brutal.

The school dropout problem is an even more striking example. At the turn of the century, when almost everyone was a "dropout," the term and the "problem" did not exist. It was not until the 1960's, when for the first time a majority of boys and girls were graduating from high school and practically all had at least some high school training, that the "dropout problem" became acute. Then, although the dropout rate was still declining, various cities developed at least fifty-five separate programs to deal with the problem. Hundreds of articles on it were published in professional journals, the National Education Association established a special action project to deal with it, and the Commissioner of Education, the Secretary of Labor, and the President all made public statements on it.[18] Obviously, if one defines the "inadequate amount of schooling line" as that which places one-fifth of all boys and girls below it, then one-fifth of all boys and girls will always be receiving an inadequate amount of schooling.

Whatever our educational standards are today, Wayland writes, they will be higher tomorrow. He summarizes the received doctrine in these words:

> Start the child in school earlier; keep him in school more and more months of the year; retain all who start to school for twelve to fourteen years; expect him to learn more and more during this period, in wider and wider areas of human experience, under the guidance of a teacher, who has had more and more training, and who is assisted by more and more specialists, who provide an ever-expanding range of services, with access to more and more detailed personal records, based on more and more carefully validated tests.[19]

To a large extent, then, our urban problems are like the mechanical rabbit at the racetrack, which is set to keep just ahead of the dogs no matter how fast they may run. Our performance is better and better, but because we set our standards and expectations to keep ahead of performance, the problems are never any nearer to solution. Indeed, if standards and expectations rise *faster* than performance, the problems may get (relatively) worse as they get (absolutely) better.

Some may say that since almost everything about the city can stand improvement (to put it mildly), this mechanical rabbit effect is a good thing in that it spurs us on to make constant progress. No doubt this is true to some extent. On the other hand, there is danger that we may mistake failure to progress as fast as we would like for failure to progress at all and, in panic, rush into ill-considered measures that will only make matters worse. After all, an "urban crisis" that results largely from rising standards and expectations is not the sort of crisis that, unless something drastic is done, is bound to lead to disaster. To treat it as if it were might be a very serious mistake.

This danger is greatest in matters where our standards are unreasonably high. The effect of too-high standards cannot be to spur us on to reach the prescribed level of performance sooner than we otherwise would, for that level is by definition impossible of attainment. At the same time, these standards may cause us to adopt measures that are wasteful and injurious and, in the long run, to conclude from the inevitable failure of these measures that there is something fundamentally wrong with our society. Consider the school dropout problem, for example. The dropout rate can never be cut to zero: there will always be some boys and girls who simply do not have whatever it takes to finish high school. If we continue to make a great hue and cry about the dropout problem after we have reached the point where all those who can reasonably be expected to finish high school are doing so, we shall accomplish nothing constructive. Instead, we shall, at considerable cost to ourselves, injure the boys and girls who cannot finish (the propaganda against being a dropout both hurts the morale of such a youngster and reduces his or her job opportunities) while creating in ourselves and in others the impression that our society is morally or otherwise incapable of meeting its obligations.

In a certain sense, then, the urban crisis may be real. By treating a spurious crisis as if it were real, we may unwittingly make it so.

CHAPTER TWO

The Logic of Metropolitan Growth

. . . within a very recent period three new factors have
been suddenly developed which promise to exert a powerful
influence on the problems of city and country life. These
are the trolley, the bicycle, and the telephone. It is impossible to foresee at present just what their influence is to
be on the question of the distribution of population; but
this much is certain, that it adds from five to fifteen miles
to the radius of every large town.

It is by such apparently unimportant, trifling, and in-
conspicuous forces that civilization is swayed and moulded
in its evolutions and no man can foresee them or say
whither they lead. . . .

— F. J. Kingsbury, 1895

Much of what has happened — as well as of what is happening — in the typical city or metropolitan area can be understood in terms of three imperatives. The first is demographic: if
the population of a city increases, the city must expand in one
direction or another — up, down, or from the center outward. The
second is technological: if it is feasible to transport large numbers
of people outward (by train, bus, and automobile) but not upward
or downward (by elevator), the city must expand outward. The
third is economic: if the distribution of wealth and income is such
that some can afford new housing and the time and money to
commute considerable distances to work while others cannot, the
expanding periphery of the city must be occupied by the first group
(the "well-off") while the older, inner parts of the city, where most
of the jobs are, must be occupied by the second group (the "not
well-off").

The word "imperatives" is used to emphasize the inexorable, constraining character of the three factors that together comprise the logic of metropolitan growth. Indeed, the principal purpose of this chapter is to show that, given a rate of population growth, a transportation technology, and a distribution of income, certain consequences must inevitably follow; that the city and its hinterland must develop according to a predictable pattern and that even an all-wise and all-powerful government could not change this pattern except by first changing the logic that gives rise to it. The argument is not that nothing can be done to improve matters. Rather, it is that only those things can be done which lie within the boundaries — rather narrow ones, to be sure — fixed by the logic of the growth process. Nor is it argued that the only factors influencing metropolitan development are those that relate to population, technology, and income. Countless others also influence it. Two of these other factors are of key importance, even though they are not part of the logic of the process. They will be discussed in the following two chapters (on class culture and race).

This chapter, highly schematic, describes in a generalized way how most American cities, small as well as large, have developed and are still developing, but it does not describe completely (or perhaps even accurately) how any *particular* city has developed. The city under discussion here is a highly simplified model. Its residents have no class, ethnic, or racial attributes (they will acquire them in the next two chapters). They are neither rich nor poor; instead, they are "well-off" or "not well-off," depending upon whether or not they can afford to buy new homes and to commute a considerable distance — requiring, say, half an hour or more — to work.

If the reader finds himself perplexed and irked at an account of metropolitan growth that deals only with demographic, technological, and economic factors, ignoring such others of obvious importance as racial discrimination, he is asked to be patient. This simplification is for analytical purposes, and the necessary complications — but *only* the necessary ones — will be introduced later on. The method is to start with the simplest possible model of urban growth and then (in the next two chapters) to elaborate on it.

The logic of metropolitan growth began unfolding the moment

the cities were founded and it has not changed since. More than a century ago, in 1857, a select committee of the state legislature described the forces that were shaping New York. These were, as the committee made clear, the same forces that had always been shaping it. And they were the same ones that are shaping it and other cities still:

As our wharves became crowded with warehouses, and encompassed with bustle and noise, the wealthier citizens, who peopled old "Knickerbocker" mansions, near the bay, transferred their residence to streets beyond the din; compensating for remoteness from their counting houses, by the advantages of increased quiet and luxury. Their habitations then passed into the hands, on the one side, of boarding house keepers, on the other, of real estate agents; and here, in its beginning, the tenant house became a real blessing to that class of industrious poor whose small earnings limited their expenses and whose employment in workshops, stores, and about the wharves and thoroughfares, rendered a near residence of much importance. At this period, rents were moderate, and a mechanic with family could hire two or more comfortable and even commodious apartments, in a house once occupied by wealthy people, for less than half what he is now obliged to pay for narrow and unhealthy quarters. This state of tenantry comfort did not, however, continue long; for the rapid march of improvement speedily enhanced the value of property in the lower wards of the city, and as this took place, rents rose, and accommodations decreased in the same proportion. At first the better class of tenants submitted to retain their single floors, or two and three rooms, at the onerous rates, but this rendered them poorer, and those who were able to do so, followed the example of former proprietors, and emigrated to the upper wards. The spacious dwelling houses then fell before improvements, or languished for a season, as tenant houses of the type which is now the prevailing evil of our city; that is to say, their large rooms were partitioned into several smaller ones (without regard to proper light or ventilation), the rates of rent being lower in proportion to space or height from the street; and they soon became filled, from cellar to garret, with a class of tenantry living from hand to mouth, loose in morals, improvident in habits, degraded or squalid as beggary itself.[1]

What was happening in New York (and elsewhere as well) was the expansion of the city outward under the pressure of growth at its center. Typically, land closest to the point of original settlement (always the point most accessible to waterborne transportation) became the site of the central business district. Great accessibility to wharves, markets, shops, and offices, and later to railheads, meant that commercial and industrial activities had to be located there; the closer a site was to the most accessible center, the more it tended to be worth. Accordingly, most people lived on the outskirts of the central business district, where land prices were not prohibitively high. Only the very rich, to whom the price of land did not matter, and the very poor, who occupied undesirable sites near factories and wharves and endured great overcrowding, lived in the very center of the city.

As the central business district grew, it absorbed the residential neighborhoods adjacent to it. The people who lived in them were pushed outward into unsettled or sparsely settled districts where land prices were still low. To say that they were "pushed" makes it sound as if they went against their wills. Probably most were glad to go. Those who owned their homes profited from the rise in prices; they could sell an old house close to the business district for enough with which to build a new and bigger one at the periphery of the city.

Much of the housing taken over in this way was torn down to make room for factories, stores, and offices. Some, however, was converted to more intensive residential use. When the only transportation was by horse, almost everyone lived within walking distance of his job in the central business district. Even afterward, when one could take a trolley to work, factory workers and office and store clerks generally preferred to pay relatively high rents for crowded quarters from which they could walk to work rather than spend the time and money to commute from neighborhoods where rents were lower. The central business district was therefore ringed with rooming houses and tenements. These establishments could afford the expensive land because they used it intensively. At the end of the last century, for example, some lodging houses in Chicago accommodated (if that is the word) as many as a thousand lodgers a night.

As the populations and income of the city grew, so did the number and proportion of those (the "well-off") who could afford new homes. In the nature of the case, most new homes had to be built at the periphery of the expanding city, where there was vacant land. Until the end of the Civil War, transportation in all large cities was by horsecar;[2] therefore, new housing had to be fairly close in and consisted largely of "three-deckers" (upper-story porches decking the front and rear of four-story tenements). Soon, however, it became feasible to build farther out. The first elevated steam railroads were built in New York in the 1870's, and twenty years later every sizable city had an electric trolley system.[3] Railroads and trolleys enabled more people to commute and to commute larger distances; the farther out they went, the cheaper the land was and the larger the lot sizes they could afford. One- and two-family houses became common.

Wherever this outward movement of the well-off passed beyond the legal boundaries of the city, it created special problems. As early as 1823, Cincinnati officials complained that people living on the edge of the town did not contribute their fair share of taxes, and a few years later the council of St. Louis, which had the same problem, petitioned the state legislature to enlarge the city to include the settlers just beyond its borders who had "all the benifits [sic] of a City residence without any of its burdens."[4] Many cities were enlarged, thus postponing — in some instances almost to the present — the emergence of an acute problem of city-suburb relations. The motives that impelled people to move outward were essentially the same, however, whether the boundaries of the city were near in or far out, and the strength of the outward movement seems to have been roughly the same in every era and in every place. The "flight to the suburbs" is certainly nothing new.[5]

The movement of the well-off out of the inner city was always regarded (as it had been by the select committee in New York) as both portent and cause of the city's decline. The well-off were sure that without their steadying and elevating influence the city would drift from bad to worse and become "the prey of professional thieves, ruffians, and political jugglers."[6] As a committee of leading Bostonians explained in the 1840's:

An individual's influence is exerted chiefly in the place where he resides. Take away from the city a hundred moral and religious families, and there will be taken away a hundred centers of moral and religious influence, though the constituted heads of those families spend the greatest part of their time in the city, and hold in the metropolis the greatest proportion of their property. Those who remove their residence from the city, remove also their places of attendance on public worship, and the children of those families are removed from our primary and higher schools, public and private. . . . They are not here to visit the poor and degraded, and by their example and conduct to assist in resisting the tide of iniquity that is rolling in on us.[7]

People said that they moved because the city was no longer habitable: they could not stand its dirt, noise, and disorder, not to mention the presence near them of "undesirable" people. (When they moved beyond the borders of the city, they added political corruption and high taxes to this list.) Actually, they would have moved anyway, although not in all cases quite so soon, even if the inner city had been as clean and fresh as a field of daisies. They would have moved sooner or later because, as the city grew, the land they occupied would have to be used more intensively. Or, to put it another way, they would have moved because only the very rich could afford to forego the advantage of much cheaper land on the outskirts.

As the well-off moved outward, the "not well-off" (meaning here those who could not afford new houses or the time and money to travel half an hour to work) moved into the relatively old and high-density housing left behind. Indeed, it was in part the pressure of their demand for this housing that caused the well-off to move as soon as they did. The result in many places was to thin out the most overcrowded districts ("rabbit-warrens," the reformers of the 1880's called them) adjacent to warehouses, factories, stores, and offices.

Had the supply of the not well-off not been continually replenished by migration from abroad and from the small towns and farms of this country, the high-density tenement districts would have emptied rapidly at the end of the last century as incomes rose and more people moved outward. As it happened, however, immigration continually brought new workers who, for at least a few years — until they, too, could move on — were glad to take refuge in the housing that the others had left behind.

Heavy as it was, migration to the city seldom fully offset the decentralizing effect of the commuter railroad and the trolley and of the expansion of commercial and industrial land uses near the city's center. In many cities the densest slums were either displaced by stores, offices, and factories or drained to reasonable densities by improvement of transportation, or both. The Basin tenement area of Cincinnati, for example, lost one-fourth of its population between 1910 and 1930, a period of rapid growth for the rest of the city. In Chicago, New York, and Philadelphia much the same thing happened.[8]

In the first half of the twentieth century the process of growth was accelerated by changes of technology, although its character was not changed in any essential way. Invention of the mechanical refrigerator, along with a vast increase in the variety of inexpensive canned foods, reduced the number of boardinghouses and restaurants. Dispersal of factories was brought about by the use of heavy-duty power transmission cables and, even more, of the assembly line (horizontal processes required more land). Probably of equal importance was the introduction of cheap and rapid highway transportation.[9] By 1915 nearly 2.5 million automobiles were in use; five years later there were 1.1 million trucks. The automobiles facilitated the creation of residential neighborhoods still farther out from the central business district, and the trucks cut factories loose from railheads (and thus from the center of the city also). Stupendous sums were spent for automobiles and for highways, in effect subsidizing the development of the hinterland.

The federal government gave outward expansion a further push when during the Depression it created the Federal Housing Administration. As was noted in the previous chapter, FHA's assistance (and later the Veterans Administration's as well) went mostly to those who bought new homes. For the most part these were in outlying neighborhoods of the central city or in the suburban ring, the only places where vacant land was plentiful. Had it been disposed to do so, FHA might have stimulated the renovation of existing housing and thus the refurbishing of the central cities. If it had done this, it would have assisted many of the not well-off, a category that included most Negroes as well as other minority group members. In fact, it did the opposite: it subsidized the well-off who wanted to leave the central city, while (by setting neighborhood and property standards that they could not meet) refusing to help the not well-off to renovate their central-city houses.[10]

The Depression slowed down but — thanks to the FHA — did not stop the outward movement of the well-off. It did, however, interrupt and even reverse the flow into the city of the not well-off. In the 1920's more than four million immigrants had come from abroad, the great majority of them settling in the larger cities. There also had been a considerable movement of Negroes from the rural South to the large cities of the North, especially New York. (The Negro population of New York more than doubled in this decade, rising from 152,467 to 327,706, and Harlem, which had only recently been occupied by outward-bound, second-generation Jews and Italians, was suddenly transformed.[11]) When the Depression struck, people not only stopped coming to the city but left it in large numbers to go "back to the land" and back to the old country. Now, partially drained and no longer being replenished, the inner city began to stagnate. Neighborhoods that had been packed a few years before were more or less depopulated; people who lived in them no longer expected to follow the "tenement trail" out of the city. They seemed to have been left permanently behind and it appeared to some people that a new and serious problem had arisen. As Edith Elmer Wood explained in a bulletin written for the Public Works Administration in 1935:

The blighting effect of slums on human lives and human character was less acute during the period of immigration and rapid population growth than it is now. Newcomers sought the cheapest and therefore the worst housing, literally pushing out, and necessarily into something better, the last previous immigrant wave. They were able to afford the move because rapidly expanding population meant rapidly expanding jobs. . . . Living in the slums was a temporary discomfort, cheerfully endured, because of an animating faith that prosperity and comfort were just ahead. . . .

Since immigration stopped, all that has changed. The situation has become static. A superior family climbs out here and there, but it is the exception, not the rule, and for every one that goes up, another must come down. Discouragement or bitterness has taken the place of hope. It is only recently that we have seen a generation reach manhood and womanhood which was born and bred in our city slums, which has known no home but a dingy tenement, no playground but the city streets. And worst of all, it has little hope of attaining anything better except by the short-cuts of crime.[12]

The "defense boom" and then World War II quickly filled the inner city to overflowing once again. Now the well-off could not move away because of controls on residential construction; at the same time, large numbers of workers, most of them unskilled, came from small towns and farms until all the inner city housing that could possibly be used was occupied. A huge amount of new factory capacity was built in two or three years, most of it at the periphery of the city but within its borders. Had this expansion taken place under normal circumstances, most of the new factories would have been located in the suburban ring, beyond the borders of the city. The effect of the war, therefore, was to slow down somewhat the decentralization of the city.

As soon as wartime controls were lifted, the logic of growth reasserted itself. A huge pent-up demand on the part of the well-off, whose numbers had been swelled by formation of new families, wartime prosperity, and the home-loan provisions of the "G.I. Bill of Rights," burst forth in a mass exodus from the city to the sub-urbs: between 1940 and 1950 some 2.3 million persons moved out of the twelve largest central cities. Not all of these people went to the suburbs, of course, and 2.3 million was only 12 percent of the total population of these cities; nevertheless, the sudden outward surge was unprecedented in scale. As had happened before, when the well-off left, the not well-off moved into the housing left behind. The most nearly well-off of them took the best of it and left the hous-ing that they vacated for others below them on the income ladder, who in turn passed their housing down to still others. Many of those in this housing queue — practically all those at the "far" end of it — were Negroes (in New York, Puerto Ricans also; in Los Angeles, Oakland, and some other cities, Mexicans also).

The heavy, rapid Negro migration to the city in the war and postwar years changed the situation markedly. In 1940 nearly three-quarters (72 percent) of the nation's Negroes lived in the South; twenty years later a little more than half (54 percent) lived there. The Negro had always been rural, but by 1960 he was urban: one-half of all Negroes lived in central cities; in the 1950 to 1960 decade in every one of the fifty largest central cities, the percentage of Negroes in the population rose.[13]

Massive as it was, this new migration into the large cities did not quite offset the movement of the well-off out of them. Consequently, by 1960 there was ample housing of a sort for most of those seeking it. Much of it was of a very good sort, built only thirty or forty years before and still structurally sound. All that was wrong with much of it was that it was out-of-date, aesthetically and otherwise, by the standards of the well-off — standards that had risen rapidly during the war and postwar prosperity. The not well-off very quickly occupied the better housing that came on the market. In the past, the least well-off had lived in compact, high-density districts. Now they spread out in all directions, leapfrogging neighborhoods here and there, covering miles and miles.[14]

By no means all of the well-off left the city. Some who could afford any rent lived in luxury apartments, a gold coast along the central business district. The number of such people was bound to grow, but not enough to change the inner city fundamentally. In the outlying neighborhoods, heads of families often remained even when they could afford to move; people getting along in years saw no point in moving from neighborhoods in which they had lived so long and to which they had become attached. It was their children and their boarders who moved away to the suburbs. On the lower East Side of New York in the early 1960's there were still some neighborhoods occupied mainly by remnants of the Jewish immigration of the early 1900's and the Puerto Rican immigration of the 1920's,[15] but the population of such neighborhoods was thinning out. The later migrants, mostly Negroes (and in New York, Puerto Ricans), had in most cases come to the city as young adults or children and were a remarkably fast-growing and fast-spreading population.

Looking at the neighborhoods they had left a decade or two before, suburbanites were often dismayed at what they saw — lawns and shrubbery trampled out, houses unpainted, porches sagging, vacant lots filled with broken bottles and junk. To them — and, of course, even more to the scattering of "old residents" who for one reason or another remained — these things constituted "blight" and "decay." To the people who were moving into these neighborhoods from old tenements and shanties, however, the situation appeared in a very different light. Many of them cared little or nothing for lawns and had no objections to broken bottles; they knew, too, that the more "fixed up" things were, the higher rents would be. What mattered most to them was having four or five rooms instead of one or two, plumbing that worked, an inside bathroom that did not have to be shared with strangers down the hall, and central heating. To the least well-off, "blight" was a blessing. They were able, for the first time in their lives, to occupy housing that was comfortable.

Although the appearance of neighborhoods declined as they were occupied by lower-income groups, the quality of housing in the central city as a whole improved dramatically. Housing was repaired and improved on a wholesale scale during the postwar years, some of it by government programs but more of it through the normal processes of consumer spending. Although differences in Census definition make precise comparisons impossible, more than half the housing in metropolitan areas that was substandard in 1949 was put in sound condition during the next ten years through structural repairs or by plumbing additions. At the end of the decade, some families still lived in housing that was appallingly bad, but their number was now small and getting smaller every year.[16]

The improvement resulting from the repair of substandard housing and the handing down of good housing by the well-off was widespread. This fact can be seen from the gains made by Negroes, the worst-housed group in the population, as shown in the table.

PERCENTAGE OF NEGRO FAMILIES
OCCUPYING SUBSTANDARD HOUSING[17]

Metropolitan Area	1950	1960
New York	33.8	23.0
Chicago	59.3	25.4
Philadelphia	42.8	13.8
Los Angeles	19.0	6.2
Detroit	29.3	10.3
St. Louis	75.0	39.4
Washington, D.C.	33.9	13.6
San Francisco–Oakland	25.6	14.9

By discarding housing that was still usable, the well-off conferred a great benefit upon the not well-off. Like many benefits, however, this one had hidden costs: in order to use the discarded housing, one had to live where it was; all too often this meant living where there were not enough jobs.

The central business district — and with it the central city as a whole — had long been losing its monopoly of accessibility. As the population at the periphery of the city grew, there was increasing support for large stores and other facilities that could compete with those of the central business district. People no longer had to go downtown for almost everything. At the same time, improvements in transportation, especially the building of expressways and of major airports that were some distance from the city, made it easier than before to get from one part of the metropolitan area to another without going downtown. Also, manufacturing always tended to move outward to cheaper land; beginning in the early 1930's, increases in plant size and improvements in materials-handling techniques hastened this movement. More and more manufacturers wanted single-story plants with horizontal material flows and aisles wide enough to permit mechanical handling of materials. This usually compelled them to move their operations to a less congested area close to a center of long-distance truck hauling.[18] After the Second World War, much manufacturing, and much retailing and wholesaling as well, moved out of the city.

The central business district retained its advantage of accessibility with respect to activities involving frequent face-to-face communication. Top executives had to be near to each other and to the bankers, lawyers, advertising men, government officials, and others with whom they dealt frequently; consequently, they kept their headquarters downtown. The rest of their operations — factories as well as record-keeping — they sent to the suburbs, where land was cheaper and clerical help easier to find, or to other areas altogether.

By far the biggest concentration of jobs for the unskilled was still in or near the central city. Service workers (for example, watchmen and elevator operators) were concentrated downtown, and "laborers" worked in the nearby industrial suburbs. There were not enough such jobs to go around, however, now that so high a proportion of the city's population consisted of the unskilled. Most of the *new* jobs for the unskilled, moreover, were in the suburban ring; that was where almost all the growth was taking place. Unskilled workers, most of whom lived near the downtown part of the central city, would have been happier had the jobs not moved outward. The outward movement of jobs did not leave them stranded, however; except in three or four of the largest metropolitan areas, a worker could travel from his inner city dwelling to a job anywhere on the outer perimeter of the metropolitan area in no more than half an hour. The radial pattern of highway and rail transportation, although not planned for the purpose, was ideal from the standpoint of workers who were characteristically needed for a few days first in one suburb and then in another, the second being perhaps on the opposite rim of the metropolitan area from the first. "Reverse commuting" — that is, traveling from an inner city residence to a suburban job — became common among the unskilled workers of the central city. The advantage of living near the center of a radial transportation system may have been a major cause — conceivably as great a one as racial discrimination — of the failure of many workers to move to the suburbs.[19]

At some future time — a very distant one perhaps — the logic of metropolitan growth will have to change. Conceivably, the urban population may stop growing, or technology may change so as to make it cheaper to build upward than outward, or government may redistribute income to such an extent that everyone can afford to buy a new house and to commute a considerable distance to work. If none of these changes occurs, the supply of vacant land into which the metropolis can expand will run out. None of these changes seems likely to occur in the foreseeable future, however. Essentially the same logic that shaped the growth of the city in the past may therefore be expected to shape that of the metropolitan area in the future. It is, in fact, already clear that the urban population will grow: the children of the postwar baby boom are already reaching adulthood, and a new, "second-generation" baby boom may be about to begin. Migration to the cities from the rural South will not be as great as it was during and after the war, but it will be substantial. In 1960 there were slightly less than half as many Negroes on farms and in rural areas as there had been in 1950, and a relatively high proportion of these people were too old to migrate or had long since decided not to. The birthrate in the rural South, however, was high — high enough to keep a large stream of migrants moving to the cities.[20]

Immigration from abroad will also contribute to the cities' growth. In 1968 it accounted for more than one-fifth (22.1 percent) of the total United States population increase; about half the immigrants were unskilled or semiskilled workers and their families.

If present trends continue, there will not only be more people in the cities in the next two or three decades, but a higher proportion of them will be well-off. By the year 2000, according to the Council of Economic Advisers, the average American family will have an annual income of about $18,000 (in 1965 prices).[21] In this very affluent society, housing will probably be discarded at an even faster rate than now, and the demand for living space will probably be greater. In the future, then, the process of turnover is likely to give more and better housing bargains to the not well-off, encouraging them to move ever farther outward and thus eventually emptying the central city and bringing "blight" to suburbs that were new a decade or two ago. To the "pulling" effect of these bargains will be added two "pushing" ones: the physical deterioration of housing in the central city (which, being the oldest, has been in use the longest) and the clearance activities of urban renewal and public works programs, which are expected to displace between half a million and two million families between 1965 and 1975. Among those moving outward from the central city will be large numbers of Negroes. Efforts to keep them in the central city where their voting strength can be exploited are bound to fail, as are efforts to distribute them throughout white neighborhoods. In their quest for living space and jobs, well-off Negroes, like the well-off in other groups, will move into the suburban ring, in some places leapfrogging white suburbs to create their own and in others occupying suburbs vacated by better-off Negroes or whites. As better-off suburbanites make ready to move farther out into the suburban ring in search of larger lots, they will relax zoning and other restrictions that have excluded the less well-off from suburban communities; as the need to find customers for their "downgraded" properties grows, less and less exhortation will be needed to convince them of the soundness of the principle of open occupancy. Despite these movements, however, large numbers of Negroes will continue to live in the central city for at least several decades.

If there is any check on outward expansion, it is probably the limited supply of vacant land. This supply will be used up faster than ever, not only because more people will be able to afford land, but also because they will be able to afford larger lots. (In the New York metropolitan region, for example, the next six million people to move to new homes in the outlying suburbs are expected to take as much land as the previous sixteen million took. Two-thirds of the land in these suburbs is now zoned for single-family houses on lots of a half acre or more.[22]) It will be many years before the frontier of vacant land is reached, however. (Even in the New York region, where the demand is greatest, the supply is expected to last for at least another generation.[23]) And when it is at last reached, the outward movement will not stop abruptly; instead, two- and three-acre lots will probably be subdivided into half-acre ones, permitting movement from the older, higher-density rings of settlement to continue for some time. As the supply of vacant land diminishes, however, the price of it will rise, and this will dampen the desire to use it lavishly. That the outlying suburbs of New York and other cities are zoned for large lots therefore indicates little about the density at which they will actually be built; the zoners there may not have anticipated how costly land would become and how sobering an effect this would have upon prospective buyers. In fact, the dampening effect of higher land prices in the suburbs has been operating for some time. Of the new dwelling units started in 1966, 32.8 percent were in apartment houses for three or more families; ten years before, the comparable figure was only 8.7 percent.

As the price of vacant land in the suburbs goes up, that of land and buildings in the central city will go down. As was pointed out earlier, the central business district — and with it the central city as a whole — has been losing the monopoly of accessibility that made its land so valuable. As the exodus of commerce, industry, and population continues, the value of real estate in the central city will decline. Urban renewal will tend to slow this down: so long as it appears likely that the government will buy deteriorating property at its present market value, that value is not likely to fall. In a few favored parts of a city, renewal may hold values steady. But it probably cannot hold them steady throughout the whole of a large city — and it certainly cannot steady them in *all* large cities. The amount of subsidy that this enterprise would require is far beyond what anyone would consider tolerable.

If the populations of the inner cities are not again replenished by low-income immigrants — an uncertain condition, since, as the example of Cuba shows, a Latin American dictator may at any time send hundreds of thousands fleeing north — the time will come when cleared land in the depopulated central city will be worth less than vacant land in the heavily populated suburbs. When this time comes, the direction of metropolitan growth will reverse itself: the well-off will move from the suburbs to the cities, probably causing editorial writers to deplore the "flight to the central city" and politicians to call for government programs to check it by redeveloping the suburbs.

Recently, some tendencies toward recentralization have appeared.[24] First, advances in electronic data processing are making some offices into "paper-processing factories"; these employ unskilled workers at the bottom of the white-collar occupational ladder in jobs such as key punch operator. Second, "the computer and the recent technological advances in teleprocessing and time-sharing have also strongly reinforced the ability of a business enterprise to retain its head office and management in a centralized location in the face of ever wider decentralization of operations."[25] Third, huge expenditures are being made on scientific research and development. Much of this work does not require great land space, is independent of manufacturing and materials locations, and is best done in close proximity to universities.

The central city is not at all likely to regain its old monopoly on accessibility, however. At most, it will be one of several nuclei in a metropolitan area over which business activity and residential occupance are, as compared to the "old-fashioned" city, rather evenly and thinly spread.

Despite recentralizing tendencies, it is idle to talk of bringing large numbers of the well-off back into the central city. For the city to compete as a residential area with the suburbs, large districts of it would have to be completely rebuilt at very low densities. This is out of the question so long as people are living in these districts. To be sure, the government might build new housing somewhere else (where?) for the residents of the old neighborhoods and move them to it, forcibly if necessary. It might then tear down the existing structures and put up new ones, creating neighborhoods that would attract the well-off back from the suburbs. This plan would be fantastically expensive, of course, since it would mean destroying a great deal of useful housing, as well as stores, factories, churches, schools, and other facilities. Doing this would be insane if the purpose were nothing more than "civic patriotism" or the wish to confer benefits on the well-off.

A case might perhaps be made for a wholesale exchange of population between the central city and the suburbs on the ground that the preservation of democratic institutions requires it. But if such were the purpose, the redeveloped central city could not be occupied solely or even mainly by the well-off — rich and poor, black and white, would have to be settled in proximity to one another, sharing schools and other facilities, the object being to improve the quality of the community by their association. An undertaking of this sort would have the justification of aiming at an important public good. Whether it would, within reasonable probability, secure that good is doubtful, however. For one thing, it would be hard to give the well-off the space necessary to bring them back from the suburbs and still have room for the large number of the not well-off who would have to be accommodated. If, as is all too likely, one of the requirements of the well-off was that they be insulated from "undesirables," then obviously the reoccupation of the city by them could not be brought about on terms that would serve any public purpose. Even on the most favorable view of the possibilities — that is, assuming that stable, integrated neighborhoods could be created — the wisdom of, in effect, throwing a large part of the city's physical plant on the scrap heap might well be questioned.

To build "new towns" (actually small cities) when doing so

involves abandoning or underutilizing existing facilities would be an even more costly venture since not only housing, schools, churches, and stores, but everything else as well — factories, streets, water and sewer lines — would have to be built new from the ground up. Here again, one may say that if the object is to create an integrated community, and if that object can be attained in this way and in no other that entails smaller costs (so that abandoning existing streets, sewer lines, and the like is unavoidable), the money is well spent. That the undertaking would be immensely expensive is beyond question, however.[26]

The impracticability of attracting large numbers of the well-off back into the central city before land prices there have become competitive with those in the suburbs (and without the use of large subsidies) can be seen from New York City's experience with a "demonstration" project. This project involved two blocks on West Ninety-fourth and Ninety-fifth streets near Central Park. The owners of the brownstone buildings in these blocks were given the choice of either bringing their buildings up to a high standard or selling them to someone — either a private purchaser or the City — who would. In May 1960, the letters to the owners went out. Nearly ten years later (September 1969) the City had bought eighteen of the buildings. Four of them were offered for sale to qualified bidders at auction in 1963, but only one was bid upon and that by only one bidder. In 1965 the City announced that it had arranged negotiated sales to eighteen "sponsors" who would rehabilitate the buildings and create a racially integrated neighborhood. The sponsors would pay from $21,000 to $34,000 for the buildings, which was about 10 percent less than their estimated market value. Since they were in very poor condition ("nothing but four walls," said Mrs. Kenneth B. Clark, who with her husband was one of the sponsors), rehabilitation costs would be high — about $15,000 per floor, making the total cost of a building (all were either four or five floors) at least $80,000.[27] By the end of 1967, only four buildings had actually passed out of the City's hands, and all but one of the original sponsors had withdrawn; for some of the buildings as many as three sponsors had come and gone. By the summer of 1969, the City still had possession of seven buildings. The cost of rehabilitation had by now risen to about $20,000 per floor, and the City was hoping to sell the remaining buildings at about 50 percent of their current market value. Of course, even if the buildings had all been bought up immediately at market prices, nothing much would have been "demonstrated," for the City's real problem was not to induce a few very prosperous families to live near the center of Manhattan but to bring tens of thousands of moderately well-off families back to such unglamorous places as Brooklyn and the Bronx.

The three imperatives listed at the beginning of this chapter — namely, rate of population growth, technology of transportation, and distribution of income — place stringent limits on policy. Except as it may relax one or more of them and so change the logic of metropolitan growth, government — even the wisest and most powerful government — must work within the limits set by these imperatives. It may hasten or delay the unfolding of the logic of growth and it may make such adaptations — very important ones sometimes — as are possible within it. But given the premises, it cannot prevent the conclusions from following.

Consider the case of New York City. The state legislative committee of 1857, whose report was quoted earlier, confidently asserted that "wise and simple laws," if only they had been adopted in time, would have checked or prevented the evils it deplored. With such laws, it said, "the city of New York would now exhibit more gratifying bills of health, more general social comfort and prosperity and less, far less expenditure for the support of pauperism and the punishment of crime." It blamed the authorities of an earlier time for not having passed the necessary laws; those authorities, it said, "were unmindful of the future public good, precisely as we, in our day and generation, are pertinaciously regardless of our posterity's welfare."[28]

Perhaps the authorities were unmindful of the future public good. Whether they were or were not does not matter much; they could not, in any case, have changed the imperatives of population growth, transportation technology, and income level, and it is these factors that account not only for their failure to change the pattern of growth but also for the failure of authorities in later times as well, including, of course, the committee of 1857 itself.

What, one wonders, are the wise and simple laws that would have saved the situation if only they had been made soon enough? The idea of controlling land use by a zoning ordinance is a recent one, but suppose that when Manhattan was first settled an ordinance had limited the spread of warehouses, factories, and other objectionable land uses. If such an ordinance had been made and enforced, the old Knickerbocker mansions would still be standing — but there would be no city. Nor, if *all* towns had made and enforced such ordinances, would there be cities anywhere. If towns are to grow into cities and cities into metropolises, old residential districts necessarily must decline and disappear.

Suppose, again, that in the city's earliest days the authorities had enacted a housing code requiring the demolition of all substandard dwellings. (The committee of 1857 did, in fact, propose a regulation against the renting of cellars.[29]) Such a code, if enforced, would have prevented the city from growing fast and from ever becoming a metropolis.[30] In order to grow fast, the city had to become a center of warehouses, shops, and factories, which meant that it had to have a plentiful supply of cheap labor, which meant that it had to have a plentiful supply of housing that such labor could afford. If all the housing had been decent by the standards of the time, some of the labor required for the city's growth could not have afforded to live in the city at all.[31]

It may be argued that if the city had insisted, adequate housing would have been provided and the extra cost in effect added to the wage bill and so passed on to the consumer. But no city could have added very much to its wage bill without worsening its competitive position vis-à-vis other areas. Had all places provided adequate housing, the city would have been under a cost handicap, and its development would have been impeded accordingly. The fundamental fact was that it would have cost more to provide adequate housing in the city than elsewhere. (To be sure, had the extra costs been imposed upon the affluent *regardless of where they lived,* the city would not have been handicapped, but because of political boundaries and other institutional arrangements this was not a real possibility.)

If society had been willing to accept a curtailment of the rate of economic growth for the sake of preventing overcrowding and bad housing in the city, it could have prevented people who could not support themselves properly from coming to the city at all. By restricting the supply of labor in the city, the authorities could have forced the price of it up. Keeping the farm boys on the farms and stopping immigration of all but skilled workers from abroad could have checked or prevented the evils that the committee deplored. But, of course, the growth of New York would also have been checked or prevented. The old Knickerbocker mansions might still be there, but the Statue of Liberty would not be.

It was impossible both to allow unrestricted immigration and to eliminate substandard housing. If free to do so, people would come to the cities from the rural backwaters of this country, and from abroad, and they would keep on coming until the opportunities in the city as they perceived them were no better than those in the places where they were. Since opportunities in much of the world were extremely poor, the movement into the city was bound to be massive and to continue almost indefinitely if allowed. Improving conditions in the city while allowing migration to continue freely could have no effect but to establish the final equilibrium at a different point — i.e., one at which *more* of the poor would have come to the city. As Jacob A. Riis wrote in *The Poor in Great Cities* (1895), if it were possible for New York to "shut her door against the immigration of the world and still maintain the conditions of today, I should confidently predict a steady progress that would leave little of the problem for the next generation to wrestle with. But that is only another way of saying, 'if New York were not New York.' "[32]

If the authorities had been able to find a miraculously cheap and fast means of transporting large numbers of people from the factory district to the outskirts of the city, the evils that the select committee deplored would easily have been ended. For a time, in fact, reformers in New York thought the subway might accomplish wonders. ("If the happy day ever comes when a poor man can be carried to the green fields of Long Island, New Jersey, or Westchester County for five cents, then a wonderful change will take place," one of them wrote.[33]) The subway and the trolley did put an end to "rabbit warrens," but in the large cities it was still necessary, despite the new transportation technology, for many people to be crowded together close to the factories, stores, and offices. In 1893 a member of the American Economic Association declared that the confident belief of a few years before that rapid transit would solve New York's housing problems was now seen to be a vain hope.[34]

So long as large numbers of workers had to live near their jobs, it was impossible to avoid high rents and overcrowding in the large cities, a conclusion that the reformers of every generation fought manfully against but finally had to accept. It was impossible, a city commission concluded in 1900, to design a tenement house that was both adequate and commercially feasible; moreover, legislation to require the conversion of existing tenements to other uses was not practicable.[35] And in 1955 a mayor's committee estimated that about a million persons (268,000 families) would be displaced if the multiple-dwelling code was strictly enforced.[36]

Redistributing income was another possibility, and it, too, was tried. Subway and highway construction was subsidized, as was the purchase of new homes. Insofar as these and other measures put people in the class of the well-off who would otherwise not have gotten there so soon, they hastened the decongestion of the city. But since they had to be paid for by taxes — taxes that were not imposed only on the super-well-off — these measures must have had some contrary and offsetting effect as well. In any event, migration into the city always replenished at least partially the "class of tenantry living from hand to mouth, loose in morals, improvident in habits, degraded and squalid as beggary itself." Redistribution of income could not eliminate poverty in the city so long as opportunities in any part of the world were conspicuously worse off than in the city, and so long as people were free to move to it.

CHAPTER THREE

The Imperatives of Class

. . . the dominant aim of our society seems to be to middle-class-ify all of its members.

— John Dollard, 1937

T HE logic of growth does not explain all that needs explaining. For one thing, it does not explain why the city expanded outward as fast as it did. When they moved, the well-off were strongly impelled by economic forces to move outward — first to the outlying neighborhoods of the central city, then to inlying suburbs, and later to outlying ones. But the well-off did not have to move as soon as they did or in such numbers. If the trolley car and then the automobile were causes of their moving, they were also effects of their desire to move. (Philadelphia was the "city of homes" long before rapid transit was invented, Adna F. Weber pointed out apropos of this in 1899.[1]) Also, the logic of growth does not explain why a considerable proportion of the well-off failed to move at all. In 1960, for example, about 22 percent of families in the central cities had incomes large enough to buy a new house.[2] In fact, the median family income in the central cities was only 16 percent less than in the suburbs. Obviously, some families evaluate the advantages of central city versus suburban living differently than do others. Furthermore, the logic of growth does not explain the existence of slums. A slum is not simply a district of low-quality housing; rather, it is one in which the style of life is squalid and vicious.[3] The logic of growth *does* require that, in general, the lowest-income people live in the oldest, highest-density, most run-down housing, which will be nearest to the factories, warehouses, stores, and offices of the inner, or downtown, part of the central city; however, nothing in the logic of growth says that such districts must be squalid and vicious.

To account for these features of metropolitan development in the United States, a second explanatory principle must, so to speak, be placed over the first one. This is the concept of class culture. The purpose of this chapter is to show how certain styles of life that are learned in childhood and passed on as a kind of collective heritage operate (within limits set by the logic of growth) to give the city its characteristic form and most of its problems. It is one of the main contentions of this book that the class cultures of the city, no less than its logic of growth, set limits on what the policymaker can accomplish.

American sociologists usually define social class in terms of "prestige" or "standing": an individual belongs to one or another class (the number of classes and the names they are given differ from one writer to another) depending upon whether he is "looked up to" or "looked down on" by the consensus of the community.[4] Frequently, an index of easily measured attributes — for example, income, education, occupation, and housing type — is treated as an indicator of prestige or standing. It generally turns out that the people put in the same prestige class share the same outlook and style of life, one that is learned in childhood and that constitutes a "life style" for them. That is, the prestige classes turn out to be cultures, or rather (since the outlook and style of life of each class is a *variant* of one common to all) subcultures.[5]

The class subcultures have been described by many sociologists, although never with the rigor and completeness of an ethnographic report (a fact that leaves some social scientists in doubt as to whether they are really subcultures).[6] There is general agreement as to their characteristics, and what follows in the next few pages is essentially a summary of what sociologists have reported about them. It differs from most other accounts, however, in that each class subculture is characterized as having a distinctive psychological orientation toward providing for a more or less distant future.

In the analysis to come, the individual's orientation toward the future will be regarded as a function of two factors: (1) ability to imagine a future, and (2) ability to discipline oneself to sacrifice present for future satisfaction.[7] The more distant the future the individual can imagine and can discipline himself to make sacrifices for, the "higher" is his class. The criterion, it should be noted, is ability, not performance. Later on (in Chapter 10) it will be explained how a person may be psychologically capable of providing for the future and yet not do so. For the present, however, his time horizon may be thought of as a function of his class culture alone. The reason for defining class in terms of orientation toward the future is that this conception seems to lend itself better than any others to analysis of the kinds of problems that are of special interest to the policymaker.[8]

The class subcultures have numerous secondary characteristics associated with this primary one (the existence of a *pattern* of characteristics justifies the term *subculture*); most of these secondary characteristics are probably caused, directly or indirectly, by the primary one, but this is a question that need not be treated here. In any case, each subculture displays distinctive attitudes toward — for example — authority, self-improvement, risk, and violence, and distinctive forms of social organization, most notably of family organization. For the purposes of this book, however, the *defining* characteristic of a class subculture is — to repeat — the one primary factor; namely, psychological orientation toward providing for the future.

For present purposes it will suffice to describe four subcultures — those of the upper, middle, working, and lower classes — and to describe them schematically as ideal types.[9] In other words, what follows are generalized models of subcultures, which do not necessarily describe the cultural traits of *particular* individuals. The four subcultures should be thought of as bands (rather than points) on a continuous scale or spectrum — bands that sometimes blend and overlap so that there can exist "in-between" positions equally characteristic of "adjoining" subcultures.

It must again be strongly emphasized that this use of the term *class* is different from the ordinary one.[10] As the term is used here, a person who is poor, unschooled, and of low status may be upper class; indeed he *is* upper class if he is psychologically capable of providing for a distant future. By the same token, one who is rich and a member of "the 400" may be lower class: he *is* lower class if he is incapable of conceptualizing the future or of controlling his impulses and is therefore obliged to live from moment to moment. In general, of course, there is at least a *rough* correspondence between being, for example, upper class in the present sense and upper class as ordinarily defined: this is because people who are capable of providing for a distant future tend by that very circumstance to get education (as distinct from schooling) and with it wealth, status, and power. Similarly, people incapable of looking ahead for more than a day or two or of controlling their impulses are likely to be poor, unskilled, and of low status for this very reason.

It should also be emphasized that behavior can rarely be explained solely in terms of class subculture. The individual belongs to other subcultures besides the class one — age group, occupational group, and ethnic group subcultures, for example. Moreover, culture is by no means the only determinant of his behavior; in many situations thorough knowledge of an individual's culture(s) would not help an observer make "interesting" predictions about his behavior.

Strong correlations have been shown to exist between IQ score and socioeconomic status, and some investigators have claimed that these correlations are largely attributable to genetic factors.[11] These considerations suggest the possibility that one's ability to take account of the future may often depend mainly upon one's biologically inherited intelligence. The assumption being made here, however, is a contrary one — namely, that time horizon is a cultural (or subcultural) trait passed on to the individual in early childhood from his group.

The Upper Class. At the most future-oriented end of the scale, the upper-class individual expects a long life, looks forward to the future of his children, grandchildren, great-grandchildren (the family "line"), and is concerned also for the future of such abstract entities as the community, nation, or mankind. He is confident that within rather wide limits he can, if he exerts himself to do so, shape the future to accord with his purposes. He therefore has strong incentives to "invest" in the improvement of the future situation — i.e., to sacrifice some present satisfaction in the expectation of enabling someone (himself, his children, mankind, etc.) to enjoy greater satisfactions at some future time. Future-oriented culture teaches the individual that he would be cheating himself if he allowed gratification of his impulses (for example, for sex or violence) to interfere with his provision for the future.

The upper-class individual is markedly self-respecting, self-confident, and self-sufficient. He places great value on independence, curiosity, creativity, happiness, "developing one's potentialities to the full," and consideration for others. In rearing his children, he stresses these values along with the idea that one should govern one's relations with others (and, in the final analysis, with one's self) by *internal* standards rather than by conformity to an externally given code ("not because you're told to but because you take the other person into consideration").[12] The upper-class parent is not alarmed if his children remain unemployed and unmarried to the age of thirty, especially if they remain in school.[13] He does not mind being alone; indeed, he requires a good deal of privacy. He wants to express himself (he may carry self-expression to the point of eccentricity), and, in principle at least, he favors self-expression by others. He takes a tolerant, perhaps even an encouraging, view of unconventional behavior in sex, the arts, and politics. He is mindful of the rights of others and wants issues to be settled on their merits and by rational discussion. He deplores bigotry (which is not to say that he has no prejudices) and abhors violence.

It will be seen that two features of this culture — the disposition to postpone present satisfaction for the sake of improving matters in the future and the desire to "express one's personality" — are somewhat antagonistic. Upper-class (that is, future-oriented) culture permits the individual to emphasize either theme. If he thinks that his means (money, power, knowledge, and the like) are almost certainly adequate to maintain him and his "line" throughout the future he envisions, the future-oriented individual has no incentive to "invest" (that is, trade present for future satisfaction) and may therefore emphasize self-expression. If, on the other hand, he thinks that his means may *not* be adequate (he will think this, of course, no matter how large his means if his plans for the future are grand enough), he is likely to emphasize self-discipline so that he may acquire the larger stock of means that he thinks he needs. Insofar as he chooses the expressive alternative, the upper-class individual's style of life may resemble the present-oriented one of the lower class. But whereas the lower-class individual is capable *only* of present-oriented behavior, the upper-class one can choose. He may, for example, do some things that require a high degree of skill, discipline, and judgment, living the rest of the time from moment to moment. Even if he lives from moment to moment all the time, he does so by choice — it is his "thing," his mode of self-expression. By contrast, the "true" present-orientedness of the lower class is both unrelieved and involuntary.

The upper-class individual feels a strong attachment to entities (formal organizations, the neighborhood, the nation, the world) toward which he stands, or wants to stand, in a relation of fellowship. He sees the "community" (or "society") as having long-range goals and the ability to shape the future. He tends to feel that it is one's responsibility to "serve" the community by assisting in efforts for its improvement — perhaps because, his own goals being long-range ones, he has a stake in the future of the community. At any rate, he tends to be active in "public service" organizations and to feel a strong obligation (which he does not always act upon, of course) to contribute time, money, and effort to worthy causes.[14] (In the South the upper-class attitude in these matters is different. As W. J. Cash remarked, the aristocratic ideal of the planter became corrupted by frontier individualism, which, "while willing enough to ameliorate the specific instance, relentlessly laid down as its basic social postulate the doctrine that every man was completely and wholly responsible for himself."[15])

The Middle Class. The middle-class individual expects to be still in his prime at sixty or thereabouts; he plans ahead for his children and perhaps his grandchildren, but, less future-oriented than the ideal typical member of the upper class, he is not likely to think in terms of "line" or to be much concerned about "mankind" in the distant future. He, too, is confident of his ability to influence the future, but he does not expect to influence so distant a future as does the upper-class individual, nor is he as confident about the probable success of his efforts to influence it. The middle-class individual's self-feelings are a little less strong than those of the upper-class individual; he is also somewhat less desirous of privacy. Although he shows a good deal of independence and creativity and a certain taste for self-expression, these traits rarely lead to eccentricity. He is less likely than the upper-class individual to have means that he considers adequate to assure a satisfactory level of goal attainment throughout his anticipated future. Therefore, "getting ahead" — and the self-improvement and sacrifice of impulse gratification that it requires — will be more likely to take precedence with him over "the expression of one's personality." In the lower middle class, self-improvement is a principal theme of life, whereas in the upper middle class, self-expression is emphasized. Almost without exception, middle-class people want their children to go to college and to acquire the kind of formal training that will help them "get ahead." In matters of sex, the middle-class individual is (in principle, at least) "conventional," and in art and politics, too, he is more ready than the upper-class individual to accept the received opinion. He has regard for the rights of others; he deplores bigotry and abhors violence. He does not, however, hold these attitudes as strongly as do members of the upper class.

The middle-class individual does not feel as strong a sense of responsibility to the community as does the upper-class one, and he defines the community somewhat less inclusively. He wants (in principle, at least) to "belong" to a community and to be of "service" to it, and accordingly he joins organizations, including "service" ones. (In the lower middle class, the taste for public service and reform is relatively weak: the individual usually votes against public improvements that will not benefit him directly.) The middle-class individual, however, is less willing than the upper-class one to give time, money, and effort for public causes.

The Working Class. The working-class individual does not "invest" as heavily in the future, nor in so distant a future, as does the middle-class one.[16] He expects to be an "old man" by the time he is fifty, and his time horizon is fixed accordingly. Also, he has less confidence than the middle-class individual in his ability to shape the future and has a stronger sense of being at the mercy of fate, a "power structure," and other uncontrollable forces. For this reason, perhaps, he attaches more importance to luck than does the middle-class individual. He is self-respecting and self-confident, but these feelings are less marked in him than in the middle-class individual and they extend to a somewhat narrower range of matters. As compared to the middle-class individual, he is little disposed toward either self-improvement or self-expression; "getting ahead" and "enlarging one's horizon" have relatively little attraction for him. In rearing his children, he emphasizes the virtues of neatness and cleanliness, honesty, obedience, and respect for external authority. (As David Riesman has observed, the problem in the working class is not, as in the upper middle class, to stimulate children; rather, it is to control them — "to teach them faith, respect, and obedience, rather than independence of mind and development of talents."[17]) If his children do not go to college, the working-class individual does not mind much. In his relations with others, he is often authoritarian and intolerant, and sometimes aggressive. He is not only a bigot but a self-righteous one. Violence and brutality are less shocking to him than to middle-class persons; indeed, he regards them — up to a point — as normal expressions of a masculine style. To the working class, the middle class appears somewhat lacking in masculinity, and the upper class — a male member of which may even weep under stress — appears decidedly feminine or "queer."

The working-class individual's deepest attachment is to his family (most of his visiting is with relatives, not friends). However, his relationship to his wife and children is not as stable or as close — for instance, does not involve as much companionship — as these relationships tend to be in the middle class.[18] Privacy is of little importance to him: he likes to have people around, and the noises and smells that they make seldom bother him (when he goes on vacation it is not to the country, which he finds too quiet and lonely, but to crowded resorts). The sense of sharing a purpose with others is not as important to him as it is to members of the upper classes, and when he joins an organization it is more likely to be for companionship and "fun" than for "service" or civic improvement. He may vote, especially if someone asks him to as a favor. His opinions on public matters are highly conventional (it does not seem to occur to him that he is entitled to form opinions of his own), and his participation in politics is motivated not by political principles but by ethnic and party loyalties, the appeal of personalities, or the hope of favors from the precinct captain.

The Lower Class. At the present-oriented end of the scale, the lower-class individual lives from moment to moment. If he has any awareness of a future, it is of something fixed, fated, beyond his control: things happen *to* him, he does not *make* them happen. Impulse governs his behavior, either because he cannot discipline himself to sacrifice a present for a future satisfaction or because he has no sense of the future. He is therefore radically improvident: whatever he cannot consume immediately he considers valueless. His bodily needs (especially for sex) and his taste for "action"[19] take precedence over everything else — and certainly over any work routine. He works only as he must to stay alive, and drifts from one unskilled job to another, taking no interest in the work.

The lower-class individual has a feeble, attenuated sense of self; he suffers from feelings of self-contempt and inadequacy, and is often apathetic or dejected. (In her discussion of "very low-lower class" families, Eleanor Pavenstadt notes that "the saddest, and to us the outstanding characteristic of this group, with adults and children alike, was the self-devaluation."[20]) In his relations with others he is suspicious and hostile, aggressive yet dependent. He is unable to maintain a stable relationship with a mate; commonly he does not marry. He feels no attachment to community, neighbors, or friends (he has companions, not friends), resents all authority (for example, that of policemen, social workers, teachers, landlords, employers), and is apt to think that he has been "railroaded" and to want to "get even." He is a nonparticipant: he belongs to no voluntary organizations, has no political interests, and does not vote unless paid to do so.

The lower-class household is usually female-based. The woman who heads it is likely to have a succession of mates who contribute intermittently to its support but take little or no part in rearing the children. In managing the children, the mother (or aunt, or grandmother) is characteristically impulsive: once they have passed babyhood they are likely to be neglected or abused, and at best they never know what to expect next. A boy raised in a female-based household is likely at an early age to join a corner gang of other such boys and to learn from the gang the "tough" style of the lower-class man.[21]

The stress on "action," risk-taking, conquest, fighting, and "smartness" makes lower-class life extraordinarily violent. However, much of the violence is probably more an expression of mental illness than of class culture. The incidence of mental illness is greater in the lower class than in any of the others. Moreover, the nature of lower-class culture is such that much behavior that in another class would be considered bizarre seems routine.[22]

In its emphasis on "action" and its utter instability, lower-class culture seems to be more attractive to men than to women. Gans writes:

The woman tries to develop a stable routine in the midst of poverty and deprivation; the action-seeking man upsets it. In order to have any male relationships, however, the woman must participate to some extent in his episodic life style. On rare occasions, she may even pursue it herself. Even then, however, she will try to encourage her children to seek a routine way of life. Thus the woman is much closer to working class culture, at least in her aspirations, although she is not often successful in achieving them.[23]

In the chapters that follow, the term *normal* will be used to refer to class culture that is not lower class. The implication that lower-class culture is pathological seems fully warranted both because of the relatively high incidence of mental illness in the lower class and also because human nature seems loath to accept a style of life that is so radically present-oriented. This is not the main reason for using the word *normal,* however. Rather, it is that *some* word is needed to designate the sector of the class-cultural continuum that is not lower class, and no other word seems preferable on the whole.

From the beginning, the cities of the United States have had upper, middle, working, and lower classes. The relative strength of the various classes has varied greatly from time to time and place to place, although the nature of the class cultures has not. At the beginning of the nineteenth century, the free population of the United States was predominantly middle class. Most were descendants of English and American yeomen, artisans, and tradesmen, a stratum of society that had long had good opportunities to better its condition and had been confident of its ability to do so.[24] The native American inherited a culture that gave prominent place to the future-oriented virtues of self-discipline and denial, industry, thrift, and respect for law and order. He was sure that these virtues would be rewarded by success; he expected to "get on" and to "improve himself" in material and other ways. The Puritans had come to America with the intention of establishing ideal communities — "a city upon a hill" — and the millennial impulse, still powerful, took many forms in the first half of the nineteenth century. In the towns and cities, most early Americans, especially those of English origin, were skilled craftsmen or tradesmen. Of the few in New England who were day laborers, nearly all could read and write and nearly all voted.[25]

The number of working- and lower-class people was by no means insignificant, however, especially in the cities. In every sizable city there were transient laborers — and in the seaports, sailors, and in inland cities like Cincinnati and St. Louis, boatmen, wagoners, and drifters, who, like Huckleberry Finn's father, lived from hand to mouth, worked only when they had to, drank and fought prodigiously, felt no tie to the community, and left their women and children behind to fend for themselves or to be looked after at public expense once they had moved on.[26] In every city there also were unassimilated immigrants from countries — Catholic ones — whose cultures tended to be present- rather than future-oriented. It is safe to say, however, that transients and Catholic immigrants did not comprise the whole of the working- and lower-class population. In Boston, for example, which in 1817 had only about four hundred Catholics, the native American residents must have patronized the city's two thousand prostitutes (one for every six males above the age of sixteen), hundreds of liquor shops, and the gambling houses open night and day. It must also have been the native Bostonians who denied the mayor, Josiah Quincy, reelection after he waged a vigorous war on vice.[27]

Eventually, as immigration increased, the working and lower classes — especially the latter — did come to consist disproportionately of Catholic immigrants. In 1832, for example, the South Boston Almshouse held almost twice as many immigrants as natives. "To see anything like indigence or idleness," a visitor to New England from abroad wrote a few years later, "we must penetrate into the purlieus in the seaport towns, occupied by the Irish laboring population." The districts inhabited by the Irish and the Negroes formed, he said, "a painful contrast to the general air of cleanliness and comfort."[28]

After 1840 immigration increased rapidly, the immigrants coming mainly from peasant cultures — first Irish and then, after 1885, southern Italian and eastern European — that were more present-oriented than those of New England, Great Britain, and northern Europe. Coming from places where ordinary people had never had opportunities to rise by effort and enterprise, these immigrants tended to believe that the world was ruled by fate and that only a miracle or a great piece of luck could change their situation. The idea of self-improvement — and even more that of community improvement — was unfamiliar and perhaps even unintelligible to them. They were mainly concerned about survival, not progress; how to get food, drink, and shelter for the day was what preoccupied them. Their motive in coming to this country was apparently less to improve their general condition than to escape the threat of immediate starvation. "The emigrants of this year are not like those of former ones," the *Cork Examiner* noted during the peak of the Irish emigration, "they are now actually *running away* from fever and disease and hunger. . . ."[29]

Among the native Americans it was a rare day laborer who could not read, write, and cipher; among the peasant immigrants it was a rare one who could. The immigrants from present-oriented cultures were slow to see the advantages of education and of self-improvement generally. Even to some sympathetic observers it appeared that many of them would as soon live in hovels and shanties as not. Unlike the native Americans and the more future-oriented immigrants from England and northern Europe, the peasant immigrants seldom patronized the free mechanics libraries. Very few became skilled workers. In part, perhaps, this was because employers, most of whom were native, were prejudiced against them; in part also, however, it was probably because the present-oriented outlook and style did not suit the requirements of work and organization.

It was symptomatic of these different attitudes toward self-improvement and "getting on" that compulsory school attendance laws were adopted only after large-scale peasant immigration got under way. In Massachusetts, for example, the first such law was passed in 1852 and required all children between the ages of eight and fourteen to attend for twelve weeks each year. Until then it had been taken for granted that anyone able to go to school would not fail to do so.

The Jewish immigrants were very different from the peasant peoples. Like the native Americans, they were future-oriented. They believed, as had the Puritans, who were in many ways like them, that they were under a special obligation to assist in the realization of God's plan for the future. The idea of making sacrifices in the expectation of future rewards came naturally to them. Even more than the native American, the Jewish immigrant worked to acquire the capital (not only money and other material goods but also knowledge, skill, character, attachment to family and community, etc.) that would enable him to rise. Jacob A. Riis wrote:

> The poorest Hebrew knows — the poorer he is, the better he knows it — that knowledge is power, and power as the means of getting on in the world that has spurned him so long, is what his soul yearns for. He lets no opportunity slip to obtain it. Day- and night-schools are crowded with his children, who learn rapidly and with ease. Every synagogue, every second rear tenement or dark back-yard, has its school and its school master, with his scourge to intercept those who might otherwise escape.[30]

The future-oriented ideal diffused rapidly throughout the population. In the latter half of the nineteenth century the whole nation seemed suddenly seized with a passion for self-improvement: in every city and in thousands of towns and villages there were lyceum discussions, Chautauquas, evening lectures, and the like. Self-improvement implied community improvement, and the native American (originally Puritan) idea that it was everyone's obligation to do what he could to bring the millennial hope to fulfillment and to create "a city on a hill" became the generally accepted doctrine of "service." To immigrants like the Jews, whose native culture was future-oriented, these tendencies were highly congenial, but to others — notably the Irish — they were alien and distasteful. Eventually, however, all the immigrant groups succumbed to the native American, future-oriented ideal. Even Negroes, whose isolation as slaves and then as Southern farmhands might, one would think, have excluded them from the culture almost altogether, were drawn toward the ideal. Although they traveled at very different rates of speed, all ethnic and racial groups were headed in the same cultural direction: from less to more future-oriented.

Movement upward along the scale of class culture tended to follow increases in income and opportunity. Those people sacrificed the present for the future who had reason to think that doing so would be in some sense profitable, and the greater the prospective rewards, the more willing they were to accept the discipline and to put forth the effort required. People generally had good grounds for believing that the future-oriented virtues would pay off. To be sure, not many rose from rags to riches, as the mythology claimed, but it was very common for the son of an unskilled laborer to become a semiskilled or a skilled one and for *his* son to emerge as a manager, teacher, or professional.[31]

It is not clear, however, whether those who moved up the occupational, income, and status ladders did so because they had absorbed a more future-oriented culture. It is possible, for example, that Patrick Kennedy, who came to this country a laborer in 1848 and was still one when he died, was present-oriented and that it was because his son, Patrick Joseph, was somehow affected by the future-oriented atmosphere of Boston that he (the son) became a leading saloonkeeper and ward politician and — *mirabile dictu* — had the foresight to send *his* son, Joseph P., to the Boston Latin School and then to Harvard College. But it is also possible that the original Patrick was just as future-oriented as his son and that he remained a laborer all his life because the circumstances of his time and place made rising too difficult for him. It makes a great difference whether one supposes that (1) the American environment instilled in the immigrant a more future-oriented view; (2) it merely gave scope to those individuals whose view was such to begin with; or (3) it produced both effects.

From every ethnic group, including, of course, the native American, some individuals were born into the lower class and others dropped into it from above. The more present-oriented a group's culture was, the larger the proportion of its members who became lower class (similarly, the more future-oriented a group's culture, the higher the proportion who entered the upper classes). The Irish, for example, contributed heavily to the lower class as compared to the Jews. From 1885 to 1890, persons born in Ireland comprised 12.6 percent of the population but accounted for 60.4 percent of the almshouse, 36.7 percent of the workhouse, and 15.5 percent of prison inmates; Jews from Russia and Austria-Hungary were 3 percent of the population but accounted for none of the almshouse, 1 percent of the workhouse, and 1 percent of the prison inmates.[32] Very likely, the present-orientedness of the Irish and the future-orientedness of the Jews had important indirect effects as well. The Anglo-Saxon Protestant elite, for example, probably discriminated against people who showed little disposition to get ahead and in favor of those who showed much.

The lower the individual was on the cultural scale, the greater the obstacles in the way of his moving up occupationally or otherwise and the less his motivation to try. At the very bottom of the scale, the desire to rise was altogether lacking — and those in the lower class rarely if ever climbed out of it. Moreover, the obstacles in the way of rising — many of which were due to the distaste future-oriented people had for the manners and morals of the extremely present-oriented — were all but insuperable. Some families doubtless remained lower class for many generations, but most probably died out within two or three.

Each class culture implies — indeed, more or less requires — a certain sort of physical environment. It follows that a city (or district within a city) which suits one culture very well is likely to suit another very poorly or not at all.

To an upper-class individual, having a great deal of space at one's disposal is important both practically and symbolically. Being by oneself a good deal — and therefore having room enough for privacy — is essential to the development of a well-defined self; in the middle and upper classes, but not in the working class, it is thought essential that each child have a room of his or her own. The higher a family is on the class culture scale, the wider the expanse of lawn (or in the case of an apartment house, the thicker the walls) that it wants between it and the neighbors. Similarly, the higher the commuter is on the scale, the more important it is to him to ride to work in solitary splendor. For the lower-middle-class person a car pool will do — it is better than the bus; the upper-middle-class person, however, finds even that distasteful.

In the middle- and upper-class cultures, one's house and grounds afford opportunities for self-improvement and self-expression.[33] To the upper-class individual, it is the latter value that is usually more important: the house is the setting for and the representation of his family line ("house"). The middle-class individual is more likely to value his house for giving scope to his impulse to improve things — not only physical things (the house and grounds) but also, and especially, his own and his family's skills, habits, feelings, and attitudes. (The do-it-yourself movement is at least in part an expression of the middle-class taste for mastering skills and "expressing one's personality.") The middle-class individual — particularly the *lower*-middle-class one — also regards the house as a means of improving his social status; having a "good address" helps one rise in the world.

In the upper- and middle-class cultures, the neighborhood and community are as important as the house and are hardly to be separated from it. It is essential to live where there are good schools, for otherwise the children might not get into good colleges. Other community facilities — parks, libraries, museums, and the like — are highly valued, as are opportunities to be of "service" by participating in civic organizations. The middle- or upper-class individual wants to feel that his local government is honest, impartial, and efficient. At the upper end of the scale, especially, he wants a sense of "belonging" to a "community" — that is, of standing in a fellowship relation to his neighbors (even though he may never see them) and thus of constituting with them a moral entity — not unlike the Puritan congregation of visible saints in the seventeenth century. This desire to belong to a community partly accounts for the exclusiveness of the "better" neighborhoods and suburbs. The exclusion of all who are not parties to the covenant (in the language of Puritanism) is a precondition of fellowship: a community, after all, consists of people who feel a sense of oneness. Where the principle of exclusion appears to be — and perhaps is — racial or ethnic, the neighbors are likely to see that in the pursuit of one of their values they have infringed upon another. Those who feel most strongly the obligation to be of "service" and to act "responsibly" — upper-middle and upper-class Jews, especially — often resolve the conflict by sponsoring a strenuous community effort to bring a certain number of Negroes (or whatever group is being discriminated against) into the neighborhood.[34]

To the working class, a different set of values to accord with its life style governs the choice of physical arrangements in the city. Space is less important to the working-class family than to the middle- or upper-class one. It prefers being "comfy" to having privacy; it is thought natural for children to sleep two or three to a room or perhaps even to a bed. Having neighbors — even noisy ones — down the hall or in a house that is adjoining or almost adjoining is taken for granted. The working-class individual has few deep friendships with his neighbors, but he likes knowing who they are and he likes seeing — and even hearing — their goings-on. (It was because the Italian working-class residents of Boston's West End took this interest in one another that Herbert J. Gans called his account of them *The Urban Villagers*.) From the working-class point of view, middle- and upper-class neighborhoods are dull and lonely. Riding to work by oneself is no fun either; the working-class person prefers a car pool but does not mind a bus or subway.

When he must choose between more and better community facilities on the one hand and lower taxes on the other, the working-class individual usually chooses the latter. He will be satisfied if his children graduate from high school, and any school that is not a blackboard jungle will do. Parks and libraries matter to him even less than schools. He has no desire to participate in community improvement projects and no wish to feel himself part of a community, except perhaps an ethnic one. If his neighbors are a mixed lot, some being hardly sane and others less than respectable, that does not concern him: he is likely to take the attitude that so long as they do not interfere with him, they can do or be what they please.

To this last statement an important qualification must be attached. The working-class individual is likely to become ugly and aggressive if members of an ethnic or racial group that he dislikes begin to "take over" his neighborhood. He is more apt to be prejudiced than are members of the middle class and much less apt to conceal his prejudice. There is no talk in working-class neighborhoods about "responsibility for reducing racial tensions."

In some areas the movement of factories to the suburban ring has led to the building of residential suburbs that are working class. Physically, these look much like middle-class ones, but in style of life the two differ sharply. The working-class suburbanite's house is not a way station on the road to something better, as is often the case with the middle class. He is also less likely than is his middle-class counterpart to forego his favorite TV program in order to collect for the Heart Fund or "serve the community" in some other way.[35]

The lower-class individual lives in the slum and sees little or no reason to complain.[36] He does not care how dirty and dilapidated his housing is either inside or out, nor does he mind the inadequacy of such public facilities as schools, parks, and libraries: indeed, where such things exist he destroys them by acts of vandalism if he can. Features that make the slum repellent to others actually please him. He finds it satisfying in several ways. First, it is a place of excitement — "where the action is." Nothing happens there by plan and anything may happen by accident — a game, a fight, a tense confrontation with the police; feeling that something exciting is about to happen is highly congenial to people who live for the present and for whom the present is often empty. Second, it is a place of opportunity. Just as some districts of the city are special-

ized as a market for, say, jewelry or antiques, so the slum is specialized as one for vice and for illicit commodities generally. Dope
peddlers, prostitutes, and receivers of stolen goods are all readily
available there, within easy reach of each other and of their
customers and victims. For "hustlers" like Malcolm Little (later
Malcolm X) and the youthful Claude Brown, the slum is the natural
headquarters. Third, it is a place of concealment. A criminal is less
visible to the police in the slum than elsewhere, and the lower-class
individual, who in some parts of the city would attract attention, is
one among many there. In the slum one can beat one's children, lie
drunk in .the gutter, or go to jail without attracting any special
notice; these are things that most of the neighbors themselves have
done and that they consider quite normal.

Although it is the lower class that gives the slum its special
character, lower-class people are by no means the only ones who
live in it. Some blocks may be occupied only by the lower class, but
in the district as a whole, the majority of residents may well be
working-class and not a few middle-class. These are people whose
incomes do not correspond to their class culture; in some cases they
are the victims of bad luck — the death of a breadwinner, for
example — but more often they are in the slum because racial discrimination, past or present, has deprived them of normal opportunities for education and employment.

For these working- and middle-class slum dwellers, life in the
slum is a daily battle to preserve life, sanity and self-respect. They
must send their children to schools where little or nothing is taught
or learned and where the children are in constant physical and
moral danger; they must endure garbage-filled alleys and rat-
infested halls; if they shop in nearby stores, they must pay high
prices for poor selections of inferior goods (the prices are often high
only for them — for the lower class, which demands credit even
though its credit rating is very poor, the same prices may actually be
low); they must suffer the risk of annoyance and even of serious
hardship by being mistaken for members of the lower class by
policemen, teachers, landlords, and others, who either cannot dis-
cern or do not trouble to look for the clues to class differences
among the poor.

To the normal people who live in the slum, the worst feature of life there is fear. Many slum dwellers, Patricia Cayo Sexton writes, "live in a generalized state of fear — of being robbed, knifed, attacked, bullied, or having their children injured. This fear colors their whole lives: their ability to learn, to work, to stay sane and healthy, to venture out of their apartments or block, to live openly and freely, to be friends with their neighbors, to trust the world, outsiders, themselves."[37]

Within the limits set by the logic of growth, the mix of class cultures more than anything else determines the city's character and the nature of its problems. Almost everything about the city — population density, per capita income, the nature and quality of housing, the crime rate, the dropout rate, the level of public services, the tenor of race relations, the style of politics — depends in some way and to some extent upon the class composition of the population. When this changes, either in a neighborhood or in the city as a whole, almost everything else changes accordingly. And except as they are compatible with the realities of class culture in the city, the most carefully contrived efforts of public and private policymakers cannot succeed, for the mix of class cultures is a constraint as real as those of income, technology, or climate. It is necessary, therefore, to form the best estimate one can of the direction that change in the class system will take.

For at least a century there has been a general movement upward on the class scale from every class except possibly (a question that will be considered in Chapter 10) the lowest. A century ago the urban population was heavily working class; now it is heavily middle class. The process of "middle-class-ification," as Dollard called it, is undoubtedly continuing at an accelerating rate and will in a few decades have reduced the working class to a very small proportion of the whole population. The upper middle class has meanwhile been increasing rapidly in its relative strength, especially since the Second World War. Eventually, the distribution of population along the class scale may be decidedly bimodal, the largest concentration being in the upper middle class and the next largest (much smaller than the first) in the lower class.

No hard data bear on these predictions. Census data on education, income, and occupation cannot be made to yield more than very approximate measures of the size of classes as defined here.[38] There are, however, many indirect indicators that are to some extent relevant. One can see evidence of the process of "middle-class-ification" in changes that have occurred in the occupational structure (in 1900, 28 percent of the work force was in skilled occupations; in 1940, 43 percent; in 1964, 58 percent); in the decline of the saloon, the poolhall, and the brothel, and the rise of the family television set (the 1880 Census counted 517 brothels in Philadelphia, and Jane Addams complained at about the same time that in some wards of Chicago, there was one saloon to every twenty-eight voters);[39] in the ever-greater sensitivity of the public to brutality such as the beating of suspects by policemen — commonplace even half a century ago — and wife and child beating ("If screams resounded through a tenement-house it was taken for granted that the child deserved all it got and more"[40]); in growing concern for civil rights (not only of Negroes but also those of women, juveniles, and persons accused of crimes); in the tendency to widen the sphere of such rights (homosexuals and hippies now receive official protection in some cities as a matter of right); in increased public support for plans to eliminate inequalities of income and opportunity (the "war on poverty" is supposed to benefit not only the poor but the old, the young, the physically disabled, the "culturally deprived," and in general the "powerless"); in the decline of the political machine and the rise of a politics of principle and ideology (in the eyes of the New Left any politics that does not allow full self-expression by all is defective); and in the growth of a mass audience for serious literature, music, and art (readers, listeners, and viewers are counted now by the millions, whereas a generation or two ago they were counted by the thousands).

The mass movement from the working into the middle class and from the lower middle into the upper middle class accounts as much as anything for the general elevation of standards that, as was contended in Chapter 1, makes most urban problems appear to be getting worse even when, *measured by a fixed standard,* they are getting better. The new standards are those of a higher class. It is because the process of "middle-class-ification" has given great numbers of people higher perspectives and standards that dissatisfaction with the city is so widespread. The city that was thought pleasant when most people were working class is thought repellent now that most are middle class, and it will be thought abhorrent when, before long, most are upper middle class.

The ascendancy of the middle and upper middle classes has increased feelings of guilt at "social failures" (that is, discrepancies between actual performance and what by the rising class standards is deemed adequate) and given rise to public rhetoric about "accepting responsibility" for ills that in some cases could not have been prevented and cannot be cured. The dropout, for example, in turning his back on education "is telling us that we never really connected with him, that in our preoccupation with others we never gave him enough time or attention."[41] This is typical. In the upper-middle-class view it is always society that is to blame. Society, according to this view, could solve all problems if it only tried hard enough; that a problem continues to exist is therefore proof positive of its guilt.

In this tendency to find society responsible for all ills, including those that are a function of rising standards, two dangers appear. One is that the allegation of social guilt may lead the individual to believe that he can do nothing to help himself. The dropout, for example, may feel himself excused from all effort once it has been established that he was never given enough time or attention, just as the juvenile delinquent may excuse himself when it has been established that he is the product of wrong social conditions. The other danger is that many people will take the talk of social guilt seriously and conclude that the society is one for which they can have no respect and in which they can place no trust. Such condemnation is mainly to be expected in those sections of society — the upper classes, especially their youth — that are most alive to moral issues, and in those other sectors — notably the poor and the minority groups — that have obvious grounds for thinking themselves victims of social injustice. To the rhetoricians, the guilty society will be "not worth saving." To those who have known all along that it is society's fault that they are at the bottom of the heap, the case will be that much clearer and their righteous anger that much hotter.[42]

CHAPTER FOUR

Race: Thinking May Make It So

. . . Being from America made me intensely sensitive to matters of color. I saw that people who looked alike drew together and most of the time stayed together. This was entirely voluntary; there being no other reason for it. But Africans were with Africans. Pakistanis were with Pakistanis. And so on. I tucked it into my mind that when I returned home I would tell Americans this observation; that where true brotherhood existed among all colors, where no one felt segregated, where there was no "superiority" complex, no "inferiority" complex — then voluntarily, naturally, people of the same kind felt drawn together by that which they had in common.

— Malcolm X

THE most conspicuous fact of life in the city is racial division. A hundred times a day there are confrontations between black and white, and almost every day an explosion turns part of some city into a battleground. The residential suburbs are mostly white — often "lily-white"; the central cities, especially their older, more deteriorated parts, and above all their slums, are predominantly or entirely black. Many observers see little reason to hope for improvement. The city, they say, has always exploited, humiliated, and degraded its immigrant groups. But whereas all the others eventually have been able to escape their oppressors by joining them, the Negro, marked as he is by skin color, can never do so. For him, in this view, the city is degradation without hope. "The dark ghettoes," writes Kenneth B. Clark, "are social, political, educational, and — above all — economic colonies. Their inhabitants are subject peoples, victims of the greed, cruelty, insensitivity, guilt, and fear of their masters."[1]

The view to be developed here is altogether different from this one. The existence of ethnic and racial prejudice both past and present is a fact too painfully evident to require assertion. Being subject to prejudice, however, it is clear in retrospect, was not the main disadvantage of the Irish, Jews, Italians, and others. Nor is it the *main* one of the Negro — not to mention the Puerto Rican and the Mexican — today. The other minority groups once lived in the oldest parts of the inner city — and the Negro lives in them now — not so much because they were looked down on (although, of course, they *were*) as because they had low incomes. It was because they were *poor* that they had to come to the city, and being poor they could not afford good housing on the outskirts of the city or in the suburbs, nor could they afford to commute to the factories, stores, and offices where they worked. Similarly, the neighborhoods in which the other groups lived were often squalid and vicious — as the Negro slum is now — not because they were subject people, victimized and degraded by the city (although there was an element of that, too), but because every wave of immigration brought many whose culture was lower-class.

Today the Negro's *main* disadvantage is the same as the Puerto Rican's and Mexican's: namely, that he is the most recent unskilled, and hence relatively low-income, migrant to reach the city from a backward rural area. The city is not the end of his journey but the start of it. He came to it not because he was lured by a cruel and greedy master but because he was attracted by job, housing, school, and other opportunities that, bad as they were, were nevertheless better by far than any he had known before. Like earlier immigrants, the Negro has reason to expect that his children will have increases of opportunity even greater than his. If he lives in a neighborhood that is all-black, the reason is not white prejudice simply, and in some instances it may not be that at all. This physical separation may arise from various causes — his having a low income, his being part of a wave of migration that inundated all of the cheap housing then available (had more been available, more migrants might well have come to take it), his having cultural characteristics that make him an undesirable neighbor, his inclination to live among his own kind. The example of Orientals, groups whose mean income and education are now higher than those of the white Protestant and possibly of the Jew, proves that acceptance and upward mobility need not depend upon the absence of distinguishing physical characteristics.

The misfortune, amounting to a tragedy, is not that Negroes got to the city but that they got there so late and then in such great numbers in so short a time. It is likely that had they moved to the city in large numbers in the decades between the Civil War and the First World War, most Negroes would long since have entered the middle class. Those who *did* come north in this period did enter it soon: Philadelphia and Cleveland, for example, had predominantly middle-class Negro communities before the turn of the century. Unfortunately, however, mob violence against them in the cities and job discrimination in favor of European immigrants kept most away. There would doubtless be slums in the central cities today even if there had been a large-scale movement of Negroes three or four generations ago, but the slums would not be all-black and they would not be surrounded by all-white suburbs. Therefore, one very serious danger — that of economic and class-cultural problems being mistaken for racial ones — would not exist.

Almost everything said about the problems of the Negro tends to exaggerate the purely racial aspects of the situation. (The same is true of what is said of the Puerto Rican, the Mexican, and other groups, but discussion here will be limited to the Negro.) "Purely racial" factors mean, first, prejudice on racial grounds (not only prejudice against but also prejudice *for* — that is, racial pride) and, second, whatever cultural characteristics pertain to a racial group *qua* racial group. The importance of these factors is exaggerated implicitly by any statement about the Negro that fails — as almost all do — to take account of the many other (nonracial or contingently racial) factors that are at work along with the purely racial ones. These nonracial factors include, especially, income, class, education, and place of origin (rural or urban, Southern or not). No doubt the effect of these factors on the Negro has been increased by the operation of racial ones in the background: for example, the lack of education that in large measure accounts for the Negro's handicaps is itself to be explained largely by racial discrimination past and present. (On the other hand, there are groups — rural Southern whites, for example — whose handicaps are much like the Negro's and must be explained entirely by nonracial factors.) In any case, there is no *a priori* reason to assume (as is too often done) that the causes operating in the *evolution* of a problem over time ("historical" causes) must be identical with those operating to *perpetuate* that problem at any given time ("continuing" causes). The concern here is with the continuing causes of the Negro's problems, which, it will be argued, are seldom purely racial and very often have little or nothing to do with race. In short, what will here be called the Statistical Negro — that is, the Negro when all non-racial factors have been controlled for — is a very different fellow from what will be called the Census Negro.[2] In some respects the Statistical Negro is indistinguishable from the white, and in all respects the differences between him and the white are smaller than those between the Census Negro and the white.

For example, the Census Negro has a birthrate about one-third higher than does the white. If, however, women who have lived on Southern farms are left out of account, the Negro birthrate does not differ significantly from that of the white. If, in addition, women with less than a high school education are omitted, the Negro rate is actually a little lower than the white.[3]

The school dropout rate among Census Negro adolescents is almost twice that among whites. But when the occupation of parents is controlled for, this difference is much reduced, and with children of white-collar parents it almost disappears.[4]

At all educational levels the Census Negro earns less than the white. On the average, however, he has achieved less well in school (in the schools of the Northeast he is 3.3 years behind the white in achievement by grade 12;[5] moreover, many Negroes attend schools having a "social promotion" policy by which children are promoted whether they have learned anything or not). It is likely that if differences in the educational achievement of graduates were fully taken into account, racial prejudice would be found to have much less significance for earnings differences than otherwise appears; indeed, it may be that the Statistical Negro graduate earns fully as much as the white.

Unemployment rates are persistently higher for Census Negroes than for whites. About half the differential in rates is to be accounted for by differences between the two groups in their distribution by occupation, education, age, and region, however. These differences are largely the result of historical discrimination, of course, but the fact is that *present* discrimination by employers on the basis of color accounts for much less unemployment than the gross figures would suggest.[6] One important factor behind unemployment differentials is place of residence: boys and girls who live in districts where there is a relative surplus of unskilled workers are at a manifest disadvantage whatever their color. Occupation and income of parents is another: boys and girls whose parents own businesses or "know people" have an advantage in finding jobs. Class culture is still another factor: lower-class youths are less likely than others to look for jobs, and the lower their class culture the less acceptable they are to employers. Even after correcting for everything possible, something is left that must be explained on racial grounds, especially job discrimination. Still, considering all these other factors, white prejudice and any specifically Negro characteristics account for much less of the difference in employment rates than would otherwise appear.

The income of the Census Negro is low as compared to that of the white. However, when one controls for region of origin, rural or urban origin, and education, the difference is greatly reduced. Much of what looks like "racial" poverty is really "rural Southern" poverty.[7]

The Census Negro spends as much as a third more for housing than do whites at a given income level but "it is far from clear that the residential segregation does in fact lead to higher housing prices for equivalent quality for Negroes."[8] Studies made in Chicago show that when differences in income, occupation, location, and some other variables are taken into account, the Negro's housing costs are not very different from the white's. In Chicago, at least, the Statistical Negro pays about the same rent and lives at about the same density as the white.[9]

The proportion of Negro children in households without a father present is very high. Whether it is higher than among whites of the same income, education, rural-urban origin, and class culture is not clear, however. An investigation conducted just before the First World War in the then predominantly Irish Middle West Side of New York found that about half the families there were father-less.[10]

Sexual promiscuity in the Negro slum is notorious. This is largely if not wholly a class characteristic, however. In another report on the predominantly Irish Middle West Side of half a century ago, mention is made of "the hopelessly unmoral attitude of the neighborhood," where "boys as young as seven and eight actually practice sodomy."[11]

Negro youths in the slums are prone to violence, but here again it is unlikely that any racial factor is at work. *All* lower-class youths are prone to violence. Charles Loring Brace, a social worker of the 1880's, remarked that the youth gangs then plaguing New York consisted mainly of the American-born children of Irish and German immigrants. He went on to say:

> The intensity of the American temperament is felt in every fibre of these children of poverty and vice. Their crimes have the unrestrained and sanguinary character of a race accustomed to overcome all obstacles. . . . The murder of an unoffending old man . . . is nothing to them. They are ready for any offense or crime, however degraded or bloody.[12]

The arrest rate of the Census Negro is undoubtedly higher than that of the Statistical Negro. According to economist Belton Fleisher, it is being of low income, not being black, that is most important in disposing one toward the kinds of crimes that juveniles commit.[13] Probably the same is true for most other kinds of crimes as well. Most crimes are committed by lower-income and lower-class people, and many Negroes fall into these categories. Also, Southerners as such are more given to violence than are other Americans, and the proportion of Negroes who are of Southern origin is of course high.

The argument here is not that purely racial factors are of little or no importance. It is all too obvious that racial prejudice enters into every sphere of life. Cultural differences (apart from *class*-cultural differences) — and conceivably even biological ones as well — also account in some degree for the special position of the Negro, as they do for that of every ethnic group. If there is something about Jewish culture that makes the Jew tend to be upwardly mobile, there may be something about Negro culture that makes the Negro tend not to be. Strangely (considering the great number of sociologists and social anthropologists produced by American universities in the last two or three decades and considering the importance of the problem), very little is known about the personality and culture of the Negro or of other racial and ethnic groups in the city.[14] Eventually, systematic study may reveal deep cultural differences among ethnic groups. It is very unlikely, however, that any differences in racial (or ethnic) culture will have as much explanatory importance for the matters under discussion here as do differences in income, education, place of origin, and — above all — class culture.

One way to estimate the importance of racial prejudice in the city is to ask how matters would change if overnight all Negroes turned white (or, if it be preferred, all whites black), thus making job and housing discrimination on color grounds impossible. If this were to happen, the Negro would in some ways be better off. But it is easy to overestimate the speed with which improvements in his situation would occur as well as the number of people who would be benefited in the short run.

If, overnight, Negroes turned white, most of them would go on living under much the same handicaps for a long time to come. The great majority of New Whites would continue working at the same jobs, living in the same neighborhoods, and sending their children to the same schools.

There would be no sudden mass exodus from the blighted and slum neighborhoods where most Negroes now live. By and large, New Whites would go on living in the same neighborhoods for the simple reason that they could not afford to move to better ones. Most of them would still be near the bottom of the income scale and would therefore buy or rent the cheapest housing on the market, which is to say the oldest, most run-down housing in the highest-density districts of the inner city. After a few years many would be living on the same blocks with Old Whites of the same (low) income level as themselves, but this change would be of slight importance, since the neighborhoods would be about as poor as before. In the very worst sections, New Whites would be an overwhelming majority for a long time to come, the reason being that Negroes constitute most of the poorest of the poor. Stores, schools, churches, and other community institutions and facilities there would still be segregated. For example, New White children would go to school only with New White children, and the slum school would remain a slum school. Negro incomes are growing as fast as white, but while Negroes are increasingly well-off *absolutely,* the gap remains nearly constant in *relative* terms.

With the end of racial discrimination, some New Whites would quickly climb the job and income ladder and then leave the slums and the blighted areas. Unfortunately, however, these would be few in number; the end of racial discrimination would not improve the job situation of most New Whites in the first generation at least. They would earn as little as before because they would still be unskilled. As for the well-trained, many would gain by the end of prejudice, but many would lose by it too. At present, most Negro professionals and politicians (the latter meaning all who act in representative capacities *qua* Negroes) have an advantage in not having to compete with whites; of the middle-class Negroes who do compete with whites, some receive a premium for being black. By putting them into competition with Old Whites, the end of racial discrimination would, in the short run at least, hurt perhaps as many New Whites as it would help.

It may be objected that in the absence of racial discrimination the Negro would soon become as well educated as the white and would then move into what are now "white" occupations. Although this would happen to some extent, there would not, unfortunately, be enough such movement to change the situation fundamentally. The reason is that while the New Whites were raising their educational level, the Old Whites would also be raising *theirs;* since the Old Whites would have a big head start, the gap between them and the New Whites would only widen if both groups made the same percentage increases in their rates of progress. The disparity between white and nonwhite levels of educational attainment, Otis Dudley Duncan calculates, "can hardly disappear in less than three-quarters of a century."[15]

How painfully slow any improvement in the occupational position of the Negro relative to that of the white is likely to be may be judged from the experience of the past few decades. In the 1940's the relative occupational position of Negro males improved by 5 percent on an index representing the main occupational categories, and in the next decade there was a further improvement of 1 percent. The total improvement, however, erased only about one-fifth of the gross difference that existed to begin with.[16] Of course, racial discrimination was widespread in the 1940's and 1950's, but there was less of it than there had been before. After twenty years the relative (but not the absolute) disadvantage of the Negro was almost unchanged. Special programs that will greatly change this prospect may perhaps be devised, although no very promising ones have appeared as yet.

One circumstance that would tend to hold the New White back is the size of his family. There were 60 percent more youths dependent on their parents among poor Negroes than among poor whites living in central cities in 1966; this situation was a consequence of the age distribution and birthrate of the Negro population and would not be affected by the end of prejudice and discrimination. Having more dependents and a lower income, the New White's disadvantage would still be compounded: that is, the amount of capital *per child* that he could invest in education and training would be much less than that available to the Old White.[17]

Finally, it must be said that many New Whites would suffer indignities and humiliations not so different from those to which the Negro now is subject. The treatment that the lower-class white receives is in many ways like that of the victim of racial prejudice — and a larger proportion of New Whites would be lower class. In one respect their new (class) status might be harder to bear than their former (racial) one; for the victim of race prejudice can take some comfort, however small, in the knowledge that he is being treated unjustly.

Much of what appears (especially to Negroes) as race prejudice is really *class* prejudice or, at any rate, class antipathy. Similarly, much of what appears (especially to whites) as "Negro" behavior is really lower-class behavior. The lower class is relatively large among Negroes; it appears even larger than it is to those whites who fail to distinguish a Negro who exhibits outward signs — lack of skill, low income, slum housing, and so on — which in a white would mark him as lower class, from one whose culture is working, middle, or even upper class but whose opportunities have been limited by discrimination and whose income is low.

How much outward resemblance there is between class antipathy and racial prejudice may be seen from sociologists' accounts of the treatment often accorded to the white lower class. A. B. Hollingshead, for example, describes in *Elmtown's Youth* the social structure of a "typical" Midwestern county seat, the population of which in 1940 was white (there was only one Negro family) and consisted mostly of native-born Protestants, many descended from "old American stock." In this all-American community, nearly a quarter of the population had the status of pariahs. Class V (lower-class) families "are excluded from the two leading residential areas. . . . Employers do not like to hire them unless labor is scarce or they can be induced to work for low wages. . . . Class V persons are almost totally isolated from organized community activities. . . . They knew that their children were discriminated against in the school system by both the teachers and the pupils. . . . The Class V's get the bad jobs, such as helping in the junk yards and hauling garbage and ashes. . . . Class V persons give the impression of being resigned to a life of frustration and defeat in a community that despises them for their disregard of morals, lack of 'success' goals, and dire poverty."[18]

Hollingshead summarizes the community's view of the lower class — "the scum of the city" — as follows:

They have no respect for the law, or themselves.

They enjoy their shacks and huts along the river or across the tracks and love their dirty, smoky, low-class dives and taverns.

Whole families — children, in-laws, mistresses, and all — live in one shack.

This is the crime class that produces the delinquency and sexual promiscuity that fills the paper.

Their interests lie in sex and its perversion. The girls are always pregnant; the families are huge; incestual relations occur frequently.

They are not inspired by education, and only a few are able to make any attainments along this line.

They are loud in their speech, vulgar in their actions, sloppy in their dress, and indifferent toward their plight. Their vocabulary develops as profanity is learned.

If they work, they work at very menial jobs.

Their life experiences are purely physical, and even these are on a low plane.

They have no interest in health and medical care.

The men are too lazy to work or do odd jobs around town.

They support the Democratic party because of the relief obtained during the depression.

This group lives for a Saturday of drinking or fighting. . . .[19]

The community's view of the lower class is not, apparently, based entirely on prejudice. Class V parents, Hollingshead says, are "indifferent to the future":

They will leave a job casually, often without notice . . . . 8 percent of the mothers and 46 percent of the fathers had been convicted once or more in the local courts. . . . Serial monogamy is the rule. . . . one-fifth to one-fourth of all births are illegitimate. . . . The mean [number of children] is 5.6 per mother. . . . Disagreements leading to quarrels and vicious fights, followed by desertion by either the man or the woman, possibly divorce, is not unusual. . . . The burden of child care, as well as support, falls on the mother more often than on the father when the family is broken. . . . Before the sixteenth birthday is reached . . . 75 percent of the class V's have left school. . . .[20]

If something like one-quarter of the population of a typical Midwestern town is (more or less correctly) perceived in this way, it should not be surprising that a sizable part of the population of a large city is perceived (also more or less correctly) in the same way. Racial and ethnic prejudice obviously do not account for the low status of so many Elmtown people. Why, then, should the same attitudes be attributed to racial prejudice when the Class V's are

Negroes (or Puerto Ricans or Mexicans or whatever) rather than white, Protestant, native-born Americans?

Obviously, racial prejudice is manifested when, as often happens, the Negro is automatically regarded as lower-class simply on the basis of his skin color or when he is treated as if he were lower-class even though it is clear that he is not. But to treat the lower-class Negro exactly like the lower-class white is not, on the face of it, to show racial prejudice.

Although, in principle, it is easy to distinguish racial prejudice from class prejudice as well as prejudice ("an irrational attitude of hostility on the basis of supposed characteristics," according to the dictionary) from justifiable antipathy (a rational attitude of hostility on the basis of objective characteristics), doing so in practice would usually require a wisdom greater than Solomon's. Concretely, racial and class prejudice are usually inextricably mixed, and so are prejudice and justifiable antipathy. Consider the following:

A Negro drifter not long ago was arrested for breaking into a liquor store and swiping a bottle. He smashed the neck, took a swig and was caught with the goods, so to speak inside him. Two policemen carted him off to the station house for booking. He was a moderately difficult prisoner, swaying around as they tried to fingerprint him. But he had joshed them into a good mood and all three were making something of a joke about the fingerprinting. The Negro then shoved a bit, saying "C'mon you m_____r f_____ers." The cops immediately turned upon him and beat him up. The word he had used is not a word to which lower-middle-class Irishmen or Italians take kindly — even in jest, and especially from a Negro (although that particular epithet is a commonplace of lower-class Negro speech).[21]

In a case like this, it is impossible to say what part was played by "racial prejudice." Negroes may be convinced that the drifter would not have been beaten if he had been white. On the other hand, readers of *Elmtown's Youth* may well conclude that a white, Protestant, "old-stock American" of Class V would have gotten exactly the same treatment.

Obstacles of many kinds, some insuperable, are placed in the way of Negroes who want to move into white neighborhoods. This fact, however, does not adequately explain the existence of neighborhoods that are wholly or almost wholly black. In many inner-city areas Negroes now constitute the main body of low-skilled, low-paid labor; this in itself would account for their being the main body of residents in the poorer parts of the city. No doubt, also, many Negroes *prefer* black neighborhoods and would live in them even if their opportunities to live in white ones were excellent (which, to repeat, they generally are not). A careful poll of Negro opinion in a sample of non-Southern metropolitan areas and in New York, Chicago, Atlanta, and Birmingham revealed in late 1964 that hardly any Negroes wanted to live in neighborhoods that were mostly white.[22] The detailed findings are presented in the table.

TYPE OF NEIGHBORHOOD NEGROES PREFER*
(in percent)

Neighborhood	Metro	N.Y.	Chic.	Atl.	Birm.	Total
Mostly Negro	55	52	68	74	69	62
Mixed or no difference	38	35	25	18	27	31
Mostly white	4	9	5	5	1	4
Don't know	3	3	4	2	3	3
Total	100	100	100	100	100	100

Source: Gary T. Marx, *Protest and Prejudice*, p. 176.
* If all equally well kept up.

The practice of calling all Negro neighborhoods "segregated" and "ghettoes" misrepresents the situation seriously and perhaps dangerously. In the technical language of many sociologists, a Negro neighborhood would be called segregated even if every family in it had recently turned down an excellent opportunity to live among whites; it is "unevenness in the distribution of white and Negro households" within a neighborhood, whatever the motive or cause of the unevenness, that constitutes segregation for the sociologist.[23] The lay reader, unaware that the word is used in a Pickwickian sense, supposes that the "ghetto" studied by such sociologists and described in the newspapers must be the result of white prejudice. That it *may* be, partly or wholly, the result of circumstances (namely, that large numbers of unskilled Negro workers came all at once to the inner city and occupied all the low-cost housing then available) or of the Negroes' own preference is not likely to occur to him. Negroes, hearing incessantly that they are "segregated" and that they live in "ghettoes," are given additional grounds for supposing that they are in all cases "forced" to do what they would sometimes — perhaps often — do of their own accord as a matter of course. One can only conjecture, but it seems plausible that the universal practice of using "ghetto" and "segregated" in reference to any all-Negro neighborhood tends to condition Negroes to the idea — which is usually a half-truth at most — that white prejudice "forces" them to live in poor housing and among other Negroes. If this is so, the semantic confusion goes a long way toward making bad matters worse.[24]

One of the few studies to shed light on *why* Negroes live apart from whites was published in 1964 by a team of researchers from Brandeis University.[25] They made the study for the Boston Urban Renewal Administration, which wanted to know how many of the families in the Washington Park neighborhood — a middle-income "ghetto" — were likely to remain there if the neighborhood was rehabilitated. When interviewers first talked to the families, they assumed that most of them would want to move to predominantly white neighborhoods. There was nothing to stop them from doing so. The renewal agency had given them lists of housing that they might rent or purchase in white neighborhoods at prices they could afford. Moreover, most of them were very dissatisfied where they were; they strongly criticized the neighborhood schools and they complained also of inadequate shopping facilities, insufficient police protection, and noise and disorder in the streets. Since they could easily leave the "ghetto," it was reasonable to expect them to do so.

In fact, only thirty-three of the families (13 percent) did leave, and of these only nine left the Negro community. A large majority of the families did not even look at the housing listed as available. Some did not look at it because they were sure that they would be turned down on one pretext or another if they decided that they wanted it, but most were just not interested. (Incidentally, the few who inspected the listed housing encountered no prejudice.)

The main reason why the Washington Park people did not move, the researchers finally concluded, was that they had good housing at bargain prices where they were. They were paying a median rent of $85 per month, which was only 12 percent of their income. The carrying charges on a house in the suburbs would be between $125 and $150. Most of the families could afford this much — two-thirds of them had incomes of over $7,800 — but they preferred to use their money for other things. As the researchers put it, "One might describe them as having been 'spoiled' by their current low costs of housing."[26] In this respect the Negroes were just like the Italians in the West End of Boston whom Gans had studied a few years before. "People were so used to paying low rents," Gans found, "that their whole mode of life was adjusted to them. Any apartment that rented for more than $50 for five or six rooms was thought to be outrageously expensive."[27]

Another reason why most of the Washington Park people chose not to move was that they wanted to be near friends and relatives. This motive, too, may have had little or nothing to do with race: Gans's Italians also liked being near friends and neighbors — that was why he called them "urban villagers." In every large city ethnic groups of the second, third, fourth, and even later generations — Irish, German, Scandinavian, Polish, Jewish, and Italian, among others — lived in self-imposed isolation and sent their children to schools that were to a high degree ethnically homogeneous.

In the case of the Negro, as in that of other ethnic groups, prejudice is not the *only* force creating spatial separation. To some extent separation is also imposed by the group upon itself in order to maintain its identity and its distinctive conception of life. As Ralph Ellison has written:

. . . it is a misunderstanding to assume that Negroes want to break out of Harlem. They want to transform the Harlems of their country. These places are precious to them. These places are where they have dreamed, where they have lived, where they have loved, where they have worked out life as they could. . . . it isn't the desire to run to the suburbs or to invade "white" neighborhoods that is the main concern with my people in Harlem. They would just like to have a more human life there. A slum like Harlem isn't just a place of decay. It is also a form of historical and social memory.[28]

Even if more "segregation" is voluntary than most people realize, the fact remains that a great deal is *not* voluntary. There are many neighborhoods into which it is all but impossible for a black family to move and many more in which blacks are, to put it mildly, unwelcome. By no means all of this hostility represents *racial* prejudice, however. Some of it is simply snobbery (it is safe to say that, if the Washington Park Negroes had been blue-collar rather than white-collar, the white neighborhoods would have been less open to them), and some of it is the more or less justifiable distaste and fear that working- and middle-class people feel toward lower-class ones. (If a Negro is assumed to be lower-class simply because he is black and not because of anything he does, that, of course, is prejudice pure and simple.) This distaste and fear is probably as common among Negroes as among whites: the lower-class Negro is usually as unwelcome in or near a middle-class Negro neighborhood as in or near a middle-class white one. Still, even when these motives are added to voluntary "segregation," there is no doubt that much segregation based on race prejudice remains.

As the Washington Park case shows, it is not the absence of white faces that makes the "ghetto" objectionable to the Negro. Rather, it is the feeling that he is not perfectly free to live wherever he pleases and, also, the inadequacy of the stores, schools, playgrounds, and other facilities of his neihgborhood. Once it is established, as in Washington Park, that he can live in a white neighborhood if he wishes, and once the facilities of the neighborhood are brought up to a standard of adequacy, the Negro very often prefers to live among other Negroes.

Like everyone else, too, he prefers to live among people whose class culture is not very different from his own. The main trouble with the "ghetto" (when it is without walls) is that so many of its residents are lower or lower-working-class. This is perhaps the principal reason why its stores carry low-quality goods at high prices, why its alleys are strewn with garbage, why there are rats in the cellars, why the school is a blackboard jungle, why the streets are noisy and disorderly, why police protection is poor, and all the rest.

The middle- and upper-working-class Negro, then, if he is to be anywhere near his friends and relatives and in a community to which he feels he "belongs," must live among people whose style of life he finds repugnant. His situation differs fundamentally from that of, say, the Italian described by Gans in that the Italian belongs to a group that is predominantly working and lower-middle-class. The middle-class Italian can live in comfort and without annoyance or embarrassment in the midst of an all-Italian neighborhood because the lower class is now too small to be noticeable. By contrast, the middle-class Negro who lives in an all-Negro district can rarely avoid contact with the slum. The choice open to him is painful: he may move to a white neighborhood, paying more for housing than he is used to, cutting himself off from relatives and friends, and risking insult and even injury from prejudiced neighbors; or he may suffer the inconveniences, annoyances, and hazards of living in or near a slum.

This problem does not exist for the lower-class Negro, who usually feels very much at home in the slum, or for the upper-class one, who can insulate himself from it by living in an expensive apartment house, working and shopping downtown, and sending his children to private schools. The problem is acute, however, for middle- and upper-working-class people whose incomes and work routines do not permit much insulation, and who are often distressed at the possibility of slipping — psychologically if not physically — into a state from which they have only recently managed to emerge. This thought, one suspects, is what lies behind Kenneth B. Clark's call for a struggle "to prevent decadence from winning over the remaining islands of middle class society."[29] His rhetoric has to do entirely with the hatefulness, callousness, and brutality of whites, but what he seems to mean by "decadence" is lower-class culture. The "dark ghetto" is, in the last analysis, really the lower-class one.

The movement of the Negro up the class scale appears as inexorable as that of all other groups. The number of middle- and upper-class Negroes is in many areas already large enough to allow the formation of predominantly middle- and upper-class neighborhoods and suburbs — places large enough to support stores, churches, restaurants, and local public services of the sort that middle- and upper-class people desire. Between 1959 and 1967, the number of Negro families in metropolitan areas with incomes of $10,000 or more per year increased from 187,000 to 601,000. This suggests that the time is at hand when the Negro to whom the slum is intolerable will be able to leave it *without at the same time having to leave the society of other Negroes.*

Urban renewal, if extensive, will hasten the formation of Negro upper- and middle-class neighborhoods in two ways: first, by forcibly dislodging the lower class from neighborhoods that are chosen for rehabilitation or conservation, and second, by subsidizing the middle- and upper-working-class people who remain and by assuring them that the powers of government will be used to bring their neighborhood up to a middle-class standard and to keep it there. Both of these things happened in the Washington Park neighborhood. One resident told a member of the Brandeis research team:

> For the first two years . . . we were dissatisfied and looked forward to moving. We were particularly concerned because of the behavior of our Negro neighbors. Liquor bottles were thrown in the yard, there were fights every night in the apartments across the street and girls were raped in the neighborhood. It was not safe. But the last two years we have thought less about moving. . . . There has been an improvement in the neighborhood. Most of the low-class Negroes have moved to Dorchester; those remaining seem to have more pride in the neighborhood. We don't find liquor bottles in our yard anymore. A housing project for the elderly has been built nearby. As a result the neighborhood has been up-graded.[30]

The "upgrading" of some neighborhoods will often mean the "downgrading" of others. As more and more Negroes withdraw into middle- and upper-class communities, the concentration of the lower class in the slum will necessarily increase. Very probably the "worsening" of the slum will be seen not as a consequence of the improved position of Negroes generally, but rather as further evidence of callousness and neglect by the "white power structure." "We have absentee leadership, absentee ministers, absentee merchants," a resident of Watts complained after the riot there.[31] Apparently, he thought that this was a problem that someone — presumably the government — should do something to solve. The increasing isolation of the lower class is a problem, to be sure, but it is hard to see what can be done about it. The upper classes will continue to want to separate themselves physically from the lower, and in a free country they probably cannot be prevented from doing so.

"Whatever their origin," writes sociologist Urie Bronfenbrenner, "the most immediate, overwhelming, and stubborn obstacles to achieving quality and equality in education now lie as much in the character and way of life of the American Negro as in the indifference and hostility of the white community."[32] This observation also is true of areas other than education. Prejudice against the Negro has declined sharply since the Second World War, while his other handicaps have grown. It is not likely, however, that the Negro man-on-the-street will fully recognize the changes that have occurred; he still has the lowest-paid and most menial jobs, he still lives in the worst neighborhoods, and he still sends his children to inadequate and all-black schools. Naturally, he concludes that the same old cause — "Whitey" — is still producing the same old effects. That these effects are now being produced largely (not entirely, of course) by other causes, especially differences of education, income, and — in the case of those who are lower class — class culture is something that he cannot be expected to see for himself or to believe if it is pointed out to him, especially when the pointing out is done by a white.

Negro leaders cannot be expected to explain that prejudice is no longer *the* obstacle. Even those of them who understand that it is not are bound to pretend otherwise. Like every specialist, the Negro leader is prone to magnify to himself as well as to others the importance of his specialty, seeing every problem in terms of it. Even when he recognizes that the situation of most Negroes would not be fundamentally different even if there were no racial prejudice at all, the logic of his position as a leader prevents him from saying so. To acknowledge that nonracial factors are more important than racial ones would cool the zeal of his supporters, give aid and comfort to the enemy, and destroy his very reason for being. So long as there is *any* racial prejudice at work, the leader cannot risk seeming to tolerate it, as he would if he emphasized those other (nonracial) aspects of the situation which from a practical (but not a moral) standpoint are vastly more important. For the race leader, there is everything to gain and nothing to lose by treating all problems as if they derived solely from the racial one.

Whites, too, will find prejudice a peculiarly satisfying explanation for the troubles of the Negro. As was observed in the last chapter, it is characteristic of upper- and middle-class culture not only to try to improve oneself and one's society but also to blame oneself for not doing more and succeeding better. Members of these classes are prone to see all social problems in terms of their own moral short-comings — to say, for example, that the Negro is "forced to live in a ghetto" even when it is clear that he *chooses* to live among other Negroes.[33] The Brandeis researchers, for example, refer to Washington Park as a "ghetto" even though their main finding is that most families live there by choice. Another study reports that the question "Do you think Puerto Ricans can live anywhere they want to if they can afford the rent?" was answered "yes" by 87 percent of a sample of New York Puerto Ricans, but calls the *barrio* a "ghetto" nevertheless.[34]

The motives that produce this overemphasis on prejudice are understandable. It is graceless of the white, to say the very least, to run any risk of underemphasizing it. There is the feeling, too, that it can do no harm — and may do some good — to err on the side of seeing more prejudice than is really there. Besides, even if prejudice is not important causally, it is very important morally.

There are, however, at least two serious dangers in widespread overemphasis on prejudice as a cause of the Negro's troubles. The first is that it may lead to the adoption of futile and even destructive policies and to the nonadoption of others that might do great good. It is clear, for example, that if improving the housing of Washington Park Negroes is the goal, programs built on the assumption that the main problem is prejudice will lead nowhere.

The other, perhaps more serious danger in the overemphasis of prejudice is that it raises still higher the psychic cost of being Negro, a cost cruelly high under the best of circumstances. It is bad enough to suffer real prejudice, as every Negro does, without having to suffer imaginary prejudice as well. To refer once more to Washington Park, it is worth noting that some of the people there who did not look at the housing listed as available in white neighborhoods "knew" that Negroes could not buy it and that they would only be humiliated if they tried. In short, the overemphasis on prejudice encourages the Negro to define all his troubles in racial terms. Driving it into him that he is forced to live in a ghetto, the victim of the white man's hate and greed, and so on, makes it all the more difficult for him to feel that he is a man first and a Negro second.

CHAPTER FIVE

The Problem of Unemployment

> They keep telling you about job opportunities, this job opportunity, and that, but who wants a job working all week and bringing home a sweat man's pay?
> — Man, aged eighteen, quoted in *Youth in the Ghetto*

> Maybe we are going to have to accept that many able-bodied people are never going to be engaged in economically productive employment.
> — Welfare Commissioner of New York City, 1964

M ANY people seem to think that the employment prospect in the city is dismal, especially for the unskilled. Technological change in general and automation in particular are said to be eliminating jobs at an unprecedented rate, and it is predicted that before long there will be permanent, mass unemployment, especially of the unskilled. Historian Constance Green describes a case in point: "Where 200 hands had run the looms in a Holyoke, Massachusetts, mill in the 1930s fifteen years later the great weave shed contained two people watching the automatic machines turn out the fine fabrics. . . ."[1] Nathan Glazer, a sociologist, makes the same observation in general terms: Our society "has less and less work for people with only hands."[2] And Paul Goodman, essayist and novelist, puts it even more bluntly: "For the uneducated there will be no jobs at all."[3] Pointing out that the baby boom of a few years ago is about to produce a big increase in the work force, demographer Donald Bogue writes that unless the new workers are kept in school and trained to hold down skilled jobs, "the economy of the entire metropolitan area [of Chicago] can literally drown in a sea of unemployment and underemployment."[4] Thomas F. Pettigrew, a social psychologist, having in mind that Negroes are concentrated in unskilled sectors of the labor force, concludes that broadening of minimum wage legislation and other measures are desperately needed "not just for national prosperity but for improved race relations as well."[5]

These authorities — all first-rate in their fields — have been quoted in order to suggest how widely and seriously the nature of the unemployment problem in the cities is misunderstood. This chapter will contend that automation and technological change are not creating a serious unemployment problem and are not likely to; that the unskilled, far from facing a hopeless future, will probably maintain and improve their position relative to the skilled, and that the Negro will benefit from this trend; and that some of the measures recommended by the quoted authorities — increasing the minimum wage, for example — would make matters worse for the least employable workers, while others — keeping them in school, for example — would probably do more harm than good in most cases. The conclusion reached is not that there is no unemployment problem in the cities, but that the problem is of a different nature than is generally supposed and that it requires for its solution measures of a sort that, for reasons that will become apparent, are not likely to be put forward by persons who wish to be taken seriously.

It will be noted that none of the persons quoted above is an economist. Most economists find nothing new or fearsome in a high rate of technological change and in the substitution of new methods and machines for labor (the term *automation* is used in various senses, but it always refers to some special case of this general phenomenon). Indeed, they say that the enormous and increasing productivity of the economy is the best possible evidence that technological change leads to economic progress.

No one denies, however, that automation has caused a net loss of jobs in *particular* plants, cities, and industries. Steel, coal, and oil refining have been cited as industries in which employment has declined (by 10 or 20 percent in the 1960's) largely from this cause.[6] Some — but not all — of the cities heavily dependent upon these industries suffered from these changes. Pittsburgh, for example, was hard hit; on the other hand, Detroit produced as many cars in 1963 as in 1955 while using 17 percent fewer employees, and had an unemployment rate below the national average in 1964.[7]

To be sure, one can always find instances, like that in Holyoke, Massachusetts, where two people now do the work formerly done by two hundred. Such instances are misleading, however, since they ignore the fact that other technological changes (as well as other factors altogether) may at the same time have been *creating* jobs (although not in the same industries or cities) and that what is relevant is the number of jobs in total. According to Robert M. Solow, an M.I.T. economist who was a member of the National Commission on Technology, Automation, and Economic Progress, the question whether automation creates or destroys more jobs is unanswerable; he doubts, he says, that anyone could make a good estimate of the net number of jobs created or destroyed merely by the invention of the zipper or of sliced bread. The question is irrelevant anyway, he adds, because the total volume of employment is not determined by the rate of technological progress; a modern mixed economy "can, by proper and active use of fiscal and monetary policy weapons, have full employment for *any* plausible rate of technological change within a range that is easily wide enough to cover the American experience."[8]

If automation is not as significant as many noneconomists believe, neither is the outlook for the unskilled worker as dismal as they imagine. One would think that if society has less and less work for the unskilled, the price of unskilled labor would be declining relative to that of skilled. In fact, over the long run it has *increased*. Before the Civil War the unskilled worker earned only about one-third as much as the skilled; at the turn of the century he earned about one-half as much; now he earns two-thirds as much.[9] Conceivably, the time will come when he will earn *more* than the skilled worker. The price of unskilled labor, like that of other commodities, is determined by supply and demand; when the supply of it decreases in relation to the demand for it, its price rises. (In the South, where there is more unskilled labor than elsewhere, its price is relatively low. Similarly, in times of unemployment, when the supply of unskilled labor is large and many unemployed skilled workers are willing to do unskilled work, the demand for it is slack, and its price falls.) It follows, then, that if in the long run the supply of unskilled labor decreases relative to the demand for it and the supply of skilled labor increases relative to the demand for it, the unskilled will in due course be paid more than the skilled. As James Tobin has observed, "When there are only a few people left in the population whose capacities are confined to garbage-collecting, it will be a high-paid calling. The same is true of domestic service and all kinds of menial work."[10] Similarly, when almost everyone can program a computer, programming will be a low-paid job. In Chicago, in fact, a study showed that, in some parts of the city, the higher the grade level completed, the *more* the unemployment; one Negro neighborhood with an average grade level of 8.6 years had an unemployment rate of 3.8 percent, while another Negro neighborhood with an average grade level of 11.4 years had an unemployment rate of 20.3 percent.[11]

Changes in technology do not, on the whole, either favor or retard the employment of Negroes. Indeed, Negroes, because they are concentrated near the bottom of the occupational ladder, have obtained far greater *relative* advances in income than have whites.[12]

Among noneconomists the belief is widespread that automation reduces the demand for unskilled labor more than for other labor. On *a priori* grounds, there is no reason to expect this, however, and empirically it does not appear to be so. The impact is mixed: in some cases automation does eliminate unskilled jobs, but in others it enables unskilled workers to do things formerly done by skilled workers. In the manufacturing and service industries, many jobs done by the unskilled and the semiskilled have proved harder to automate than those done by more skilled workers.[13]

There is not much unemployment among unskilled workers. In May 1969, 94.8 percent of nonfarm laborers, 98.9 percent of farmers and farm laborers, and 96.6 percent of unskilled (private) household workers were employed.[14] (Unskilled hospital, restaurant, recreational, and custodial employees are not included because there are no current separate data for them.)

The crucial factor is not automation but the aggregate demand of the economy for goods and services. If demand is high enough, everyone who wants to work can find a job no matter how lacking in skills he or she may be. To assure full employment, aggregate demand will have to grow constantly, however, for the number of persons wanting jobs is increasing along with the population as a whole, and the average output per man-hour of work is increasing too. According to the National Commission on Technology, Automation, and Economic Progress, aggregate demand must grow by more than 4 percent a year just to keep the unemployment rate from rising; to decrease the unemployment rate, it must grow by even more. In the past, the economy has seldom, if ever, grown at a rate faster than 3.5 percent for any extended time; however, it can be made to do so, the Commission says, by positive fiscal, monetary, and manpower policies.[15]

If the labor market is kept tight, employers will find it necessary to employ people previously thought undesirable or even unemployable. On the other hand, if the labor market is allowed to become slack, they will pick and choose. The labor market, the Commission says, can be viewed

as a gigantic "shapeup," with members of the labor force queued in order of their relative attractiveness to employers. If the labor market operates efficiently, employers will start at the head of the line, selecting as many as they need of employees most attractive to them. Their choice may be based on objective standards relating to ability, or on dubious standards of race, sex, or age; wage differentials may also be important; and formal education may be used as a rough screening device. The total number employed and unemployed depends primarily on the general state of economic activity. The employed tend to be those near the beginning and the unemployed those near the end of the line. Only as demand rises will employers reach further down the line in their search for employees.[16]

Those near the far end of the line — that is, those considered least desirable by employers — tend to be teen-agers and other young people with little education and little or no job experience, members of the lower class (who cannot be depended upon from one day to the next), and victims of racial and other prejudice. At the very end of the line, of course, are those who have *all* these handicaps — lower-class-Negro-teen-age-dropouts. In May 1969, when the general unemployment rate was down to 2.9 percent, the rate among adult men was only 1.8 percent, but that among eighteen- and nineteen-year-old white males was 4.9 percent and that among eighteen- and nineteen-year-old white females was 9.8 percent. The rates for nonwhite males and females of these ages were 19.4 percent and 28.6 percent, respectively. Among still younger teen-agers and dropouts, the rate was even higher.[17]

As is apparent from these figures, a reduction of only 1 percent in the general unemployment rate would make a big difference to those near the end of the hiring line. If the general rate were brought down to about 2 percent (which must be close to the absolute minimum, since some workers are always in the process of moving from one job to another), then probably even those at the end of the line would receive job offers.

In the United States the general yearly unemployment rate has never, except in wartime, fallen below 3.2 percent. Therefore, the rate of unemployment among the least-wanted workers is normally very high.

Economists disagree as to why we do not come closer to achieving full employment. For one thing, some say, public opinion does not give the President or anyone else the authority to carry a fiscal and monetary policy into effect. A President can only recommend actions needed to maintain the necessary high level of aggregate demand; other bodies, especially Congress and the Federal Reserve System, pursue frequently unrelated and perhaps contradictory policies of their own. Even without these bodies to contend with, public opinion might prevent a President from taking the necessary steps. Strange as it may seem, Presidents have on occasion failed even to propose tax cuts thought urgently necessary for fear of the reaction from righteously indignant taxpayers.

A second reason why we do not reduce unemployment to the barest minimum, some economists say, is that the measures required would worsen the nation's international balance of payments problem. This fear, according to James Tobin, a member of the Council of Economic Advisers under President Kennedy, stems from a widespread and irrational attachment to the dollar.

In the final analysis what we fear is that we might not be able to defend the parity of the dollar with gold, that is, to sell gold at thirty-five dollars an ounce to any government that wants to buy. So great is the gold mystique that this objective has come to occupy a niche in the hierarchy of U.S. goals second only to the military defense of the country, and not always to that. It is not fanciful to link the plight of Negro teenagers in Harlem to the monetary whims of General de Gaulle. But it is only our own attachment to "the dollar" as an abstraction which makes us cringe before the European appetite for gold.[18]

The third reason economists give for a needlessly high rate of unemployment derives not from mythology but from interests that are real. A reduction in unemployment must be paid for by an increase in the consumer price level. One economist has estimated that the price of three million jobs that were brought into being in 1965 and 1966 was a 5 percent increase in the consumer price index.[19] In 1968, when unemployment was down to 3.5 percent, prices rose by 3 to 4 percent. Getting the rate down to, say, 2 percent would almost certainly entail a politically unacceptable amount of inflation. Inflationary pressure would arise in part from the tendency of employers in a tight labor market to raise the wages of their preferred workers rather than look for workers among the unemployed; these wage increases would spread by "contagion." Letting some people remain unemployed serves the same function as does "holding the line" on the wages of those who are employed, or carrying on bond-purchase drives among consumers: all are ways of preventing people from bidding up the price of a fixed stock of goods and services. Tolerating unemployment is in fact a particularly effective way of curbing inflation when the unemployed are people who, if employed, would by their labor add less to the total stock of goods and services than they would subtract from it by the increases in their consumption that their greater incomes would permit. In the last analysis, there is a fundamental conflict of interest between the Negro teen-ager at the end of the hiring line and those people (ones on fixed incomes, especially) who stand to lose by inflation.

Some economists, on the other hand, disagree with this analysis. In his presidential address to the American Economic Association in 1968, Milton Friedman maintained that there is *no* steady rate of inflation that would reduce the average level of unemployment.[20] He acknowledges that by speeding up inflation one may reduce unemployment, but he points out that it is impossible to continue speeding it up indefinitely. Whenever the rate of inflation stabilizes, he claims, people will grow accustomed to the new rate and unemployment will return to its former level or to an even higher one. In Friedman's opinion, the reason for the high rate of unemployment is not unwillingness to tolerate inflation; rather, it is that certain laws and practices (to be described presently) make it unprofitable for employers to employ certain kinds of labor.

At first glance it may appear that the people near the end of the hiring line are there solely because they are young, unskilled, victims of racial prejudice, and so on. On reflection, however, it will be seen that, except in a recession, when skilled workers bid for unskilled work, there is no reason to expect a higher rate of unemployment among the classes of labor that are the least capable (the inexperienced, the unskilled, and so on) than among those that are the most capable. This is because the attractiveness of a class of labor to an employer depends not solely upon its capability (real or imagined) but also upon its *price*. A lazy worker, for example, is more attractive to an employer than an energetic one, provided that his wages (and the other costs involved in using him) are low enough to more than compensate for his lesser productivity. To state the matter generally, those at the end of the hiring line are there not because of an absolute incapability (real or imagined) but because *the price of their services is so high that it is unprofitable to employ them.* If their price were low enough, they would move to the head of the hiring line, forcing some more "attractive" (i.e., more attractive in all but price) workers to the rear. In practice, the price of the least capable (real or imagined) would have to be very low indeed in order for this to occur; it might even have to be negative, employers being paid to take the workers they found least attractive, but this does not invalidate the principle involved.

The reason why low-quality labor is so high priced is that numerous laws and institutional arrangements, all supposed to benefit the worker, make it so. Minimum-wage laws are among the worst offenders. Enacted by the federal government[21] and by thirty-three states, Puerto Rico, and the District of Columbia, these laws forbid an employer to pay a worker in a covered occupation less than a certain wage ($1.60 an hour under the federal laws in 1968)[22] even though the alternative may be not to employ him at all. Originally, minimum wage was an approach to curbing prostitution: the laws applied only to women and were passed by some states shortly after the federal government adopted the Mann Act (1910). ("Economic needs," a lady reformer explained, primly but not cogently, "impel many a girl toward a personally degrading life.")[23] Later, Northern textile manufacturers joined with labor unions to support federal minimum-wage legislation in order to reduce Southern competition by raising the price of its labor. Although the minimum is redefined upward from time to time, it is never set high enough to affect most wage workers.[24] Those who *are* affected are the previously low-paid and low-productivity ones, but not all of them; many of the very lowest-paid are in occupations — agriculture, for instance — not covered by the laws.

A principal effect of the minimum wage is to "injure some of the lowest-paid workers by forcing them into even lower-paid occupations exempt from the act, one of which is unemployment."[25] An employer who does not have to compete with other employers for labor may pay his workers less than their labor is worth in production; in his case the effect of the minimum wage may be to raise wages without creating unemployment. But the number of such employers is negligible: workers today move around by car and otherwise and usually have a variety of job alternatives. This being the case, the effect of the minimum wage is not to cause an employer to raise wages (except as he may have been about to do so anyway); rather, it is to cause him to eliminate all labor that now costs more than it is worth in his productive process. Some work that would be done if the price of this labor were lower is left undone. Other work is done in ways that economize on low-productivity but high-cost labor; labor-saving methods are tried, machines are substituted for labor, and a somewhat higher quality of labor is hired at the somewhat higher wage set by law, leaving the least productive with fewer and worse opportunities than before.

When the minimum wage was raised from 75 cents to $1.00 (March 1, 1956), the Bureau of Labor Statistics studied the response of employers in low-wage industries. A majority of plants reported doing one or more of the following: increasing expenditures for machinery and equipment, changing plant layout or work procedures, discharging some employees, or changing product line.[26] After an increase in the minimum, the unemployment rate among the workers least attractive to employers — Negro teen-agers — jumps, as the chart shows. The only people who gain (leaving aside the rare situations in which an employer does not have to compete for labor) are the relatively skilled and well-paid workers who make and sell the machines or do other things to replace the low-productivity worker who has been priced out of the market by the law-makers.

Trade unions tend to produce the same effects, some think on an even larger scale than does national minimum-wage legislation; by forcing the price of low-productivity (and other) labor above the value of labor to employers, unions cause less of it to be employed. In New York City's highly unionized construction industry, for example, the union scale for unskilled building laborers as of July 1, 1964, was $4.65 an hour for a thirty-five-hour week, plus pensions and insurance. (Incidentally, this compares to $5.35 for skilled workers.) One effect of overpaying the unskilled workers was to cause fewer of them to be employed; the construction industry is vigorous in its effort to find techniques — for example, diamond drills that will go through concrete — by which it can economize on labor. Another effect is to restrict the jobs to a favored few, mostly workers in a relatively good position to get jobs elsewhere. Young people, for example, are practically walled out of the construction industry by the union's minimum-age and educational requirements (in 1960, only slightly more than 2 percent of the men were under twenty years of age, while about 14 percent were sixty or older). Negroes, too, have great difficulty getting into apprenticeship programs.

The seniority provisions now common in union contracts also discriminate against the low-productivity worker. Knowing that he will be permitted to promote only from within, an employer does his

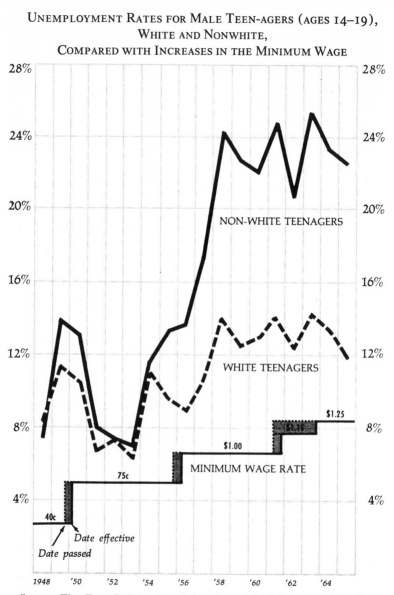

UNEMPLOYMENT RATES FOR MALE TEEN-AGERS (AGES 14–19),
WHITE AND NONWHITE,
COMPARED WITH INCREASES IN THE MINIMUM WAGE

NON-WHITE TEENAGERS

WHITE TEENAGERS

$1.25

$1.15

$1.00

MINIMUM WAGE RATE

75c

40c

Date effective

Date passed

1948   '50   '52   '54   '56   '58   '60   '62   '64

Source: The Free Society Association, Inc., *The Minimum Wage Rate, Who Really Pays: An Interview with Yale Brozen and Milton Friedman,* Washington, D.C., April 1966. *Source of chart data:* Bureau of Labor Statistics, U.S. Department of Labor. Reprinted by courtesy of The Free Society Association, Inc.

best to hire only those whom he can afford to promote eventually. Therefore, the worker who is perfectly capable of pushing a brush around the factory floor but not of doing much else will not get a job. The employer cannot risk having to put him in charge of an expensive machine or in a supervisory position someday.[27]

Occupational licensure is another way in which the law says that some labor must either be overpaid or else not employed. By restricting entry into certain occupations to those who have passed a course of training — by requiring, for example, that in order to cut hair one must graduate from a barbering school that provides at least one thousand hours of instruction in "theoretical subjects" and then go through an apprenticeship,[28] or that a television repairman or garage mechanic pass a rigorous examination and post a bond[29] — the cities and states reduce employment opportunities for the workers whose possibilities are most limited.

Local, state, and federal agencies are all under pressure to "set an example of enlightened wage policy," that is, to pay labor more than it is worth. This policy injures workers at the bottom of the heap by giving others not at the bottom an incentive to take jobs they otherwise would avoid. Early in 1965 some three thousand persons took examinations for 125 jobs as coin collectors for Boston's metropolitan transit system. The jobs could have been done by workers who were not capable of doing much else, but because the wages were set higher than need be — $3.00 an hour plus various fringe benefits — low-capability workers had to compete for them against workers who could have been better employed. Naturally, the low-capability workers lost out; they remained unemployed while those who got the jobs wasted ability doing what less-able people could have done as well.[30]

After the Watts riots it was pointed out that the city's civil-service system had contributed to the Negroes' employment problem. Operating on "merit" alone, it had established such high education qualifications for employees that most Watts residents could not get civil-service jobs even as common laborers. This outcome would have been impossible had the city not been overpaying its employees; the Watts residents would have had little or no competition for the jobs if the only qualification had been ability to perform the task and if the wage rate had not been above the market.

Opinion is another factor that often causes overpricing of — and therefore unemployment of — low-value labor. In every locale people have a common idea of the lowest wage it is "reasonable" to expect workers to accept even if the alternative is to remain unemployed. Frequently, this "informal" minimum wage is higher than the legal one. And frequently it calls for paying wages only a philanthropist could afford. In Detroit, for example, auto companies pay unskilled production workers a very high wage — $3.17 an hour in 1966 (as compared to $4.17 for the skilled worker) — and this high rate is taken by unskilled workers in all industries as the model of what is "fair" and "decent." The auto workers' wages are high not because unskilled workers are more valuable in the auto industry than elsewhere, but because the power of an aggressive union (the UAW) has forced them up. Unskilled workers not lucky enough to get one of the small number of good union jobs — especially workers in low-paying enterprises, such as laundries and car parking lots — earn less than half as much as the auto workers. Naturally they are angry at the injustice of it all. They suppose that they are being underpaid, not that the others are being overpaid.

Working for less than the informal minimum — "for peanuts" — destroys a man's standing in whatever circle he moves in and undermines his self-respect. Some men prefer to go on welfare. In the summer of 1965, when a federal youth employment project in Detroit proposed paying seventy youths the legal minimum wage while training them for better-paying jobs, it could find only thirty who would accept its offer.[31] The legal minimum, then $1.25 an hour, was "peanuts." Three years later, the Labor Department made a $3,104,044 grant to train and find jobs for 970 "hard-core" unemployed in Detroit, but there was some question whether enough men could be found to accept training. The city had about thirty thousand eligibles, about ten thousand of whom were considered extreme cases. However, the trainees were to receive only $1.60 an hour during training and $2.30 an hour afterward. A laid-off auto worker, it was pointed out, would receive from the state and the company more take-home pay than a man putting in forty hours a week at $2.30 an hour.[32]

Illicit enterprises, too, tend to have the effect of setting an informal minimum wage for unskilled labor that has no relation to the market value of such labor and that other employers cannot afford to pay. As a result, the young "dropout" loses face and self-respect unless he is either a "hustler" or an idler; the suggestion that he be paid what his work is worth is tantamount to an insult. Asked why he did not go downtown and get a job, a Harlem youth replied:

Oh, come on. Get off that crap. I make $40 or $50 a day selling marijuana. You want me to go down into the garment district and push one of those trucks through the street and at the end of the week take home $40 or $50 if I'm lucky? Come off it. They don't have animals doing what you want me to do. There would be some society to protect animals if anybody had them pushing those damn trucks around. I'm better than an animal, but nobody protects me. Go away, mister. I got to look out for myself.[33]

In the final analysis, it is middle-class opinion that sets the informal minimum wage for low-value labor, and it does so, of course, on the basis of its own notion of what is reasonable. Unemployment compensation and other welfare programs explicitly recognize an informal minimum: no applicant for assistance may be required to accept "unreasonable" offers of employment, which is to say that no one may be required to work for what he is worth to his employer if this is much under what the general (middle-class) opinion considers "fair."

One important reason, then, why the number of jobs for very low-value labor is declining — why, for example, fewer shops make occasional deliveries, fewer part-time messengers are hired, fewer people are paid to mow lawns and shovel sidewalks — is not, as Paul Goodman contends, that the system is "tightly organized and highly urbanized,"[34] but rather that those who might do these jobs have been told by parents, welfare departments, and the ever more affluent middle class generally that the small amounts they could earn by doing them are "peanuts" — too little for a self-respecting person to bother with.

Even if the total supply of jobs is large, there is likely to be (except perhaps in the very long run) some chronic unemployment among the unskilled workers who are concentrated in the inner city. For one thing, factories have long been moving from the inner to the outer city and from the city to the suburbs and beyond. Also, since the Second World War, large numbers of unskilled workers have moved into the inner city. (In 1929 two-thirds of all production jobs were in central cities; now well under half are there. The number of unskilled workers in the central cities, meanwhile, has risen.[35]) As the previous chapters have pointed out, economic, class-cultural, and racial factors tend to prevent some factory workers from following their jobs out of the city. Of particular importance are the relative abundance of cheap housing in the central city as compared to the suburbs and the inability or unwillingness of some workers to commute to jobs in the suburban fringe.

Next to high transportation costs and the need for space, the overpricing of low-value labor explains why factories have left the inner city so rapidly. In many instances employers have gone to the suburbs in order to build new plants that would enable them to take advantage of labor-saving methods and devices.

Almost all new growth in employment since the war has occurred in the service, as opposed to the goods, sector of the economy (trade, finance, insurance, and real estate; personal, professional, and repair service; and general government).[36] This shift from factory employment has probably been injurious to the unskilled and to members of minority groups: the criteria for selecting service workers are more likely to be "subjective" and thus unfair to — or at any rate unfavorable to — those whose attributes are considered undesirable. No one cares if a factory worker speaks crudely, scratches himself in the wrong places, or is physically unattractive; if he can read signs like DANGER — NO SMOKING and if he keeps his part of the assembly line moving, little else matters. In many service jobs, on the other hand, it is essential that the service worker "make a good impression" on the middle-class people he serves. If ethnic, racial, class, or other characteristics render him unattractive in their eyes, he is for that reason unemployable. The problem is not that he is unskilled, but that he is aesthetically objectionable — he spoils the decor, so to speak.[37] Unions and minimum-wage legislation encourage the shift from factory to service employment, which entails these disadvantages for the least attractive workers. By raising relative wages in the goods industries, they cause a reallocation of resources into the service industries.

It would appear that the way to solve the employment problem in the city is to allow the price of all labor, including the least valuable, to fall to a level at which it will all be purchased. If a ditchdigger's work is worth no more than $1.00 an hour to anyone and if a fifteen-year-old dropout's work is worth no more than 50 cents an hour, these should be their wages. The point is that low-value labor must be priced no higher than it is worth if those who can use it are to have an incentive to do so.

It will be objected that to require the low-value worker to work for what he is worth to an employer is to condemn him and his family to poverty. This does not follow. Much low-value work is done not by breadwinners but by persons, especially married women and teen-agers, who want to supplement an income already above the poverty line. But even if this aspect is disregarded, the objection is not a weighty one. Theoretically, at least, there is no reason why a family (or unattached person) earning too little could not be subsidized from public sources so as to bring its total income up to a level deemed adequate. This arrangement has an obvious advantage to the public: whatever the worker earns, however little, reduces the cost of his support.

The main beneficiaries, however, would be the workers themselves. A job can be much more than a source of income. It can be an opportunity to learn things, to test one's ability to stand up to strains, to get out of the house and away from home, and to feel that one is a part, however small, of a worthwhile undertaking. Especially for a male, the job (along with other things) helps establish one's identity and supports one's self-respect. Obviously, a job that pays "peanuts" is no aid to self-respect; on the contrary, having such a job entails a loss of it. Other, nonmonetary advantages accrue even from a poor job, however, and if everyone were expected to work for what his work is worth, the lowest paid would have at least somewhat less cause for embarrassment than they have now.

The idea of pricing low-value labor into the market is not worth serious consideration, however; it is hopelessly Utopian. Trade unions are not about to stop trying to get their members paid more than their work is worth. Minimum-wage laws will not be repealed; instead, the minimum rate will be pushed steadily upward (Bayard Rustin, the Negro leader, has said that he would gladly trade the whole war on poverty for an increase to $2.00 in the minimum wage). Occupational licensure will not be dropped so long as various occupational groups can gain by restricting entry and raising prices. Nor is the idea that one should not work for "peanuts" (even if that happens to be all that one's labor is worth) likely to lose its hold. On the contrary, the informal minimum is likely to rise at an accelerating rate: as the standard of living of the affluent goes up, more and more low-pay, no-future jobs will be thought to be beneath the dignity of even the poorest and the least able.

If low-value labor cannot be priced into the market, what can be done to make the best of a bad situation? One familiar suggestion is to train the unskilled, the idea being that if the price of low-value labor cannot be brought down to its value-in-production, then its value-in-production should be raised up to its price. In practice, however, this can seldom be done simply by teaching the worker new skills. What makes the kind of labor here under discussion valuable to the employer is usually not so much possession of *skills* (the ones needed are mostly manual and can be learned on the job by almost anyone who will try); rather, it is possession of certain qualities — reliability, motivation to learn, and adaptability to the demands of the work situation. Perhaps this fact helps to explain why the federal government's Manpower Development Training program has not achieved more.[38] (According to one study, those who completed training got only 13 to 23 percent more employment in the year following their training than did a control group of friends, neighbors, and relatives who received no training.)[39] Of course, even if training programs succeeded in making employees more productive, they would not make them more employable if their wages were made to rise even faster than their productivity; as was emphasized before, it is overpricing of labor that is the principal obstacle to its employment, and skilled labor, too, can be overpriced.

Another possibility — one that has natural appeal to small-city mayors and Chambers of Commerce — is to offer tax exemptions and other subsidies to induce factories to stay in the city or to move back to it from the suburbs. For this approach to work, the subsidies offered must be quite large — large enough, at least, to offset the added costs to the employer of using the overpriced labor and to make up for the loss of accessibility and the other advantages that would be gained by moving. As a practical matter, city governments are very rarely able to offer subsidies large enough to have much effect, which may be just as well anyway, since in the long run the city must adjust to becoming a center for services and exchanges rather than for the production of goods. To race for manufacturing jobs, says Wilbur R. Thompson in his *A Preface to Urban Economics,* is to swim against the current, especially if it is unskilled and semiskilled jobs that are sought.[40] Even so, it might cost the public less to subsidize the return of factories to the city than to support workers who are permanently unemployed. There is an important danger, however, that a job-creation program may attract more migrants from the rural South. Indeed, it is possible, as Kain and Persky have pointed out, that more migrants might come than there are jobs created, and unemployment in the city would actually increase.[41]

One main problem in opening job opportunities for the unskilled in the inner city "ghetto" is that most of those who are unemployed or intermittently employed have habits or cultural characteristics incompatible with employment in steady, high-paying jobs. As Michael J. Piore, an M.I.T. economist, points out, they leave their jobs without notice, sometimes steal, are frequently absent or late, are insubordinate, and so on.[42] Learning the skills needed for the job is not especially difficult for them (most of the "good" jobs in these areas are semiskilled, requiring only manual skills); what *is* difficult for them is to accept the discipline of regular work in accordance with definite work rules. Efforts to overcome these problems have not been encouraging. Men accustomed to a street-corner style of life, to living off women on welfare, and to "hustling" are seldom willing to accept the dull routines of the "good" job. Moreover, Piore says, fitting such workers into the factory routine often creates pressures and tensions that are hard for management to cope with (for example, a policy of tolerating offenses by Negroes against shop rules that whites have been severely punished for violating may cause resentment, and relaxing the rules for *all* workers may cause production to fall off to an intolerable extent). Employers may circumvent these difficulties, Piore suggests, either by having separate plants for workers who are not used to industrial discipline, these being isolated from the normal industrial relations dynamic, or by using such special plants as "feeders" to supply other company plants with those workers who prove able to adapt to the normal rules and routines.

If there is a surplus of unskilled workers in the big cities, perhaps the thing to do is to assist them to move to places where their long-run prospects are better — from Harlem, say, to rural areas upstate or to the centers of space-age industry in Southern California. This idea seems plausible until one considers that in many places employment opportunities for the unskilled are even worse than they are in the big cities. It is hard to justify moving workers from Harlem until other workers whose job situations are even worse have been moved from, say, Appalachia. As a practical matter, moreover, it is often impossible to persuade workers to leave the city even when doing so would be to their material advantage.[43] People who have lived in a big city all their lives are apt to find a small one intolerably dull, and if, as is usually the case, they are accustomed to a neighborhood with a certain class and ethnic character, then another — even a "better" one — lacking this character may not suit them at all. Finally, an unpleasant fact must be taken into account: places to which the government might propose moving the workers would fight the idea tooth and nail, for the workers usually would be people whose income, class, and race (they would be Negroes in most cases) would make them unwelcome. Considering that the number of persons who might need relocation runs to many hundreds of thousands, government programs of this kind offer little hope.

A more practical approach is to make it easier for the unskilled or semiskilled worker living in the inner city to get to the suburban ring, where the new jobs are. At present, bus and train schedules are often better arranged to carry suburbanites to the city than to carry city workers to the suburbs. Most low-income city dwellers do not own automobiles, while public transportation to the suburbs is frequently poor and sometimes expensive. A study of fourteen metropolitan areas showed that the fare from the central city to the closest suburban area ranged from 30 cents one way in one metropolitan area to 65 cents in another, and that the average city resident working in the suburbs must spend at least an hour a day in travel. For a Harlem resident, it costs $40 a month to take public transportation to work in an aircraft plant in Long Island, in a parts plant in Yonkers or Westchester, or in a basic chemical plant or shipyard on Staten Island. The public-transit cost from Bedford-Stuyvesant to the same places is nearly $50 a month.[44]

Another way to improve the job situation of the unskilled would be to eliminate the barriers that discourage them from moving from the inner city to the suburban ring. The inner city is the focus of radial transportation lines extending in almost all directions to the outer perimeter of the metropolitan area. Therefore, casual workers — domestics, for example — generally find it the most logical place to reside. There are, however, some suburban areas where it would be advantageous for these workers to live, and if free to do so, many workers would move there from the inner city. They seldom are free to do so, however; in the name of health, safety, and the maintenance of local property values, suburban building codes and zoning regulations commonly set housing standards so high as in effect to exclude low-income people. If such standards were relaxed to allow use of the cheapest housing that can reasonably be called safe — mobile homes, for example — some unskilled workers would move to the suburbs rather than commute or (the only alternative for some) be unemployed or underemployed. All interferences with the freedom of workers to live where they please, whether in the inner city or in the suburban ring, tend to contribute to unemployment.

It must be recognized, however, that so long as there exists a large stock of relatively cheap housing in the inner city, and so long as it is relatively easy to commute from the inner city to the suburban ring, most unskilled workers will prefer to live in the inner city. Apart from housing and transportation, there is another consideration: Negroes (like members of other minority groups) will not in general move to places where they will be cut off from the social life of their group. Once enough families to constitute a "critical mass" have moved to a particular place, the growth of population there may be very rapid; establishing the critical mass presents a real difficulty, however.

Eventually, the logic of metropolitan growth will of itself cause the low-earner to move to the suburban ring. As always, he will replace the well-off, who themselves will be moving still farther out, leaving behind housing better than that which the low-earners presently occupy. As was pointed out in Chapter 2, many suburbs built after the war will be "downgraded" and ready for occupancy by the not well-off in the next decade or two. In the meantime, of course, the older housing in the central city will be wearing out. That low-earning workers will eventually reach the suburban ring does not necessarily mean that they will find jobs, however. By the time they arrive, some factories will have moved still farther out. Moreover, many jobs will have been eliminated altogether by suburban employers who could not wait for workers to arrive.

For at least the next decade or two, then, the supply of low-value labor in the inner city is likely to exceed the demand for it (at the wages asked). Unemployment will probably be greatest in the inner-city districts where the unskilled are concentrated, especially in those districts from which the suburban ring is relatively inaccessible. It can also be expected to remain severe among those groups with the highest proportion of low-value workers: the young, especially teen-agers and, above all, dropouts. Even in the entire absence of racial prejudice by employers, the unemployment rate in Negro districts would for these reasons remain higher than anywhere else. At the end of 1968, after many months of full employment nationally, the rate in the "ghettoes" was generally estimated to be three times as high as elsewhere.

One way to provide work and on-the-job training for low-productivity workers would be to compensate private employers from public funds for the losses they would incur by employing them at the minimum wage.[45] If, for example, it costs a private employer $4,500 a year (wages at $1.40 per hour plus the cost of supervision and administrative overhead) to employ a worker who is worth to him only $1,000, he would receive $3,500. One advantage of this arrangement is that it would tap a limitless number of job possibilities; another is that employers would have incentive not to waste the labor in "make-work" projects. These advantages are probably more than offset, however, by the administrative difficulties in compensating employers correctly (that is, in paying enough to induce them to employ the workers but not much more than that). There is also the difficulty, amounting to an impossibility, of preventing employers from substituting labor that is cheap to them for that which they would normally hire.

On balance, a more feasible solution seems to be to have low-value workers employed by public agencies and nonprofit institutions. However, there are difficulties with this plan, too. Labor unions are likely to insist that the workers be paid at union rates, which may be as much as twice the minimum wage and therefore ridiculously high for the labor in question. Taxpayers will not stand for paying teen-age dropouts $3.00 or $4.00 an hour, and there would inevitably be a demand that these overpaid jobs be distributed "according to merit" on the basis of civil-service procedures. Then, of course, the jobs will go to white adults, not to Negro teen-agers.

To get around such difficulties, new agencies have been created in the federal government.[46] Through them, employing the unemployed becomes almost costless to the local taxpayer (who well knows that if the federal money is not spent in his city it will be spent somewhere else and that his taxes will be no lower). They also have the advantage of being relatively immune to union and other local pressures. Beginning in 1965, the Neighborhood Youth Corps has each year paid 90 percent of the wage of about 250,000 fourteen- to twenty-year-olds employed in projects sponsored by public and nonprofit agencies (especially community-action agencies, state agencies, and schools). The youths receive the federal minimum wage or a little more for up to thirty-two hours a week (fifteen for those still in school). For the most part, they do "make-work" jobs as file clerks, settlement house aides, and the like in nonunionized white-collar occupations. To employ large numbers of youths in "real" (that is, permanent, full-time, unionized) jobs would of course be politically impossible. New York City, which must clear tons of litter from Coney Island and other public beaches in the summer, was recently reported to be considering the purchase of several costly ($25,000 each) beach-sweeping machines. The city's sanitation workers — highly unionized and highly paid (more than $7,000 per year) — prefer the use of a few machines with high-paid operators to the employment of hundreds of low-paid youths.

To increase the employability of hard-to-employ youths aged sixteen to twenty-one, the Job Corps operates residential centers (in 1968 there were 109, with a total enrollment of nearly 33,000) where youths receive vocational training and a small cash wage. The costs of the program are high — more than $8,000 per enrollee in fiscal 1967 — and its potentialities limited. Unlike the Civilian Conservation Corps, which existed to provide work, food, and shelter when joblessness was widespread and which enrolled white working- and lower-middle-class males for the most part, the Job Corps exists at a time of full employment, and its mission is to open opportunities for those who have not had them. The enrollees are lower-working and lower class (nearly one in three was unable to read a simple sentence), and well over one-half are Negro. In the nature of the case, the Corpsmen do not learn much from each other or develop an *esprit de corps* that would give them greater confidence and self-respect. In addition, the Corps has chronic political problems. Despite efforts to prevent it, its enrollment has become preponderantly Negro, and therefore most centers are in effect segregated. Also, behavior problems that outrage middle-class opinion arise from time to time and keep the Corps in hot water. To survive, it must avoid enrolling many of the youths who presumably need it most — especially drug addicts, homosexuals, and those with criminal records. It must also regulate the enrollees' behavior in ways that youths accustomed to the freedom of the slums will not tolerate.[47] More than 40 percent of the enrollees drop out or are discharged within three months of enrollment. Those who remain in the Corps for six months or more have, on the average, slightly better employment when they leave it than they had before enrolling; on the other hand, those who drop out in less than three months have, on the average, somewhat less employment than before. According to Sar A. Levitan, ". . . no conclusive case has yet been established to justify the Job Corps on the basis of past performance."[48]

For government to be "employer of last resort," guaranteeing a job to anyone who wants one, is probably not a practical proposition. Garth L. Mangum, a specialist on manpower policy, has estimated that in 1966 there were about three million potential applicants for such jobs; employing them at $1.50 an hour would have cost about $12 billion a year.[49] A more feasible alternative, Mangum suggests, would be to guarantee employment to all within certain labor markets. This too would probably involve a huge outlay (in 1966 some 400,000 persons were unemployed in the poverty areas of thirty-seven cities), and it is hardly likely that Congress would favor the big cities in this way.

In 1968 a business-and-government effort to provide training and jobs for the "hard-core" unemployed was begun in the fifty largest cities by the National Alliance of Businessmen. In the first year of the J.O.B.S. program, 12,500 cooperating firms placed 125,000 persons. About a third of these placements involved federal training subsidies averaging $2,850 per worker; these trainees were persons who had been certified as disadvantaged by a state employment service, and the training that they received met government standards. The other two-thirds of the placements were of persons certified by the *employer;* in their training the employer was not bound by government standards. There is reason to believe that many, if not most, of this two-thirds were not much disadvantaged and did not receive much training. The subsidized placement program is to be taken more seriously, but it has not — and probably cannot — accomplish a great deal. Some high-wage companies appear to have modified their hiring standards in order to take disadvantaged workers; these companies, however, have usually interviewed applicants carefully and have "creamed off" the supply so as to get workers who are hardly less capable than those not described as disadvantaged. Low-wage companies, which have been hiring disadvantaged workers all along, now get a windfall payment from the government for doing so. J.O.B.S. has not increased the supply of jobs and it has not opened up higher-wage jobs to persons who would not ordinarily get them. The most that can be said for it is that it has redistributed the existing supply of jobs somewhat. Questions may be raised about the fairness of this policy: Why should one worker be displaced by another simply on the ground that the other is (more) disadvantaged? And why should the displacing be done under government auspices and at the taxpayer's expense? Furthermore, if redistribution of jobs occurred on a large scale, those who lost by it would presumably produce a "backlash" that would bring the program to an end.[50]

Even if there were a lively demand at high wages for all the labor in the city, however unproductive, some people would remain unemployed. Members of the lower class work only intermittently even if job opportunities are good. Providing for a future, even a week or two away, is not part of their culture; nor will they accept the discipline that a job usually imposes. Youth culture somewhat resembles lower-class culture in these respects. Teen-age boys are often strongly disinclined to work; they like to be "where the action is." Jobs that are lawful, safe, and well regulated are often more than they can stand — especially if they do not pay well. And in an ever more affluent society, those who prefer to live from hand to mouth without working find it increasingly easy to do so.

Resistance to steady work on the part of able-bodied persons is especially strong in the slums. A study of the "ghetto" labor market in Boston in 1968, for example, showed that about 70 percent of the job applicants referred by neighborhood employment centers received offers. More than half of the offers were rejected, however, and only about 40 percent of those who took jobs kept them for as long as a month. "Much of the ghetto unemployment," the author explains, "appears to be a result of work instability rather than job scarcity."[51]

In 1966 the U.S. Department of Labor made an intensive survey in slum areas of eight large cities; between a fifth and a third of the adult males expected from other statistical sources to be part of the slum population were "unfound." Of the persons who *were* found, between 10 and 20 percent of those who should have been working were neither working nor looking for work. Only one in five of these said that he would be willing to "live away from home temporarily to take training or get a job" or to "move to another metropolitan area if it meant getting a job." Adding together the unemployed, the fully employed who earned less than $56 a week, half the men aged twenty to sixty-four who were not looking for work, and half those who were "unfound," the Department arrived at "subemployment" estimates ranging from 24.2 percent for Boston's slum to 45.3 percent for the New Orleans one. "Unemployment in these areas is *primarily* a story of inferior education, no skills, police and garnishment records, discrimination [more frequently on the basis of age than of race], fatherless children, dope addiction, hopelessness."[52] "The problem," the Labor Department suggests, "is less one of inadequate opportunity than of inability, under existing conditions, to use opportunity."

CHAPTER SIX

Several Kinds of Poverty

A condition of chronic poverty is developing in the Jewish community of New York that is appalling in its immensity. Forty-five percent of our applicants, representing between twenty thousand and twenty-five thousand human beings, have been in the United States over five years; have been given the opportunities for economic and industrial improvement which this country affords; yet, notwithstanding all this, have not managed to reach a position of economic independence.

— United Hebrew Charities,
Annual Report for 1901

THE city, far from being a cause of poverty, has proved to be a remarkably efficient machine for transforming it into prosperity and even affluence. For many generations the world's "wretched refuse" (as the inscription on the Statue of Liberty puts it) has been coming to live in the city. One would expect that after so many years of immigration, incomes in the city would be much lower than anywhere else. In fact, the median income is considerably higher than in the country as a whole ($8,700 for central cities in 1967 as against $8,000 for the country as a whole), although of course considerably lower than in the suburbs ($9,400).[1]

The city's remarkable performance would be even more clearly evident if, so to speak, the books were kept on a more meaningful basis — if the city were credited with the incomes of all persons brought up in it and not debited with those of persons who grew up elsewhere. By counting the millions of suburbanites who attended city schools and got their feet on the first rung of the occupational ladder in the city and by omitting the other millions of persons of farm and rural origins, whose earning capacity was already largely fixed when they migrated, the city's role as destroyer of poverty and creator of wealth would be dramatically revealed.

The city attracts the poor — especially poor parents with numerous children — by offering better conditions of life — better food, clothing, shelter, health care, schools, and treatment from employers and officials; this is why it always has so many poor.[2] The problem of poverty in the cities is seldom of the cities' own making; it is essentially a problem made elsewhere and then brought to the city. In every generation the city largely solves the problem, only to see it posed anew by fresh arrivals.

The Social Security Administration has defined poverty as existing below a minimum income — $3,335 for a "nonfarm" family of four in 1967. By this definition a total of 26.1 million persons were counted poor in 1967, about 13.2 million of whom lived in metropolitan areas. Of these, 8.3 million lived in central cities (where they comprised 14 percent of the population) and a little less than 5 million in the suburbs (where they comprised 7 percent of the population).[3] Poverty was especially frequent among Negroes, unrelated individuals, and the old.

Some statisticians believe that most figures used considerably exaggerate both the number of persons whose incomes are low year after year and the lowness of their incomes. The poor (and the nonpoor as well) generally underreport their incomes, perhaps because they do not always know how much they receive or perhaps because they are unwilling to tell. Also, every survey catches some people who at that particular time are below their normal incomes.[4] (Thus, in 1960 it was found that in the large cities consumers with incomes under $1,000 were spending $224 for every $100 of income received and those with incomes from $2,000 to $3,000 were spending $116.)[5] Even if one takes the reported incomes as given, questions of interpretation arise. One economist, using the same figures as the Council of Economic Advisers, cut its estimate of the amount of poverty in half — from 20 percent of the population to 10 percent.[6]

A more fundamental question concerns the *definition* of poverty. According to the dictionary, "poverty" is lack of money or material possessions. But how severe a lack? *How* poor is "poor"?

For present purposes, it will be useful to distinguish four degrees of poverty: *destitution,* which is lack of income sufficient to assure physical survival and to prevent suffering from hunger, exposure, or remediable or preventable illness; *want,* which is lack of enough income to support "essential welfare" (as distinguished from comfort and convenience); *hardship,* which is lack of enough to prevent acute, persistent discomfort or inconvenience; and *relative deprivation,* which is lack of enough to prevent one from feeling poor by comparison with others.

The official poverty line obviously does not refer to destitution, although even half a century ago destitution was not uncommon. (It was estimated that in New York at the turn of the century, one person in ten was buried in Potter's Field — an indication of widespread distress, since "lying in a pauper's grave" was a disgrace most people would make almost any sacrifice to avoid.)[7] Today, however, it is probably safe to say that no one in the city is destitute. Many persons still suffer from hunger, exposure, or illness but lack of income is not the cause, or at any rate not the proximate cause, of their suffering. A cultural (or other) incapacity to make use of income is a different matter from lack of income, and destitution (as defined here) has to do with income, not culture.[8]

One might suppose, then, that the poverty line refers to want. The Council implies this by characterizing the poor as "those who are not now maintaining a *decent* standard of living — those whose basic needs exceed their means to satisfy them."[9] It is very difficult to specify, even for food, the minimum "bundle" of goods necessary to support essential welfare. It is impossible to state precisely the indispensable material prerequisites of individual happiness and social well-being. However, although the contents of the bundle might vary a good deal from one country to another and from one age to another, within a given culture and a given age the variations would not be very great. "Basic needs" do not change much from one generation to the next (if they do, they are not "basic"!); neither does a culture's idea of what constitutes a "decent," worthy, respectable, etc., mode of life. Therefore, want can be defined by a standard that changes so slowly as to be for all practical purposes fixed. One laid down by Alfred Marshall almost a century ago will serve rather well today:

> The necessaries for the efficiency of an ordinary agricultural or of an unskilled town laborer and his family, in England, in this generation, may be said to consist of a well-drained dwelling with several rooms, warm clothing, with some changes of underclothing, pure water, a plentiful supply of cereal food, with a moderate allowance of meat and milk, and a little tea, etc., some education, and some recreation, and lastly, sufficient freedom for his wife from other work to enable her to perform properly her maternal and household duties.[10]

Measured by this standard, or by one anything like it, the amount of want in the city has been steadily reduced decade by decade for at least a century. There was still considerable want twenty or thirty years ago, but today there is very little. Within another few decades there will almost certainly be none. If no one goes hungry, very few have (for reasons of income) diets that are nutritionally inadequate; as long ago as 1955 the poorest third of city dwellers' average consumption exceeded the National Research Council's recommended dietary allowances for seven of eight nutrients.[11] Almost everyone has enough warm clothing; few people live in housing that is greatly overcrowded, structurally unsafe, or otherwise injurious to essential welfare; all children can have high school education; books and records are easily obtainable (one can buy almost any book of general interest, including all the classics, for the price of a couple of packages of cigarettes); every city has a public library and the larger ones also have museums, art galleries, adult-education classes, and so on.

About health care in the city it is somewhat harder to generalize. Its quality may vary considerably among cities and even among hospitals within a city.[12] Some hospitals (including many big-city ones frequented by the poor) are favored by proximity to university medical schools and their students, but these hospitals, like most, suffer from overcrowding and understaffing. On the whole, however, city hospitals and clinics today provide health care far superior to that enjoyed by previous city (not to mention noncity) dwellers. The poor in the cities receive as many visits from physicians as do the well-off (4.82 visits per person per year in families with incomes under $2,000; 4.92 in families with incomes above $7,000) and, prior to the age of forty-five, they are somewhat less likely than the well-off to suffer from chronic conditions (after forty-five they are somewhat more likely to suffer from them).[13] Medicare and Medicaid have greatly reduced, if not altogether eliminated, the cost of health care for large numbers of the poor, including all who receive public assistance.

If one is willing to live just above the level of want — that is, having enough for essential welfare but not enough to avoid hardship — one can do so now with little effort. In Marshall's time the unskilled laborer had to work from dawn to dusk merely to escape destitution. Today, because of economic progress, technological improvement, and various welfare measures, an unskilled laborer is not likely to suffer want if he works only a few hours a day and he may not suffer it if he does not work at all.

Most of those classified by the Council of Economic Advisers as poor do not experience want. Their poverty may entail hardship, but it does not entail serious injury. They can afford nutritionally adequate diets but not the better cuts of meat; their clothing is warm and plentiful but not "the latest thing"; their housing keeps out the rain and the cold, but the bath is down the hall; their children can finish high school, but they cannot go to college unless they are unusually good scholars or athletes; they will usually be adequately cared for in case of illness — especially in case of *serious* illness — if they are willing to avail themselves of the services and facilities that are available to them.

Many — perhaps most — of those with reported incomes below the official poverty line are not undergoing hardship (or if they are, it is not because of lack of income). About 40 percent own cars, a slightly higher percentage own their own homes, more than half have savings, and of those with savings about one-third have more than $500.[14] According to Herman P. Miller, of those families with incomes below $4,000 and living in rented apartments in central cities in 1959, 95 percent of the whites and 90 percent of the Negroes had adequate housing, and the same percentages (not necessarily the same families) had a television set and access to a telephone for receiving calls. (Adequate housing in this context means an apartment free of defects that make it unsafe to live in, having hot piped water, direct access, a private kitchen with cooking equipment, a flush toilet and bath for the exclusive use of the occupants, and no more than one person per room.)[15] Almost all the poor have some furniture and appliances, and many have more than enough of both for comfort and convenience. A study of consumption patterns of several hundred families living in Manhattan housing projects and having a median income just above the poverty line ($3,300 in 1960) found that 95 percent had at least one television set; three-fourths had either a phonograph or a television-phonograph console, and 83 percent of the televisions, phonographs, and vacuum cleaners had been bought new. Of the telephones observed in these apartments (many families kept them hidden because it was against Welfare Department rules to have them), nearly one-fourth were of the extra-cost colored variety.[16]

The discomfort and inconvenience experienced by most of those classified as poor are seldom acute and persistent. But it is not even discomfort and inconvenience that mainly constitute poverty in the city today. In our society a conspicuously low income is a mark of low status. It is this — appearing to others and to oneself as inferior or of "no account" — that constitutes most poverty now. In short, the problem of poverty is not so much one of income *level* as one of income *distribution*. As Victor R. Fuchs explains:

By the standards that have prevailed over most of history, and still prevail over large areas of the world, there are very few poor in the United States today. Nevertheless, there are millions of American families who, both in their own eyes and in those of others, are poor. As our nation prospers, our judgment as to what constitutes poverty will inevitably change. *When we talk about poverty in America, we are talking about families and individuals who have much less income than most of us. When we talk about reducing or eliminating poverty, we are really talking about changing the distribution of income* [italics added].[17]

On first impression the poverty problem may not seem very difficult to solve. Even if no special measures are taken, the amount of poverty (in the sense of incomes below the poverty line as now officially defined) will gradually decrease until twenty-five to fifty years hence there will very likely be none at all.[18] If one is unwilling to wait that long, all that is necessary (so it may seem) is to redistribute income: in a society as affluent as ours there will be enough for everyone if the total is distributed properly.

There are essentially two ways of redistributing income. The first, which is altogether preferable so far as it goes, is to increase the productivity and earning power of those who are poor. This might be done by measures some of which have already been discussed — maintaining a very high level of employment, pricing labor at what it is worth so that all of it will be employed, improving workers' skills, health, and geographical mobility, and ending discrimination in jobs (and, of course, in housing) on grounds of race, age, sex, class, amount of schooling, or whatever.

These measures, however, would not eliminate poverty no matter how far they were carried; their direct and main effect is on *employable* persons, and about one-half of all poor families ("income units," strictly speaking) have no employable member. Among the most common causes of poverty (altogether accounting for about one-half of it) are old age, disability, and family dependence on women. Obviously, efforts to increase earning power would not significantly affect these causes, except perhaps in the very long run.

The other way of redistributing income is by "transfer payments" — that is, by taxing some and giving to others. This, of course, has been done on a large and increasing scale since the New Deal (but not on a scale large enough to reduce the gap between the greatest earners and the smallest). At present, social insurance, public assistance, veterans' pensions, and the compensation system involve transfers of about $40 billion a year. However, only about half this sum goes to people whose incomes were below the poverty line before the transfer. Although the $24 billion these families receive raises their total income by 42 percent, half of the families ("income units") below the poverty line receive no transfer payments at all. The "poverty gap" remaining amounts to about $12 billion. To fill it completely by expanding the present welfare system might cost about $30 billion; to reduce it by about one-half might cost about $5 billion.[19]

A much simpler method of transferring income — and one much more likely to reach its intended beneficiaries and them alone — is by means of the "negative income tax."[20] Under this plan (which economists at both ends of the political spectrum have endorsed) all families ("income units") would file income tax returns; those reporting incomes below the poverty line would then receive a payment from the government. To discourage able-bodied persons from taking unfair advantage of the plan, the government might pay only part of the income deficiency. If, for example, the "standard" income for a family of four were $5,500 and the tax rate 50 percent, a family that earned nothing would get $2,750 (50 percent of $5,500); if it earned $1,000 it would get $2,240 and thus have a total income of $3,250.

According to Milton Friedman (the originator of the idea) all the poor could be brought above the poverty line with total transfer payments much smaller than those presently made, provided that few people stopped working once they were assured of some minimum income and provided that the negative income tax were regarded as a substitute for, not an addition to, most existing welfare programs. In his opinion, the savings would amount to more than twice the cost of the negative income tax itself. The plan has the added advantages, he argues, of minimizing interference in the allocation of resources by the market and of making explicit the cost of transfers to any particular income group.

All methods of redistributing income by transfer payments are open, although not in the same degree, to the objection that they destroy incentives — that both the one whose income is to be taken and the one to whom it is to be given will have less incentive to earn because of the transfer. A very severe reduction of incentives would render the elimination of poverty impossible and would have other extremely harmful consequences for society. One main advantage of the negative income tax is that its rates might be graduated so as to enable the individual always to add to his disposable income by

earning more. At present in most states, whatever a welfare recipient earns is deducted from the assistance he receives, leaving
him no incentive to earn anything.

No one can be at all sure how strong the disincentive effects of a
proposed income transfer will be. On theoretical grounds one would
expect them to be least important at the high end of the class
cultural scale and most important at the low end. Upper- and upper-
middle-class people often find intrinsic satisfaction in their work. To
them work is a means of self-improvement, self-expression, and
"service"; sometimes it is "exciting," "fun," "a game." Such satisfactions exist, but to a relatively small degree, in the work of the
lower-middle and the upper-working classes. For the lower-working
class they amount to very little: in this subculture, one works only
because one has to. In the lower class, work is most dissatisfying
because of the discipline it entails; the lower-class person prefers
near-destitution without work to abundance with it. The evidence
(such as it is) seems to confirm these expectations. High-income
earners have been found not to be — up to now at least — much
deterred by the prospect of higher taxes.[21] On the other hand, some
low-income earners seem to be very sensitive to disincentives. That
they will not work when welfare payments are as much or more
than they could earn is to be expected, of course.[22] However, it
also appears that many poor persons will not put forth effort to get
"extras" once they have been assured of a level of living which,
while extremely low, seems to them to be "enough."

The higher the floor that is put under incomes, the greater the
number of workers who will see no reason to work. A minimum
income at or slightly above the present poverty line might induce
many working- and middle-class people to lower substantially their
level of living for the sake of not working. To the extent that living
standards are thus reduced, the cost of eliminating poverty will be
tremendously increased; conceivably, it may be more than even a
very rich society can afford.

It may seem possible to avoid the disincentive problem merely by
refusing to give a minimum income to anyone able to work. Most of
the poor would still qualify, since a large majority are in families
headed by mothers, or by persons disabled or too old to work. The

difficulty, however, is that it would be outrageously unfair to give generous support to dependent families while supporting meagerly or not at all families — including about 30 percent of the poor — in which the head works full time. An inescapable dilemma exists, for the people who need assistance most are sometimes among the readiest to stop working.

Transfer payments produce disincentives not only to work but also to save, to learn skills, and in general to provide for the future.[23] No one can know how seriously these qualities might be impaired as a result of large-scale transfer payments.

Why, it may be asked, should anyone care — so long as society can afford it — if many able-bodied people are supported at some minimum-acceptable level of living without their having to work or to worry about the future? That it is unfair for some to "ride free" at the expense of others is one answer to this question but a rather minor one. (It must be remembered, too, that if it is unfair for the poor to live without working, it is also unfair for the rich to do so — more so, in fact, since they live better.) Another answer is that the level of living of those accepting the minimum will almost certainly be lower than it otherwise would be and lower than is socially desirable.

The major lesson in the British experience seems to be that flatrate schemes, whatever the original intention, end up at the subsistence level, forcing the system to depend on a combination of insurance and welfare.[24]

Still another consideration is that, generally speaking, the experience of not working and not taking responsibility for oneself and for one's family's welfare weakens not only personal character and happiness but also the family itself and perhaps other institutions upon which the welfare of society depends.[25]

A serious difficulty exists insofar as it is relative deprivation that constitutes poverty. It is usually assumed that only great inequalities of income make people feel poor in this sense. Victor R. Fuchs, in an article cited earlier, proposes defining as poor "any family whose income is less than one-half the median family income."[26] There will always be some differences in incomes in any society, he remarks, and there is no point in defining as poor those at the lower end of the distribution unless the gap between them and the median families is large. He assumes that a gap of less than 100 percent will not be thought large. It is possible, however, that when all incomes have been brought up to at least half the median, those people with incomes below, say, three-fourths of the median will seem — to themselves or to others — as poor as those with incomes under half the median used to seem. In principle, the subjective significance of income differences may increase steadily while the objective size of the differences decreases; this process may continue right up to the point (assuming that there is one in some meaningful sense) of income equality. In other words, it is at least possible that the closer they come to income equality the more acutely dissatisfied people with relatively low incomes may feel on account of such differences as remain.

This possibility is not as remote as it may seem. The poor today are not "objectively" any more deprived relative to the nonpoor than they were a decade ago. Few will doubt, however, that they *feel* more deprived — that they perceive the gap to be wider and that, this being the case, it *is* wider in the sense that matters most. By constantly calling attention to income differences, the war on poverty has probably engendered and strengthened feelings of relative deprivation. This subjective effect may have more than offset whatever objective reduction occurred in income inequality.

Finally, it may be that poverty in the sense of relative deprivation is only incidentally related to a lack of material things, and that therefore even "equality" of income (whatever that may mean) would leave as many people "poor" — i.e., feeling deprived — as before. This conclusion is implied by some of David Caplovitz's comments on the behavior of the low-income consumers he studied. They bought console phonographs, color television sets, and so on, he says, in order to "embellish" their social status; having failed to move up the social ladder, they "compensated" by climbing symbolically through consumption of such things.[27] If he is right, no amount of income redistribution can reduce, much less eliminate, their poverty: it consists not of lack of income, but of lack of *status*. Indeed, the more far-reaching the income redistribution, the more painfully apparent it may become that such symbols as color television sets cannot provide "real" status. If what the poor really want is a reduction of the extremes of status inequality, then income redistribution, however comprehensive, cannot help much. If they want the elimination of *all* status differences, then nothing can help.

why?

There is another kind of poverty, however. Robert Hunter described it in 1904:

They lived in God only knows what misery. They ate when there were things to eat; they starved when there was lack of food. But, on the whole, although they swore and beat each other and got drunk, they were more contented than any other class I have happened to know. It took a long time to understand them. Our Committees were busy from morning until night in giving them opportunities to take up the fight again, and to become independent of relief. They always took what we gave them; they always promised to try; but as soon as we expected them to fulfill any promises, they gave up in despair, and either wept or looked ashamed, and took to misery and drink again, — almost, so it seemed to me at times, with a sense of relief.[28]

In Hunter's day these were the "undeserving," "unworthy," "depraved," "debased," or "disreputable" poor; today, they are the "troubled," "culturally deprived," "hard to reach," or "multiproblem."[29] In the opinion of anthropologist Oscar Lewis, their kind of poverty "is a way of life, remarkably stable and persistent, passed down from generation to generation along family lines."[30] This "culture of poverty," as he calls it, exists in city slums in many parts of the world, and is, he says, an adaptation made by the poor in order to defend themselves against the harsh realities of slum life.

The view to be taken here (applying the analysis of the lower class of Chapter 3) is that there is indeed such a culture, but that poverty is its effect rather than its cause. (There are societies even poorer than the ones Lewis has described — primitive ones, for example — in which nothing remotely resembling the pattern of behavior here under discussion exists.) Extreme present-orientedness, not lack of income or wealth, is the principal cause of poverty in the sense of "the culture of poverty." Most of those caught up in this culture are unable or unwilling to plan for the future, to sacrifice immediate gratifications in favor of future ones, or to accept the disciplines that are required in order to get and to spend. Their inabilities are probably culturally given in most cases — "multiproblem" families being normal representatives of a class culture that is itself abnormal. No doubt there are also people whose present-orientedness is rationally adaptive rather than cultural, but these probably comprise only a small part of the "hard-core" poor. (See Chapter 10.)

Outside the lower class, poverty (in the sense of hardship, want, or destitution) is today almost always the result of external circumstances — involuntary unemployment, prolonged illness, the death of a breadwinner, or some other misfortune. Even when severe, such poverty is not squalid or degrading. Moreover, it ends quickly once the (external) cause of it no longer exists. Public or private assistance can sometimes remove or alleviate the cause — for example, by job retraining or remedial surgery. Even when the cause cannot be removed, simply providing the nonlower-class poor with sufficient income is enough to enable them to live "decently."

Lower-class poverty, by contrast, is "inwardly" caused (by psychological inability to provide for the future, and all that this inability implies). Improvements in external circumstances can affect this poverty only superficially: one problem of a "multiproblem" family is no sooner solved than another arises. In principle, it is possible to eliminate the poverty (material lack) of such a family, but only at great expense, since the capacity of the radically improvident to waste money is almost unlimited. Raising such a family's income would not necessarily improve its way of life, moreover, and could conceivably even make things worse. Consider, for example, the H. family:

Mrs. H. seemed overwhelmed with the simple mechanics of dressing her six children and washing their clothes. The younger ones were running around in their underwear; the older ones were unaccounted for, but presumably were around the neighborhood. Mrs. H. had not been out of the house for several months; evidently her husband did the shopping. The apartment was filthy and it smelled. Mrs. H. was dressed in a bathrobe, although it was mid-afternoon. She seemed to have no plan or expectations with regard to the children; she did not know the names of their teachers and she did not seem to worry about their school work, although one child had been retained one year and another two years. Mrs. H. did seem to be somewhat concerned about her husband's lack of activity over the weekend — his continuous drinking and watching baseball on television. Apparently he and she never went out socially together nor did the family ever go anywhere as a unit.[31]

If this family had a very high income — say, $50,000 a year — it would not be considered a "culture of poverty" case. Mrs. H. would hire maids to look after the small children, send the others to boarding schools, and spend her time at fashion shows while her husband drank and watched TV at his club. But with an income of only moderate size — say 100 percent above the poverty line — they would probably be about as badly off as they are now. They might be even worse off, for Mrs. H. would be able to go to the dog races, leaving the children alone, and Mr. H. could devote more time to his bottle and TV set.

Such families constitute a small proportion both of all families in the city (perhaps 5 percent at most[32]) and of those with incomes below the poverty line (perhaps 10 to 20 percent). The problems that they present are out of proportion to their numbers, however; in St. Paul, Minnesota, for example, a survey showed that 6 percent of the city's families absorbed 77 percent of its public assistance, 51 percent of its health services, and 56 percent of its mental health and correction casework services.[33] Moreover, their misery is (or at least seems) far greater than that of the other poor — the garbage-strewn, rat-infested hovels with toilets out of order are now almost exclusively theirs. Giving them income, even in rather large amounts, is unlikely to reduce and may even increase their poverty.

Welfare agencies, recognizing the difference between "internally" and "externally" caused poverty, have long been trying first by one means and then another to improve the characters or, as it is now put, to "bring about personal adjustment" of the poor. In the nineteenth century, the view was widely held that what the lower-class individual needed was to be brought into a right relation with God or (the secular version of the same thing) with the respectable (that is, middle- and upper-class) elements of the community. The missionary who distributed tracts door to door in the slums was the first caseworker; his — more often, her — task was to minister to what today would be called "feelings of alienation."

> The stranger, coming on a stranger's errand, becomes a friend, discharging the offices and exerting the influence of a friend. . . .[34]

Secularized, this approach became the "friendly visitor" system under which "certain persons, under the direction of a central board, pledge themselves to take one or more families who need counsel, if not material help, on their visiting list, and maintain personal friendly relations with them."[35] The system did not work; middle- and upper-class people might be "friendly," but they could not sympathize, let alone communicate, with the lower class. By the beginning of the twentieth century the friendly visitor had been replaced by the "expert."[36] The idea now was that the authority of "the facts" would bring about desired changes of attitude, motive, and habit. As it happened, however, the lower class did not recognize the authority of the facts. The expert then became a supervisor, using his (or her) power to confer or withhold material benefits in order to force the poor to do the things that were supposed to lead to "rehabilitation" (that is, to a middle-class style of life).[37] This method did not work either; the lower class could always find ways to defeat and exploit the system. They seldom changed their ways very much and they never changed them for long. Besides, there was really no body of expertise to tell caseworkers how to produce the changes desired. As one caseworker remarked recently in a book addressed to fellow social service professionals:

> Despite years of experience in providing public aid to poor families precious little is yet known about how to help truly inadequate parents make long term improvements in child care, personal maturity, social relations, or work stability.[38]

Some people understood that if the individual's style of life was to be changed at all, it would be necessary to change that of the group that produced, motivated, and constrained him. Thus, the settlement house. As Robert A. Woods explained:

> The settlements are able to take neighborhoods in cities, and by patience bring back to them much of the healthy village life, so that the people shall again know and care for one another. . . .[39]

When it became clear that settlement houses would not change the culture of slum neighborhoods, the group approach was broadened into what is called "community action." In one type of community action ("community development"), a community organizer tries to persuade a neighborhood's informal leaders to support measures (for instance, measures for delinquency control) that he advances.[40] In another form of it ("community organization"), the organizer tries to promote self-confidence, self-respect, and attachment to the group (and, hopefully, to normal society) among lower-class people. He attempts to do this by encouraging them in efforts at joint action, or by showing them how to conduct meetings, carry on discussions, pass resolutions, present requests to politicians, and the like. In still another form ("community mobilization"), the organizer endeavors to arouse the anger of lower-class persons against the local "power structure," to teach them the techniques of mass action — strikes, sit-ins, picketing, and so on — and to show them how they may capture power. The theory of community organization attributes the malaise of the poor to their lack of self-confidence (which is held to derive largely from their "inexperience"); community mobilization theory, by contrast, attributes it to their feelings of "powerlessness." According to this doctrine, the best cure for poverty is to give the poor power. But since power is not "given," it must be seized.[41]

The success of the group approach has been no greater than that of the caseworker approach. Reviewing five years of effort on the part of various community action programs, Marris and Rein conclude:

. . . the reforms had not evolved any reliable solutions to the intractable problems with which they struggled. They had not discovered how in general to override the intransigent autonomy of public and private agencies, at any level of government; nor how to use the social sciences practically to formulate and evaluate policy; nor how, under the sponsorship of government, to raise the power of the poor. Given the talent and money they had brought to bear, they had not even reopened very many opportunities.[42]

If the war on poverty is judged by its ability "to generate major, meaningful and lasting social and economic reforms in conformity with the expressed wishes of poor people," writes Thomas Gladwin, ". . . it is extremely difficult to find even scattered evidence of success."[43] The Economic Opportunity Act of 1965 might require "maximum feasible participation" in the planning and conduct of programs financed under it, but the poor rarely cared to participate even to the extent of voting. In Philadelphia, for example, there was a polling place in each of the twelve "poverty areas," and the Gas Works contributed twelve trucks and drivers to carry additional voting machines from block to block; the turnout, however, was only 5.5 percent of those eligible in 1966.[44]

Although city agencies have sent community organizers by the score into slum neighborhoods, the lower-class poor cannot be organized. In East Harlem in 1948, five social workers were assigned to organize a five-block area and to initiate a program of social action based on housing, recreation, and other neighborhood needs. After three years of effort, the organizers had failed to attract a significant number of participants, and those they did attract were upwardly mobile persons who were unrepresentative of the neighborhood.[45] In Boston a "total community" delinquency control project was found to have had "negligible impact," an outcome strikingly like that of the Cambridge-Somerville experiment — a "total caseworker" project — a decade earlier.[46] Even community mobilization, despite the advantages of a rhetoric of hate and an emphasis on "action," failed to involve lower-class persons to a significant extent.[47] Gangsters and leaders of youth gangs were co-opted on occasion, but they did not suffer from feelings of powerlessness and were not representative of the class for which mobilization was to provide therapy. No matter how hard they have tried to appeal to people at the very bottom of the scale, community organizers have rarely succeeded. Where they have appeared to succeed, as, for example, in the National Welfare Rights Organization, it has been by recruiting people who had some of the *outward* attributes of the lower class — poverty, for example — but whose outlook and values were not lower class; the lower-class person (as defined here) is incapable of being organized. Although it tried strenuously to avoid it, what the Mobilization for Youth described as the general experience proved to be its own experience as well:

Most efforts to organize lower-class people attract individuals on their way up the social-class ladder. Persons who are relatively responsible about participation, articulate and successful at managing organizational "forms" are identified as lower-class leaders, rather than individuals who actually reflect the values of lower-class groups. Ordinarily the slum's network of informal group associations is not reached.[48]

He defines 4 kinds of Poverty: destitution, want, hardship and relative deprivation.

He Notes two possible policy alternatives: work or transfer payments.

His main point is that no amount of work or transfer payment programs will help the lower class poor, which he says is a relatively small amount of poor - the hardcore. The reason is that they are the incapable of either working effectively or spending appropriately, because of the cultural traits they have inherited. These traits are the cause of their poverty. For the majority of poor however, the problem is one of environment or circumstance.

"unworkly poor" — Hunter's Paupers

Schooling Versus Education

DEAR ABBY: I took my freshman year over again and I am still a freshman. In other words, I failed everything again. I admit I fooled around the first time, but I really tried to make it this time, but the work was too hard for me. My parents don't believe me. They think I let them down, but I really tried my best.

I would like to quit school and go to a trade school, but my father says I have to graduate from high school if it takes me 10 years. What can I do?

— ASHAMED

T HE most widely recommended "solution" to the problems of the city is more and better schooling. There is almost nothing that someone does not hope to achieve by this means. City planners see it as a necessary and perhaps sufficient condition for bringing the middle class back into the city from the suburbs. Almost everyone (except economists) thinks that the unschooled will be unemployable in the automated society of the future and — a *non sequitur* — that schooling will prevent unemployment. Since it can be shown statistically that the least schooled have the lowest incomes, schooling is also thought to be a cure for poverty and thus, indirectly, for the slum and the "ghetto." A proper system of education, the HARYOU manual says, is "an inescapable foundation for the reality of respect and self-respect . . . and the basis for the type of vocational and academic adjustment essential for an effective life. . . ."[1]

Education is, of course, a good thing, and no society can have too much of it. What must be questioned, however, is whether "schooling" and "education" necessarily imply one another and, more particularly, whether the kind of schooling possible under existing circumstances — for instance, the intelligence of children, their class culture, the state of the art of teaching, the character of the teaching profession, and so on — is capable of producing the desired effects. The view to be taken in this chapter is that the possibilities for improving the city by reforming its schools are sharply limited. Even if the schools were to do much better those things that it is possible for them to do, the result would hardly change the main features of the situation in the city. Nothing that can be done in the schools of the central city can significantly affect the movement of the well-off to the suburbs or reduce the amount of poverty or teen-age unemployment.[2] Nothing done in them can provide that "inescapable foundation of respect and self-respect" which HARYOU thinks would reduce racial unrest and social disorganization in general. On the contrary, the reforms that would probably be made in the name of "education" — especially requiring more children to spend more time in school — may be expected to produce results exactly the opposite of those intended; that is, they will very likely hasten the movement of the well-off from the city, increase unemployment and poverty, widen the chasms of class and race, and plunge deeper into apathy, or stir into fiercer anger, those already angry or apathetic.

There is no denying that, in general, boys and girls who graduate from high school find better jobs and find them faster than do boys and girls who do not graduate from high school, or that those who have two or three years of high school find better jobs than those who have only one.[3] The more high school one has, the less unemployment one is likely to suffer in later life and the greater one's lifetime earnings are likely to be. Economists have calculated that the individual who finishes high school gets a very high rate of return on his investment of time (represented by what he might earn if he went to work instead of to school). In 1961, according to Gary Becker, a Columbia economist, the rate was slightly more than 28 percent.[4] This rate was a good deal higher than that of a generation or so ago, and higher also than the current rate of return from a college education.

That the average graduate makes more than the average nongraduate does not mean that it would pay the nongraduate equally to get a diploma. Some who leave school could not get diplomas no matter how long they stayed, and others, even if they got them, would earn less in later life than the average graduate because of their lesser ability. (When Becker adjusted for the lower capability of dropouts, the difference between their earnings and those of the graduates was reduced by from 40 to 60 percent.[5])

In the cities (and elsewhere) the percentage of boys and girls failing to complete high school has long been declining and continues to decline. (In 1940, one adult in four had completed high school; by 1970 more than half will be graduates.) If this trend continues, a point must soon be reached below which the dropout rate cannot be reduced, for there will be *some* number of students who are simply not capable of doing high school work (unless, of course, as has happened in some places, standards are redefined so as not to require reading ability).

That, on the average, high school graduates earn more than dropouts does not necessarily mean that they earn more *because of anything that they learned in high school* (although of course it may mean that). Their greater earnings may be attributable partly or wholly to their greater quickness of mind. Suppose that all those who now graduate (average IQ 112) became dropouts instead and that all those who now drop out (average IQ 98) became graduates. If this happened, one might find twenty or thirty years hence that dropouts had higher incomes than graduates. Of course, it would be a mistake to attribute their success to their having dropped out.

The higher earnings of graduates may also be attributable in part (conceivably entirely) to their class culture. Perhaps class characteristics (for example, willingness or ability to defer gratification, accept discipline, and behave in ways acceptable to middle-class people) rather than what such youths learn in high school account for their greater employability later. Suppose, again, that middle- and upper-class children left school and lower- and working-class ones got diplomas. In this case, too, the dropouts might have higher average incomes later on.

Still another possibility is that employers attach more importance than they should to the number of years a person has spent in school and perhaps also to the value to them of what he has learned there. According to Daniel E. Diamond, a labor economist:

> There is evidence that employers often fail to test whether a particular requirement or set of requirements are justified by the actual job to be performed. For example, one of our graduate students, utilizing statistical analysis, studied the relationship between hiring requirements and job performance of bank tellers in a large New York City bank. The bank gave each job applicant a battery of psychological tests. High test scores were interpreted as evidence of potential success as a teller and low scores as evidence of potential failure. Fortunately for the bank, the test scores were not used as an automatic screening out device; although some applicants undoubtedly were denied employment because of low test scores. Discriminate analysis showed that there were no significant relationships between test scores and success on the job. Indeed, some of the test scores correlated negatively with job performance.[6]

In times of slack employment especially, employers are likely to give an automatic preference to graduates. Even if the work (e.g., wrapping packages) could be done as well by a dropout, the employer will probably prefer a graduate if he can have him at the same wage as the dropout. When the wage rate is the same, he has to find *some* basis for choosing one boy rather than another, and it is at least plausible for him to assume that a diploma is evidence of some sort of achievement, or — more likely perhaps — that there is probably "something wrong" with a boy who does not finish high school now that most do.[7]

Presumably, the enormous amount of propaganda directed at actual and potential dropouts by school authorities and by officialdom in general proceeds from the assumption that jobs require more formal education now than they did a generation or two ago and that every additional year of schooling will make a boy or girl that much more employable. The conclusion makes sense for students who are going into such work as medicine, which does require more technical training. But much work does not require more, and students who are told the contrary are being deceived and defrauded. That many *are* being told the contrary probably accounts in part for the fact that between October 1952 and March 1965 the percentage of unskilled factory workers with twelve years of schooling increased from 13.8 percent to 23.9 percent.[8] Unskilled factory work, needless to say, did not change its nature very much, if at all, in less than thirteen years.

There is every reason to try to persuade the would-be — or to-be — laborer to get as much education as he can for his own enjoyment later on. But there is no reason to encourage him to stay in school on the pretext that he will acquire skills valuable to him as a manual laborer. As Arthur Stinchcombe remarks in *Rebellion in High School:*

Is there anything that a high school can teach which employers of manual labor would be willing to pay for, if it were learned well? In general, the answer is no. Neither physical abilities nor reliability, the two main variables of interest to employers of manual labor, are much influenced by schooling. Employers concerned with securing reliable workers may require high school diplomas as evidence of good discipline. Otherwise they can train workers better and cheaper than a high school can, on the job.[9]

That earning power in later life is less affected by what is learned in high school than is generally supposed can be seen from studies of the careers of people who are of such low intelligence that they cannot have learned much in school. Such people often do about as well as "normal" ones in the job market. A sociologist in Connecticut compared the job experience of a group of "mentally deficient persons who had graduated from the special class for slow learners in the regular public schools" with that of a control group consisting of persons who had started first grade at the same time and had passed through the school system in the regular way. The two groups were approximately matched as to age, sex, nationality, religion, and father's occupation, but the subjects' IQ's ranged from 50 to 75, whereas those of the controls ranged from 75 upward. After interviewing each subject in 1948 and again in 1960, the investigator concluded: "The overwhelming majority of both subjects and controls had made acceptable and remarkably similar adjustment in all three areas: personal, social, and economic." The median weekly earnings of the subjects were $88.50, those of the controls $102.50. More than a fourth of both groups had been on the same job for twelve years. None of the subjects earned exceptionally large salaries; a few of the controls did. Employers rated the subjects somewhat less favorably than the controls on almost all criteria. The subjects also were less likely to have savings accounts, checking accounts, or telephones, or to own their own homes. *"In most respects, however,"* the investigator concluded, *"the differences in . . . economic measurements between subjects and controls are insignificant. . . ."*[10]

It is safe to say that if the subjects in this study had been known to the employers as "mentally retarded" they would not have gotten their jobs in the first place. Indeed, "mentally retarded" persons are generally to be found in institutions, and the reason in most cases is not that they are innately incapable of working but that public opinion simply takes it for granted that the "retarded" cannot work and should be institutionalized. "Normal" employees suffer loss of self-esteem when they work alongside known retardates; knowing that the retardate can do what they do — perhaps almost as well as they can do it — makes it hard for them to take pride in their work. But if the retardate is not known as such, the problem does not arise. There are societies in which more than half the population would be "retarded" if retardation were defined in the usual way by an IQ score. They manage quite well, however, because they lack a concept of retardation; in the nature of the case, the percentage of those seriously handicapped by lack of intelligence in competition with others is small. But when, as in our society, retardation is defined in terms of an objective test and the retardates' alleged incapacity is made known to all, the number of retardates is thereby enormously increased and their chances of leading normal lives enormously decreased.[11]

With dropouts the situation is much the same. Persons who have not mastered the subject matter taught in the last year or two of high school need not for that reason be much less employable than those who have. In fact, those of them who got diplomas (those, that is, who merely occupied a chair in school for the required time) are about as employable as those who actually mastered the subject matter. If we did not have the label "dropout" to hang on them, those who left school without a diploma would be about as employable as the others. It is because our society is rich and wasteful — and because it is too much on the lookout for ways of "doing good"— that it defines millions of people with IQ's between 50 and 70 as "retarded" and "needing help" (thereby implying that they are not employable and probably ought to be institutionalized) and hundreds of thousands who have not seen fit to spend twelve years in school as "dropouts" (thereby implying that they, too, need help and will be of little use to society and to themselves unless they get it).[12]

Measures to reduce unemployment and poverty by increasing the skills of workers through schooling can have only a very limited success. They cannot change the situation fundamentally; probably the best they can do is to hasten somewhat the movement up the job and income ladder of people who would move up it anyway.

A distinction should be made between a "trained" worker and an "educated" one. The trained worker has learned how to perform certain tasks of more or less complexity — to operate a machine, say, or to keep accounts. Training may mean acquiring certain manual dexterities, mastering some body of facts, or learning to apply a set of rules or to exercise discretion within some given limits. The educated worker, by contrast, (1) possesses the kind of general knowledge, especially of reading and mathematics, that will enable him to solve various new problems, and (2) has certain traits of character — especially motivation to achieve, ability to accept the discipline of a work situation, willingness to take the initiative and to accept responsibility, and ability to deal fairly with employers, fellow-employees, and others.

Training may be given entirely in school or on the job. Education, on the other hand, cannot be wholly acquired in either place. Some of what it takes to make a worker educated (especially in reading and mathematical knowledge) can only be learned from books and is usually best learned in school — or perhaps one should say would be best learned there if the school were, in fact, a place where boys and girls generally tried to learn; but the traits of character that are equally a part of education are not learned in school — or at any rate not there more than elsewhere. For the most part, they are acquired in childhood as part of one's culture.

The lower-class person cannot as a rule be given much training because he will not accept it. He lives for the moment, and learning to perform a task is a way of providing for the future. If the training process is accompanied by immediate rewards to the trainee — if it is "fun" or if he is paid while learning — the lower-class person *may* accept training. But even if he does, his earning power will not be much increased, because his class outlook and style of life will generally make him an unreliable and otherwise undesirable employee. Besides, the ability to perform tasks (that is, to do what he has been trained to do) is seldom a very rare or valuable commodity. He *would* increase his earning power greatly if he became educated (as opposed to trained); to have in high degree and in combination both general education and the traits of character mentioned above is rare and valuable. Unfortunately, however, the lower-class person acquires in childhood an outlook and style of life completely antithetical to education.

The lower-class person presents the extreme case: it is all but impossible to increase his employability by training. With the lower working class the difficulties are the same in kind but less in degree. There are also many persons who, because of racial prejudice or other externally imposed handicaps, are taken to be lower or lower working class when in fact they are not. Their abilities, motivation, and traits of character are such that they can be trained to perform tasks and sometimes educated to hold down skilled jobs. Most such people would find ways of getting the training or education somehow even if there were no schools, but not all of them would, and in any case there is much to be said for any measures that will help them. That the general problem of the low-capability worker can be solved in this way is too much to hope for, however.

Much more might be accomplished by altering jobs to fit the limitations of workers than vice versa.[13] The principle of specialization could be applied so as to make the low-intelligence and even the lower-class worker much more employable than he is at present. Cutting meat, for example, need not involve dealing with customers: the two activities could be organized as separate jobs. If employers would program work for low-capability workers in the manner that they program it for computers, the workers' job opportunities would be vastly increased. They are not likely to do so, however, so long as minimum-wage laws, union practices, and social prejudices compel them to pay more for low-value labor than it is worth. Instead, they will do the opposite — find ways to replace low-capacity workers with high-capacity ones and with machines.

To say that the school cannot change the child's class culture is to deny that it can serve what many believe to be its principal purpose. The schools, many people think, exist to liberate the child from the confines — moral and emotional as well as intellectual — of his earliest environment and to open higher horizons for him. No child is more in need of liberation than the lower-class one, and therefore it is thought that the schools are — or at any rate should be — instrumentalities for drawing this child into the larger, freer, more productive world of normal culture as well as for encouraging and facilitating the movement of the working-class child into the middle class and the middle-class child into the upper class. This seems to be what is meant when it is said that schooling provides an "inescapable foundation for the reality of respect and self-respect . . . and the basis for the type of vocational and academic adjustment essential for an effective life." This is why it is generally held that, both from the standpoint of the individual and of the society, it is impossible to have too much schooling. And this is why the inability of the schools to prepare thousands of boys and girls for skilled (or even semiskilled) work and for responsible citizenship and adulthood is counted against them as a failure and is taken as a portent of social decay and collapse.

This idea of what the schools should do contrasts strangely with the account sociologists give of what they do in fact.[14] According to this account, the school does not liberate the child from his class culture but instead confines him in it even more securely — it thickens the walls that separate him from the rest of society. The child has absorbed the elements of his class culture long before reaching school; what the school does is to "socialize" him into it more fully and to make him more aware of the differences that separate him and his kind from others. The child has "picked up" from parents and playmates an outline map of his universe, and the main features of it — the continents, so to speak — cannot be changed by anything that is said or done in school. At best, teachers can only help the child to fill in certain empty spaces on the map he brings with him to school. If the map is extremely crude or wildly inaccurate, teachers and textbooks can be of little help. Nor can they help very much if it is drawn in symbols that are incomprehensible to them. (Working-class Italian-American children studied by Gans in Boston's West End were not adept at manipulating concepts or at handling the reasoning processes in texts and lessons; instead, they were sensitive to people, used words not as concepts but to impress people, and stressed the anecdotal and the episodic — all of which led to learning difficulties in school.)[15] In extreme cases (that is, those presented by lower-class children) not much filling-in of the map is possible, and the little that is possible must take place in the street rather than in the school.

How, it may be asked, can this claim that the school furthers the socialization of a child into his class culture be reconciled with the familiar fact that in America the schools are and always have been a principal vehicle of upward mobility? The answer is that the children who are stimulated into mobility in school are ones whose initial class culture permits or encourages — perhaps even demands — mobility. The more nearly upper class the child's initial culture, the more susceptible he is to being "set in motion" by the school. At the other end of the continuum, the lower-class child's culture does not even recognize — much less value — the possibility of rising or, rather, of doing those things, all of which require some sacrifice of present for future gratification, without which rising is impossible. The lower-class child's conceptual universe lacks the dimension of time; in such a universe it would never occur to anyone to try to change things.

The circumstances that prevent the lower-class child (and in lesser degree the lower-working-class one as well) from learning in school the traits of character that contribute to education also prevent him from learning adequately how to read, write, and compute. The inadequacy of his preparation in the earliest years imposes a handicap that schools cannot overcome later on. By the age of fourteen, according to Basil Bernstein, many such children are "unteachable." Keeping them in school does not add to their knowledge; it only damages their self-respect, which is already small.[16] For the child whose class culture *does* encourage upward mobility, schooling very often has the broadening and liberating effects that it is supposed to have. But even for these children, ". . . education is but one of many factors influencing mobility, and it may be far from a dominant factor."[17]

Class-cultural factors largely account for the conspicuous difference between the slum and the suburban school. Each school has a class character imposed upon it by the social setting in which it exists; this, and not staff inefficiency, racial discrimination, or inequitable provision of resources, is the *main* reason for the virtues of one and the defects of the other. The implication is one that reformers find hard to accept — to wit, that no matter how able, dedicated, and hardworking the teachers, no matter how ample the facilities of the school or how well-designed its curriculum, no matter how free the atmosphere of the school from racial or other prejudice, the performance of pupils at the lower end of the class-cultural scale will always fall short not only of that of pupils at the upper end of the scale, but also of what is necessary to make them educated workers.

These conclusions are supported by several recent studies. The most elaborate (involving some 645,000 pupils in 4,000 public schools) was made by James S. Coleman and others for the U.S. Office of Education and published under the title *Equality of Educational Opportunity*.[18] Standard achievement tests administered to pupils at grades 1, 3, 6, 9, and 12 showed wide differences among metropolitan and nonmetropolitan areas, among regions, and among racial groups in what pupils had learned. Differences among schools accounted for very little of the differences in learning. Differences in facilities, curriculum, and staff also had very little connection with achievement. Only among Southern Negroes did low per-pupil expenditures influence pupil achievement. Such factors as pupil-teacher ratio and comprehensiveness of curriculum made little difference anywhere. Teacher quality made more difference in the achievement of children from deficient educational backgrounds — especially minority-group ones — than it made in the achievement of the more advantaged, but even this factor was not of great importance. Attributes of fellow students, Coleman and his associates found, account far more for the lower achievement of minority-group pupils than do any attributes of school facilities and slightly more than does the quality of the teachers.[19] Negro pupils did better in schools with greater proportions of white pupils, but this effect, the authors said, "comes not from racial composition per se, but from the better educational background and higher educational aspirations" generally found among white pupils.[20] The factor found to be of greatest importance in accounting for variations in achievement was "family background." Compared to this one, the factors relating to the schools themselves (facilities, curriculum, and staff) amounted to very little. "Schools," the report said, "bring little influence to bear on a child's achievement that is independent of his background and general social context."[21]

One element deriving from family background — pupil's attitude — was found to be of special significance (it accounted for more of the variation in achievement than did all other family background variables taken together and also more than did all school variables taken together).[22] Three attitudes were tested: (1) the pupil's interest in school and in reading outside of school: (2) his "self-concept," especially with regard to learning and to success in school; and (3) his sense of control of his environment. For white and Oriental pupils, self-concept was most important; for all other minority groups (Negroes, American Indians, Mexican-Americans, and Puerto Ricans) sense of control of environment had the greatest significance. Sense of control of environment was measured by pupils' responses to three statements: "Good luck is more important than hard work for success," "Every time I try to get ahead, something or someone stops me," and "People like me don't have much of a chance to be successful in life." The responses of pupils from those minority groups with lowest pupil achievement (i.e., all but the Orientals) related more strongly to achievement than did any other variable. This result, the Coleman group wrote, "is particularly impressive because this attitude has no direct logical relation to achievement."[23] Perhaps a relation is to be found in the time horizon peculiar to a child's class (and possibly ethnic) culture. One would expect that the more present-oriented the child, the less sense of control over his environment he would have.

A study conducted by the Advisory Committee on Race and Education (chairman, Thomas F. Pettigrew) of the U.S. Commission on Civil Rights, extended and reinforced some of the Coleman group's principal findings.[24] Reanalyzing Coleman's data, the Pettigrew group found that the average performance of a "disadvantaged" pupil improves when the social class (as measured by the average education of students' parents) of the school he attends is higher than his own social class. This relationship was found to be particularly strong when the disadvantaged pupil is a Negro.[25] The implication is, of course, that putting a lower-class child (whatever his race) in a middle-class school will cause him to perform better and, by the same token, that putting a middle-class one in a lower-class school will cause him to perform worse.

The Pettigrew committee also found that programs designed to improve pupil achievement by raising the aspirations of parents, the expectations of teachers, or the pupils' motivation and cultural horizons, as well as preschool programs — in short, "compensatory" programs of all kinds — have so far had no lasting effect when tried in a segregated school. The reason, the committee conjectured, is that segregation creates a moral and psychological atmosphere that makes success impossible.[26] An alternative explanation might be that the pupils participating in these programs have in most cases been lower or lower working class.[27]

On one important point the Pettigrew study came to a conclusion opposite to the Coleman one. Racial segregation in the classroom, it found, accounts to a significant extent for the poorer achievement of Negro as compared to white pupils. (Twelfth-grade Negroes in predominantly white lower-class schools perform a little over one grade level higher than do those in predominantly Negro lower-class schools.)[28] The committee inferred that the elimination of racial segregation would considerably improve the performance of the average Negro pupil. Some have questioned this inference by pointing out that Negro children who go to white schools (even to lower-class ones) are more likely than most Negroes to be middle class and that this (i.e., their class culture) rather than their going to school with whites may account for their somewhat better performance. This criticism receives some support from the fact that lower-class Negro children going to lower-class white schools perform only a little better than do lower-class Negro children going to lower-class Negro schools (twelfth-graders going to white lower-class schools have eighth-grade scores, whereas those going to Negro schools have seventh-grade ones).

These and other studies lead one to conclude that if the teachers, facilities, and curricula of all slum schools were exactly as good as those of the very best suburban ones, and if all schools were integrated, there would be almost as many low achievers as there are now.

If the view that has been taken here is correct, the principal difficulty is that the school is future-oriented, whereas the lower-class (or "disadvantaged") pupil is present-oriented. "The school," writes Bernstein, "is an institution where every item in the present is finely linked to a distant future, and in consequence there is no serious clash of expectations between the school and the middle-class child." The lower-class child, by contrast,

is concerned mainly with the present; his social structure, unlike that of the middle-class child, provides little incentive or purposeful support to make the methods and ends of the school personally meaningful. The problems of discipline and classroom control result not from isolated points of resistance or conflict but from the attempt to reorient a whole pattern of perception with its emotional counterpart.[29]

Cloward and Jones describe the American situation in much the same terms:

Our system of education places a strong stress upon doing rather than being, upon a future orientation rather than an orientation toward the present or the past, upon the notion that man is superordinate to nature rather than in harmony with it or subjugated by it, upon the notion that man is flexible and plastic and capable of change rather than that he is essentially, and perhaps immutably, evil. A child who has not acquired these particular value orientations in his home and community is not so likely to compete successfully with youngsters among whom these values are implicitly taken for granted.[30]

The implication is that the school must adapt to the mentality of the lower-class child if it is to be of use to him. "The methods and problems of teaching need to be thought out almost as though middle-class children do not exist," Bernstein says.[31] Others think that it is unfair to offer the lower-class child a choice between a middle-class education and no education at all. Cloward and Jones, for example, say that the system should not be organized "to favor children who are socialized in one rather than another part of the social structure."[32] However, the only way to avoid this is to organize some schools to give what may be called a lower-class (in contradistinction to a middle- or upper-class) education — an education for those who want to be rather than to do, whose verbal ability is very low, and who are not motivated to learn. This notion of fairness, presumably, is the basis for complaints about the fact that teachers are almost all middle-class and for objections to the efforts of the schools to teach correct (middle-class) English to children who will never have occasion to speak it. Apparently, the idea is that to be fair to the lower-class child, the schools should give him teachers, books, and subject matter appropriate to a lower-class education.

The trouble with this idea, however, is that a lower-class education is a contradiction in terms; lower-class culture is the attitudes and behavior patterns of people who have not been educated at all. To be sure, a child "learns" this culture in the sense that he learns to be improvident, undisciplined, and so on. But what he learns is not knowledge that could be taught in school even if everyone agreed that it should be. No one would write it down in books (for to do so would require a large measure of "middle-class" knowledge), no one would teach it (a lower-class teacher would not come to work regularly and would not have anything to teach in a classroom if he did), and no one would learn it (for the lower-class pupil is poorly disposed toward learning anything).

Giving a "lower-class education" can only mean giving no education at all, and this, one would suppose, can be done better on the street than in school. If, for example, it is pointless to try to teach the child correct English, it is pointless to try to teach him English at all. The only system that will not favor the child at the upper end of the class-cultural scale is one that frees the lower-class child from having to go to school at all. *All* education favors the middle- and upper-class child, because to be middle- or upper-class is to have qualities that make one particularly educable.

Perhaps critics who attack the school for its middle-class character really mean that if a strenuous enough effort were made to avoid confusing and humiliating the lower-class child, it might be possible to get him to try climbing the educational ladder. On this view, the school should not only avoid the unconscious snobbism of the middle class but ought also to make some pretense of being lower-class in order to put the child at his ease and to establish contact with him. This approach is not really to change the school's class character but only to seem to do so. The question that must be asked is: Will it work, and not merely with a few gifted teachers but with most teachers? That it is highly desirable not to offend or humiliate the child goes without saying. But whether the school, which in the nature of things must be an expression of normal (as opposed to lower-class) culture, can pretend not to be that, or could accomplish anything by so doing, may well be doubted. Such evidence as there is suggests that by the time he reaches school, the lower-class child's handicap is too firmly fixed to allow of its being significantly reduced by anything the school might do.

There is much evidence that children learn fastest in the earliest years of life. By the age of four, according to one account, general intelligence has developed as much as it will in the next fourteen years; a poor start in these first years means that the child is likely to fail throughout his school career no matter what the school may do later on to help him.[33]

These findings make it plausible to suppose that if the school is to educate the lower-class child, it must start with him much earlier than it now does. Preschool programs such as Headstart (which involved 561,000 children in 1965) apparently do not go far enough in this direction. Whatever the reason, they seem to accomplish very little. "Disadvantaged" children usually make rather large gains in intelligence-test performance after a year of preschool, but the gains are partly lost either in a second year of preschool or in the first grade. One study showed an average decrease in IQ during the second year.[34] Another showed no differences in educational achievement between children who had six months of kindergarten and children who did not and revealed that children who had been to kindergarten and later had poor teachers actually performed less well than they had before going to kindergarten.[35] Some theorists explain these findings on the ground that preschool comes too late to influence the child very deeply. Working on this assumption, one group of researchers planned a day-care center to take infants as young as six weeks.[36]

It would be premature to conclude that the lower-class child must be introduced to normal culture almost from birth if he is ever to succeed in school. The evidence, however, seems to point in this direction. Unfortunately, the prospects for fundamental reform in this direction appear very poor; in a free society infants cannot be taken from their parents on the grounds that the parents are lower-class and that the children therefore will not do well in school. Perhaps many parents could be bribed to send their infants to day care centers. Even so, however, it is by no means certain that tens of thousands of suitable "teachers" could be found to look after them.

Since the schools are not teaching much to many children after ninth grade, it would make sense to give a diploma on completion of nine grades (rather than twelve as at present) and to lower the school-leaving age to fourteen.[37] These steps would not reduce the amount of public education available to those who are able and willing to learn, but they would enable nonlearners to leave school and to do so without being stigmatized as dropouts. (Unfortunately, however, in a society in which increasing numbers of students do finish high school, *some* stigma for those who do not is inescapable.)

There are at least three compelling reasons for getting non-learners out of school. The first is to stop what one educator has called the process of "anti-education" in school and thus to prevent further injury to the nonlearners' self-respect and further lessening of their regard for the institutions of the society. As matters now stand, the pretense of the school — one that must be ridiculous to boys who will be manual workers and to girls who will soon start having babies — that it and it alone offers "opportunity" is surely one cause of youth unrest. The boy who knows that he has learned nothing since the eighth grade but that he must nevertheless sit in boredom, frustration, and embarrassment until he is sixteen or seventeen (in a few states, eighteen), when finally he will be labeled "dropout," must be profoundly disaffected by the experience. He senses that the school authorities and the whole apparatus of middle- and upper-class opinion that confine him there neither understand nor even care about the most palpable realities of his situation: that he will very likely work with his hands all his life, that he is not learning anything, that for such work he would not be helped by learning any more, and that one who works with his hands had better start early because he will be "old" by the time he is forty. To tell such a boy that he must stay in school anyway because in the future there will be no jobs for people with only hands is to tell him something that is both untrue and irrelevant. If he cannot learn, staying in school will not help, and if there are no jobs for people with only hands, supporting him will be society's problem, not his.

Rebellious behavior, Stinchcombe concluded from his study of a high school, "is largely a reaction to the school itself and to its promises, not a failure of the family or community."[38] The suggestion is that much juvenile delinquency originates in the adolescent's anger at the stupidity and hypocrisy of a system that uses him in this way. The later the school-leaving age, the more involved with delinquency the school will be. As Martin Trow has written:

The growth of educational opportunity threatens to make the greater part of terminal education in high schools coincidental with the social problems of juvenile delinquency. This is not to say that every classroom full of non-college-going students is or will be a "blackboard jungle." It does mean that the hostility toward the school characteristic of the juvenile gangs, but much more widespread than their membership, will be an increasing part of the educational problem faced by schools and teachers dealing with terminal students.[39]

The school's involvement with delinquency may become greater as the school-leaving age is delayed, not simply because there are then more students of an age to be delinquent (which is what Trow seems to mean) but also because having to stay in school after learning has stopped is itself a cause of delinquency. In Britain, the Crowther Committee reported that when (in 1947) the school-leaving age was raised from fourteen to fifteen ". . . there was an immediate change over in the delinquency record of the thirteen-year-olds (who until then had been the most troublesome age group) and the fourteen-year-olds, who took their place in 1948 and have held it consistently ever since."[40] Presumably what happened was that fourteen-year-olds, upon confinement in school, became more delinquent than fourteen-year-olds had been before. If so, one may conjecture that if they were to be confined still another year or two or three (as they are in most states of this country), they would become even more troublesome.

The frustration, anger, and contempt for authority engendered by the school may possibly enter into the personality of the individual, coloring his attitudes in adulthood and leading him to take a cynical and resentful view of the society and all its works. Conceivably, the practice of forcing the incapable and unwilling to waste their adolescent years in schoolrooms further weakens the already tenuous attachment of the lower classes to social institutions. The discovery that the school consists largely of cant and pretense may prepare the way for the discovery that the police and the courts, for example, do too.

That many lower-class pupils are also black complicates the school problem in a tragic way. Increasingly since 1960 the ideology of the civil rights movement has tended to justify and thus reinforce the Negro's resentment of the white; this has had a subtle but pervasive effect on the attitudes of the black working and lower classes, even though those classes have little or no interest in the ideology of equality or of anything else. Since 1964 (the year of the first riots) the growing "black power" movement, by accusing the "white" school system of practicing "mental genocide" against black children and by forcibly demanding "community control" of schools, has dramatized for black pupils the idea that whites are to blame for everything and that they, the pupils, ought to show their resentment by learning nothing while making life as miserable as possible for their white teachers. Not all black schoolchildren have been infected by the contagion of these ideas, but enough have been to make it doubtful that whites — even those sympathetic to the militant point of view — can in the future be even moderately successful in the inner-city schools. That white teachers can no longer teach black children would be a much less serious matter if there were plenty of well-qualified black teachers to take over. In fact, of course, there are not, and the worse the black schools become, the harder it will be to find qualified black teachers in the future.

A second reason for getting nonlearners out of the school is — paradoxical though it may seem — to give them opportunities and incentives to learn. Not everything worth learning must be (or indeed can be) learned from books and teachers, and not everyone — not even everyone with a first-rate mind — learns better from books and teachers than from other sources. Educators tend to overlook this, since they have a professional interest in booklearning and have been self-selected into their occupation on the basis of an aptitude for it. To be sure, some of the boys and girls here in question are not likely to learn much from *any* source. But if they leave school and go to work, they will learn more than they would if they stayed in school. There are additional reasons, apart from the fact that some people learn otherwise than from books, for supposing this to be so: one is that on a job a worker is usually rewarded at once if he learns something that improves his performance; the job, that is, gives incentives to present-oriented people, whereas the school gives them only to the future-oriented. Another is that in some jobs (but, alas, not in all by any means) the thing to be learned is "fun" — even a radically present-oriented person has an incentive to learn under these circumstances.

The third reason for getting nonlearners out of school is to improve the situation for learners. Here the Coleman and Pettigrew studies, which show that the attributes of other students explain variations in pupil achievement more than any other factor, are very much in point. If putting low achievers into the same classes with high achievers improves the performance of the former, it seems likely that it also worsens that of the latter when the proportion of low achievers passes a certain point. One may perhaps deem the harm done to the high achievers justified by the benefits conferred on the low achievers (especially when, as in the common case, the low achievers' initial handicap results from race prejudice and discrimination), but this consideration applies only when the low achiever is able and willing to learn. Unfortunately, he often is not — especially in the last years of high school — and in this case there is no justification for imposing upon the high achievers. Even a few troublemakers can distract and intimidate a whole class of serious students and wear almost any teacher down to the breaking point. In one slum school it was found that even the best teachers had to devote half the school day to discipline and to organizational detail.[41]

It should be emphasized that lowering the school-leaving age to fourteen need not mean giving less education to anyone. In the case of the nonlearners it is only to acknowledge what already exists. The more able and willing students would in almost all cases go on to college. Four years of high school is too much for those who will do manual work; it is not enough for those who will do work that requires education. These need at least fourteen years of schooling, and ending high school at the ninth grade would enable them to start college or other advanced training that much sooner.

An able pupil under the present system is usually ready for college after the tenth or the eleventh grade. (In one experiment, such "dropouts" did as well or better in college than classmates who spent four years in high school; moreover, "their interest in their studies is often greater than that of their contemporaries who have been exposed to the boredom which frequently accompanies high school education."[42]) The system should be changed to speed up the process of education. It is evident from European practice, as well as from that of the better schools in this country, that with proper curricula and teaching methods almost as much can be learned in a nine-year school as in the present twelve-year one. Fritz Machlup, whose conclusion this is, has remarked, "Most people *can* learn what they ever learn in school in eight years, and if they are kept there for ten, twelve, fourteen, or sixteen years they will merely learn it more slowly."[43]

There is little to be said for the suggestion (made by "Ashamed" in the letter to "Dear Abby" quoted at the head of this chapter) that nonlearners be sent to vocational (or "trade") schools. At present the main effect of such schools is to separate lower- and lower-working-class students from the others — to get them out of the way. In general, the students who go to them fare no better in the labor market by virtue of their supposedly practical training. Even in principle the contribution that such schools might make is very small. Students of low capability and motivation seldom benefit much from schooling of whatever kind, and most of those of higher capability and motivation would do better to finish "academic" high school and go on to college. The in-between group — those able to benefit from vocational but not from "academic" training — is probably very small. Moreover, it is increasingly futile to train workers in narrow occupational skills such as drill-press operation, because changes in technology render such skills obsolete very quickly. For these reasons the Project Talent research group at the University of Pittsburgh concluded that the vocational school might well be converted into post–high school technical institutes which would give about four years of highly technical training to capable students who had completed at least ten grades of general education.[44]

So long as large numbers of adolescents like "Ashamed" are kept in school for twelve grades, theirs will necessarily be, in Trow's words, "a second-class program for second-class students." And, as he adds, ". . . they will know it, and that knowledge will feed their bitterness and resentment."[45] In other words, "Ashamed" is very likely to end up being "Angry" or even "In Open Rebellion."

If large numbers of boys and girls are to be let out of school after eight grades, which in most cases would be at the age of fourteen, the question arises of how their time is to be occupied. One could argue that, even if they learn nothing in school, it is, on the whole, better to keep them there than to let them lie around in idleness or roam the streets. The young require a certain amount of looking after. Who is to look after them if not teachers?

In principle, the answer to this question is easy. At whatever age they finish school, boys and girls should go to work. The discipline of the job will more than take the place of that of the school.

Moreover, it is a better discipline. One *chooses* one's job, and therefore one's boss and fellow workers, in that (at the very least) one can always quit and look for another; the boss knows this and therefore has some incentive to make the conditions of work pleasant or at least tolerable. But if the discipline of the job is in some ways less confining than that of the school, in other ways — ones that are on the whole beneficial to the individual — it is more confining. The employee must do or produce something of value if he is to keep his job. He is not permitted, or at any rate not encouraged, to waste his time and that of others. Having to work is not really the disadvantage it is often made out to be, for nothing is so demoralizing in the long run as to know that one's energies and abilities are of no use to anyone.

The gain in income to the individual and thus to society from having nonlearners go to work instead of to school would be more than trivial. Indeed, the most costly item in schooling is not teachers or buildings but the goods and services that are not produced because the people who might produce them are in school. To a society as wealthy as ours, the loss of income from time wasted in school is of rather small importance. It is somewhat more important than dollar amounts might suggest, however, because (as was explained in Chapter 6) there are obstacles — perhaps insuperable — in the way of *giving* income to the people in question without thereby reducing their incentives to provide for themselves and thus in the long run making them worse off.

The main reason for encouraging boys and girls who leave school to go to work, however, is not to increase their incomes but to hasten their growing up — to bring them sooner into the adult world, where they will have the satisfactions of being taken seriously, of being on their own, of being responsible for themselves and indeed very soon for others as well. Stretching out childhood and adolescence is characteristic of the upper classes, and for them doing so makes good sense: the individual anticipates a long life and therefore an extended period of preparation is both a luxury he can afford and a good investment as well. The lower-class individual's situation is very different: his earning power and his capacity to enjoy what for him are the good things of life are greatest in his twenties and thirties and diminish rapidly thereafter. To force the lower classes to adapt to the practice of the upper classes in these matters is both pointless and harmful: it does not give lower-class youth the advantages that the upper classes enjoy and want others to enjoy — lower-class culture renders this impossible. Instead, it creates problems — loss of self-confidence, boredom, unrest, loss of income — for the boys and girls whose urge to grow up is frustrated and thus, of course, problems for the society as well.

As a matter of biology, youth is a time when one seeks a good deal of hard physical exercise, preferably accompanied by excitement and even danger. It is also a time when one wants and needs opportunities to find out who and what one is, and therefore to test one's qualities — endurance, skill, courage and the rest — against those of adult models. These needs are especially strong in the lower classes and they are more urgent among boys than among girls. (Youth culture is in some ways similar to lower-class culture: being present-oriented, it places high value on excitement, danger, and thrills — being "where the action is" — and low value on providing for the future.)

To be sure, the jobs that teen-agers might get would in most instances be far from exciting, like pushing a broom around a factory. Even a dull job, however, would be exciting as compared to sitting in a classroom where the subjects discussed are boring if not incomprehensible. The factory, unlike the school, is the "real" world; it is a world of adults, usually male, and of lower- or working- (as opposed to middle- or upper-) class types. In such a world even dull work has satisfactions for a youth: one stands in line with men (not "kids") to punch the time clock, one takes orders from a foreman who talks one's own language (instead of from a middle-class lady), and one learns from the boss and from fellow workers that it makes a difference whether one does one's job or not. Not all jobs for the young need be as simple and unexciting as pushing a broom, however. There is no reason why a healthy boy of fourteen or fifteen should not do work that calls for considerable strength, endurance, and bravery. Indeed, it is only in the upper classes of an affluent society that any doubt about this could arise. If, as the military asserts, eighteen to nineteen is the optimal age for a combat soldier, it is safe to say that nothing but prejudice prevents the employment of boys of that age as lumberjacks, long-distance truck drivers, longshoremen, construction workers, taxicab drivers, and the like, and of even younger ones as helpers in these occupations.

It will be objected that, whether because of prejudice or something else, employers will not hire boys and girls in their early teens; even at the high wartime employment level of 1967 the unemployment rate among teen-agers was 13 percent. This figure need only be turned around to answer the objection: if 13 percent of the teen-agers wanting jobs had not found them, then 87 percent *had* found them. The fact is that a great many boys and girls are employed: in New York City 80,314 aged fourteen to seventeen had jobs in 1960.[46] These young people, moreover, were able to get jobs despite many institutional obstacles in their way and in the way of potential employers — the late school-leaving age (sixteen in New York), licensing and union restrictions, and minimum-wage rates that overprice low-productivity labor. If these obstacles were removed, many boys and girls who are now last in line for jobs, as well as many who are not permitted to get in line at all, would move to the head of the line. Indeed, the real danger may be not that the young would be unable to find jobs but that they would find them too readily by displacing the no-longer-young. Middle- and upper-class bias in favor of education and prolonged adolescence is one reason why the young are kept in school longer than necessary; another is that unskilled adult workers prefer not to compete with them for jobs.

Even with no prejudice against the young and the unschooled, with the fullest of full employment, and with realistic pricing of low-productivity labor, there would remain some boys and girls — perhaps a considerable number — who either would not take a job or could not get one. These youths would require enough supervision to keep them "out of trouble" until they got a job or reached an age at which they would be entitled to do exactly as they pleased so long as they broke no laws. Although publicly supported institutions would have to meet this need, such institutions need not be in any sense schools. The function of supervising the activities of nonlearners simply cannot be performed well by the same institution (namely, the school) that educates the learners. The combination means poor education for learners and antieducation for nonlearners. If the schools were limited to their proper business, other institutions might be developed to meet the needs of those boys and girls who are too old to learn but too young to work.

High school, it seems fair to conclude, cannot possibly "educate" those young people whose class culture strongly disposes them not to learn. In the case of lower-class youth, enforced attendance tends to undermine what little self-respect the individual has and to aggravate his feeling, already strong, of being victimized by forces beyond his control. It must be acknowledged, however, that the alternative of allowing the lower-class youth to receive his diploma at the age of fourteen and then expecting him to go to work presents serious difficulties, too. The same class culture that stood in the boy's way in school will stand in his way elsewhere. He may not be willing to take a job even if good ones are available. Indeed, it is more than likely that he will prefer the "action" of the street to any job that he could possibly fill. If the choice is between idleness and demoralization in school and idleness and demoralization on the street, then doubtless the former is the lesser evil. It may be possible to avoid these alternatives, however, by — as James S. Coleman has suggested[47] — moving high school training out of schools and into factories and offices: that is, by giving students the option of combining work and learning. In order to do this it would be necessary for governmental bodies (in effect, school districts) to enter into contracts with private firms, specifying the kind of training to be given and the amount to be paid for it by the public. This would certainly entail a great many practical difficulties (for example, firms would tend to demand payment for giving training that their own business interest would prompt them to give anyway), but so much is at stake and the alternatives are so dismal that even serious difficulties should not be regarded as prohibitive.

CHAPTER EIGHT

Several Kinds of Crime

. . . let the policeman's club be thrown down or wrested from him, and the fountains of the great deep are opened, and quicker than ever before chaos comes again. Strong as it may seem, our civilization is evolving destructive forces. Not desert and forest, but city slums and country roadsides are nursing the barbarians who may be to the new what Hun and Vandal were to the old.

— Henry George

Warring on poverty, inadequate housing and unemployment, is warring on crime. A civil rights law is a law against crime. Money for schools is money against crime. Medical, psychiatric, and family-counseling services are services against crime. More broadly and most importantly every effort to improve life in America's "inner cities" is an effort against crime.

— The Crime Commission

THEORIES about the causes and cures of crime tend to be variations of ones about the causes and cures of hard-core poverty. One theory asserts that the criminal suffers from some malaise (such as "alienation") and must be brought into a right relation with the Deity, or — nowadays — with Society or with Self. According to another, he is frustrated by lack of opportunity; the cure is to enable him to earn by socially acceptable means the rewards (largely material) that society declares to be the indispensable marks of success. Still another theory holds that if only he had an adequate income and a proper physical environment — good housing, schools, hospitals, transportation, clean air and so on — his outlook and style of life would improve, and he would cease to commit crimes. That efforts to apply these theories have not led to the reduction of crime in the city is painfully apparent. Indeed, it is possible that they may somehow have led to an increase in crime.

In this chapter it will be maintained that crime, like poverty, depends primarily upon two sets of variables. One set relates mainly to class culture and personality (but also to sex and age) and determines an individual's *propensity* to crime. The other relates to situational factors (such as the number of policemen on the scene and the size of the payroll) and determines his *incentive*. The probability that he will commit crimes — his *proneness* to crime — depends upon propensity *and* incentive. A city's *potential* for crime may be thought of as the average proneness of persons in various "sex-age-culture-personality" groups times their number.

This view does not deny causal importance to alienation, poor housing, inferior schools, and the like. All such factors presumably help to shape class culture and personality (and therefore propensity), and may also influence the situation (and therefore incentive). However, the more "subjective" factors (such as alienation) can seldom be defined and related to crime with much precision, while the connection between crime and more "objective" factors (such as housing) can almost never be determined for the reason that countless such factors influence culture and personality on the one hand and the situation on the other.

As was remarked in earlier chapters, the policymaker usually must take certain cultural and psychological traits as given. This means that a city's *potential* for crime can, at least in the short run, be changed very little, if at all. By contrast, situational factors — and thus incentives — often can be changed according to plan. Even so, it cannot be taken for granted that the measures so often recommended — higher incomes, more schooling, and the like — tend to reduce crime; on the contrary, they may under some circumstances lead to more crime. The reason why crime rates tend to be higher in large cities than in small ones *may* have something to do with the fact that in the larger city the individual has more schooling, more income and more opportunity.[1]

Before entering into a discussion of substantive matters, it is necessary to give some further account of the analytical framework just outlined.[2]

The individual will be thought of as perceiving various action possibilities; he chooses from among them the one that he thinks will yield him the most utility. He estimates the benefits and costs to himself of acting on each alternative and chooses that which promises the largest net benefit. He counts as benefits whatever money or other material goods he expects to gain by the action, any satisfaction that he expects to take in its performance (he may, for example, enjoy hurting someone), and any indirect returns that he expects to accrue from it (for example, a gain in reputation by virtue of having performed it). Similar considerations enter into his estimation of costs (for example, he may feel displeasure at having to hurt someone or may fear loss of reputation). He counts as a cost any work required in the performance of the action or in preparation for it (for example, acquiring information about how to do it).

It may seem far-fetched to describe human behavior — above all criminal behavior — in such rationalistic terms. In fact they cannot be applied either to the behavior of the insane (who commit only a negligible proportion of all crimes) or to that of narcotics addicts when they are in need of a "fix." But except in these abnormal cases, one suspects that there is an element of calculation — usually a very considerable one — in most criminal behavior; few crimes are, strictly speaking, "senseless." (The juvenile who steals "to punish his father" almost always steals something he wants and almost always takes some account of his chances of being caught.) Criminologists generally agree that there is no such thing as a "criminal type"; presumably, they mean that people decide whether or not to do illegal things in essentially the same way that they decide whether or not to do other things.

The present scheme implies that when probable costs exceed probable benefits, an individual will not commit the crime. Indeed, he will not commit it even when probable benefits exceed probable costs if another (noncriminal) action promises to be *more* profitable.

Some important qualifications must be added, however. An individual's choice process is biased toward or against certain kinds of crime (or crime in general) by constraints deeply built into its structure. These class-cultural and personality constraints (propensity) are constants that influence his cost-benefit calculus. Conceivably, this influence might be so great that situational factors would never be decisive. In fact, of course, situational factors are commonly decisive, even among persons of strong propensity in one direction or another. An individual who would "never think of stealing" steals when the temptation becomes great enough; that is, when the situation promises great enough benefits at small enough cost. Similarly, one who thinks nothing of murder may be checked by the presence of a policeman.

The elements of propensity seem to be mainly these:

Type of Morality.[3] This refers to the way in which an individual conceptualizes right and wrong and, therefore, to the weight he gives to legal and moral rules in making choices. One whose morality is *"preconventional"* understands a "right" action to be one that will serve his purpose and that can be gotten away with; a "wrong" action is one that will bring ill success or punishment. An individual whose morality is preconventional cannot be influenced by authority (as opposed to power). One whose morality is *"conventional"* defines "right" action as doing one's "duty" or doing what those in authority require; for him, laws and moral rules have a constraining effect even in the absence of an enforcement apparatus. One whose morality is *"postconventional"* defines "right" action as that which is in accord with some universal (or very general) principle that he considers worthy of choice. Such an individual is constrained by law as such only if the principle that he has chosen requires him to be; if it requires him to obey the law only when he thinks that the law in question is just, he is, of course, not under the constraint of law at all.

Ego Strength. This refers to the individual's ability to control himself — especially to his ability to adhere to and act on his intentions (and therefore to manage his impulses) and to his ability to make efforts at self-reform. One who is radically deficient in ego strength cannot conceive or implement a plan of action; he has a succession of fleeting resolves, the last of which eventuates in action under the pressure of circumstances.

Time Horizon. This refers to the time perspective an individual takes in estimating costs and benefits of alternative courses of action. The more present-oriented an individual, the less likely he is to take account of consequences that lie in the future. Since the benefits of crime tend to be immediate and its costs (such as imprisonment or loss of reputation) in the future, the present-oriented individual is *ipso facto* more disposed toward crime than others.

Taste for Risk. Commission of most crimes involves a certain amount of risk. An individual who places a very low (perhaps even a negative) value on the avoidance of risk is thereby biased in the direction of crime.

Willingness to Inflict Injury. Most crimes involve at least the possibility of injury to others and therefore a certain willingness on the part of the actor to inflict injury. It may be useful to distinguish among (a) individuals with a distaste for inflicting *any* injury ("crimes without victims" would still be open to them, of course); (b) those with a distaste for injuring specifiable individuals (they might steal from a large enterprise, but they would not cheat the corner grocer); (c) those with a distaste for doing bodily (but not necessarily other) injury to people; and (d) those with no distaste for inflicting injuries, along with those who positively enjoy inflicting them.

These several elements of propensity tend to exist in typical combinations. In general, an individual whose morality is preconventional also has little ego strength, a short time horizon, a fondness for risk, and little distaste for doing bodily harm to specifiable individuals. The opposites of these traits also tend to be found together.

It also happens that individuals whose propensity toward crime is relatively high — especially those with high propensity for *violent* crime — tend to be those whose situation provides the strongest incentive to crimes of the common sorts. The low-income individual obviously has much more incentive to steal than does the high-income one. Similarly, a boy has much more incentive to "prove he is not chicken" than does a girl. In general, then, high propensity and high incentive go together.

With respect to both propensity and incentive, there are very important differences between: (1) males and females, (2) persons of different class cultures, and (3) the young and the not-young.

The most striking of these differences is that between males and females. In all class cultures and in all age groups women commit relatively few crimes. (That most of the crimes they do commit are sex-related suggests that even in these they may merely be accomplices.) In general, women seem to be more future-oriented than males, better able to control their impulses, more adverse to risk, and less disposed to inflict physical injury. Be this as it may, in all class cultures their *incentive* to most kinds of crime is clearly less than that of males. Far from being under pressure to be "tough" and to prove that they have "been around," they are, even in the lower class, expected to be frail and "domestic." They are also less likely to be in the role of provider — a role that increases both motive and opportunity for the most common crime, stealing. Moreover, their relative lack of physical strength disqualifies them from heavy criminal work as it does from other heavy work, and no doubt it has much to do with their distaste for risk and for inflicting bodily injury on others.

The difference in propensity and incentive is hardly less striking among classes than between sexes. For the lower-class individual, high propensity coincides with high incentive. Because his culture is present-oriented, he does not learn to formulate goals or to control impulses. His behavior is "decided upon" from moment to moment.

Now without havin' any intention of robbin' this guy I was crossin' the street. Actually I was crossin' the street to rob him, but it actually wasn't on my mind. If someone had asked me why I had crossed the street I couldn't a told him. I just doin' this unconscious.[4]

The morality of lower-class culture is preconventional, which means that the individual's actions are influenced not by conscience but only by a sense of what he can get away with.[5]

The general attitude toward stealing is one in which the individual feels some type of "right" to do so. It is not perceived strictly in terms of "stealing" but instead of "taking."[6]

Apparently everyone has this conception of stealing at a stage of his childhood. Most persons grow out of it, pangs of conscience making it hard for them to steal; the lower-class person, however, continues to "take" things all his life.

As the child grows older, there is a gradual change in the type of things stolen and their relative worth. There is a graduation from the candy bar to stealing from the rummage shop sale, to stealing from downtown department stores, to stealing, signing and cashing welfare checks.[7]

Infliction of bodily injury is also sanctioned — often inculcated — by lower-class culture.

The lower classes not uncommonly teach their children and adolescents to strike out with fist or knife and to be certain to hit first. Both girls and boys at adolescence may curse their father to his face or even attack him with fists, sticks, or axes in free-for-all family encounters. Husbands and wives sometimes stage pitched battles in the home; wives have their husbands arrested; and husbands try to break in or burn down their own homes when locked out. Such fights with fists or weapons, and the whipping of wives, occur sooner or later in most lower-class families. They may not appear today, nor tomorrow, but they will appear if the observer remains long enough.[8]

Because the lower-class style of life involves an unremitting search for sex and for relief from boredom, it tends to bring the individual into situations in which he is likely to violate a law. Moreover, he has little or nothing to lose — no job, no money, no reputation — by being charged with a crime. In the lower-class world it is taken for granted that everyone "gets in trouble" and may go to jail now and then. Being known as vicious and violent may give one a certain prestige in the slum, as it does in a prison. Finally, since he is unwilling or unable to keep a job or to acquire a skill, the lower-class individual's opportunities for income are relatively poor. The "wage rate" for robbery is probably low; even so, robbery may often be the best "job" open to an unskilled man who refuses to work except when the spirit moves him.

Higher up on the class-cultural continuum — in the upper-working and lower-middle classes — the situation is very different as regards both propensity and incentive. As compared to the lower class, members of these classes have little taste for violence or for risk; they are also much more able to take the future into account and to control their behavior. But what most distinguishes them from those "above" as well as from those "below" them on the class-cultural continuum is their respect for authority. They tend to accept unquestioningly whatever the authority of law, custom, religious teaching, or even "public opinion" declares. Of course, the individual sometimes does what he knows to be wrong, but when he does he feels guilty about it. The prickings of conscience weight his calculus heavily, if not always decisively, toward what he considers right and proper.

In these classes, too, incentive tends to reinforce propensity. Once he has married and settled down, such an individual can usually earn more at honest work than he could get by crime. In addition, his job, family, and circle of friends and neighbors insulate him from many temptations. He knows also that if he "got in trouble," he would lose his job and bring disgrace upon himself and his family.

It might be expected that those "highest" on the continuum — the upper-middle and upper classes — would be least prone to crime. They have the greatest ability to take account of the future and to control themselves. They tend to be more risk-adverse, and, whereas the lower class has learned in childhood to be violent, they have learned to be nonviolent — "to hammer on the Playskool Cobbler Bench but not on their brothers and sisters."[9]

There is, however, another tendency within the upper- and upper-middle-class culture that works in an opposite direction. The individual has a strong sense of self, and he attaches great importance to "developing his potentialities to the full." Insofar as he thinks that his future is sufficiently provided for (that he "has it made"), he tends to emphasize self-expression rather than self-improvement and, accordingly, present gratification rather than saving and investment; his style of life may then resemble that of the present-oriented individual, except, of course, that whereas he *chooses* to live in the present, the lower-class one lives in it because he must.

In order to develop or express his personality, the upper- or upper-middle-class person seeks out new and "rewarding" "experiences." He "owes it to himself" to try dried grasshoppers with his martinis and the equivalent with his sex, his politics, his child rearing, and all else. He feels obliged "as a responsible person" to decide for himself what is right and wrong; simply to accept the dictates of authority, including that of law, appears to him demeaning: one ought to assert oneself as an "individual" by deciding (on "rational" grounds, of course) what rules to follow. Having done so, one ought to have "the courage of one's convictions."

Such an individual is apt to try illegal as well as other "experiences." He is especially apt to do so if he thinks that the law proscribing them is "stupid" or inappropriate to the circumstances of his particular case. If he breaks the law, he is unlikely to feel guilty; on the contrary, he may take virtuous satisfaction in the thought that he has performed a public service by helping to bring a "stupid" law into disrepute.

How upper- and upper-middle-class attitudes can lead by this different route to behavior that is concretely indistinguishable from that of the lower class may be seen in the matter of drug use. According to Dr. Norman E. Zinberg, there are two contrasting motivations behind the use of drugs. One group of users, drawn mainly from the lower socioeconomic strata, are "like children" in that they "want nothing but the immediate satisfaction of pleasurable desires." The other group, drawn mainly from the middle and upper socioeconomic strata, consists of "experience seekers": "Drugs give them a sense of liberation from convention, a feeling that a level of genuine experience which is closed to them by their culture is opened for them by the drug."[10]

As with drug use, so with many crimes: the "same" act has very different meaning for the experience-seeker and the pleasure-seeker.

If it is characteristic of the upper- and upper-middle-class individual to express his personality and to seek experience, it is also characteristic of him not to want to hurt others — indeed, to want to do them good if possible. This attitude also influences the kinds of crime that he may commit. For murder, assault, and rape — violence in general — he has no stomach. He may commit an act of violence in order to further a political principle; this, after all, is what doing the "right" thing or the "just" thing may require. Euthanasia and suicide are the only kinds of killing that are really compatible with his style, however — the latter because it injures no one but the doer and the former because it is a way of doing good. Whereas rates of aggressive (i.e., nonaccidental) homicide decrease the higher one goes on the class-cultural scale, those of suicide increase.[11]

The same principle applies to other kinds of crime. Vice, for example, may attract the upper- or upper-middle-class individual both because it is "experience" and because (in his view) no one is injured by it. Under some circumstances he may steal with a clear, or almost clear, conscience. If he is a teen-ager he may "borrow" an automobile (much — some think most — auto theft is by middle-class youths), expecting that the owner will suffer nothing more than a certain amount of inconvenience on account of the theft. If he is a grown-up, he may embezzle from an organization (the larger the better) knowing that no specifiable individual will be much injured by his action. If the organization is a very large one, he may steal in the knowledge that no one will be injured at all. Who suffers if he cheats a little on his income tax?

In every social class, children, adolescents, and youths, most of them male, commit far more than their proportionate share of most crimes. About half the arrests for burglary and larceny and about 60 percent of arrests for auto theft are of persons aged eleven to seventeen, a group that includes only about 14 percent of the population. The arrest rate for violent crimes (homicide, forcible rape, assault, and robbery) is higher in the age group eleven to fourteen than in any age group above forty-five. By far the most frequent offense of the young is stealing.[12] Most of it is done by boys (the most common offenses of girls are sexual promiscuity and failure to accept parental discipline); they steal things that they "need," such as cigarettes, candy, bicycles, and presents for girl friends and mothers. (Stealing in stores increases sharply just before Christmas.) When a boy "needs" something and does not have the money to pay for it, he "takes" it. Stealing is also a way by which boys "prove" themselves by displaying qualities that they believe (not altogether mistakenly) to be manly — boldness, stamina, willingness to accept risk — in a word, "heart." Unusual achievement along these lines earns a boy prestige among his fellows. "You stole eight cars! Jeez!"

The younger the individual, the greater (other things being equal) his propensity toward crime. Children, of course, have very little ability to control their impulses or to take account of the future. Even teen-agers are typically improvident in the extreme.

Whatever money meant to them, the boys never kept it very long. When they had money, they stopped stealing and started spending. Very often they bought things they did not need, and sometimes things they did not want. They would perhaps plan in rather meticulous detail how much money they would save for what, but the money seldom lasted long enough to be spent even the next day.[13]

If ego strength and awareness of the future develop slowly, so does moral understanding. A boy has passed the stage of preconventional morality (if he is ever going to pass it) long before reaching his teens; the hold of conventional (or postconventional) morality on him is less than firm, however. Moreover, the disturbance, partly biological and partly sociopsychological, arising from the sudden eruption of sexual impulses and the compulsion to find an answer to the question: Who am I? frequently leads to confused and irrational behavior.

In the case of boys, especially, one is struck by a resemblance between the adolescent and the lower-class styles. Both emphasize the present, action, risk, defiance of authority, and the display of "masculinity." What sociologist David Matza says of the juvenile — that for him delinquency is (among other things) a way of "making things happen" and so of escaping a "mood of fatalism"[14] — is probably true also of the lower-class adult.

It is to be expected, then, that when male adolescence and lower-class culture meet in the same person, they will interact, reinforce each other, and produce an extraordinarily high propensity toward crime. At the other end of the class-cultural continuum, the situation is not altogether different: upper- and upper-middle-class people — those of them who are oriented more toward self-expression than toward self-improvement — encourage their children to "experiment" and "find themselves," a process that is likely to reinforce the natural restlessness of the adolescent and to heighten his desire to "make things happen." Describing the "cult of the present" among middle- and upper-middle-class youths, psychologist Kenneth Keniston writes:

Indeed, among the defining characteristics of American youth culture — the special world of American adolescents and young adults — are a concentration on the present, a focus on immediate experience, an effort to achieve "genuineness," "directness," "sincerity," in perception and human relations. We see this cult in both forms — as a search for external stimulation and for internal transformation — in many of the deviant behaviors of our society: in the search for adventure among delinquent gangs, in the use of drugs to break through the gates of perception, in the "beat" quest for "kicks." And in less extreme form, a similar emphasis on the present exists in the increasing American stress on consumption rather than saving, on the "rich, full life" in the present rather than the deferred goals and future satisfactions of an earlier society.[15]

Young people as such differ from the lower class as such in at least one very important respect: they dislike hurting people. When they employ violence, it is as a means rather than as an end in itself. Youth gang members, according to Walter B. Miller, see it as a means of winning "honor and glory."

Gang members fight to secure and defend their honor as males; to secure and defend the reputation of their local area and the honor of their women; to show that an affront to their pride and dignity demands retaliation. Combat between males is a major means for attaining these ends.[16]

In the overwhelming majority of cases, delinquent boys and girls cease their delinquencies when (typically in the late teens for the girls and middle twenties for the boys) they marry and settle down to jobs and to looking after children. Then things that were "fun" all of a sudden become "kid stuff." The few whose delinquency continues in adult life probably come disproportionately from the lower class. In these cases, class culture, rather than the confusions that attend rapid physical and psychological development, may have been the real cause of trouble all along.

Taking a wide and long perspective, one sees that some crime problems have been shrinking while others have been growing, and that the long-term trends are likely to continue. Taking the metropolitan area as a whole, there seems to have been (the data are very scanty) a fairly steady decline in the amount of violent crime and possibly in the amount of all common crime. Presumably, this trend is the result of the process of middle- and upper-class-ification that has been going on for a hundred years or more. A century ago the city was predominantly lower and lower-working class, whereas now it is predominantly upper-working and middle class. Movement upward on the class-cultural scale has made each generation more law-abiding, more regardful of the rights of others, and, of course, less violent than the last. Comparisons are hazardous, but there is reason to think that the rate of violent crime in the metropolitan area as a whole has declined steadily over the last century to a level about one-third lower.[17]

This long-run trend has, of course, been interrupted and even reversed in the central city and its larger, older suburbs. The tendencies described in Chapter 2 — especially the movement of the well-off out of the city and the poor into it and the decentralization of the slum — have returned these cities and suburbs to a condition probably not very different from the one that obtained a century ago. The proportion of lower and lower-working class in the central cities is probably almost as high as it was a century ago. The migrants who came to the city after the war were a young — and therefore fecund — population. Accordingly, the number of boys and young men — the most crime-prone group — is larger than before. In addition to these demographic changes, there has been an important technological one: expressways. In preexpressway days motorists had to stop frequently for lights, and police officers had good opportunities to look them over and to spot those who appeared suspicious. Now motorists drive back and forth between the central city and the suburbs without stopping and at such speeds that no one can tell whether they are suspicious-looking or not.

The greater proportion of youths and lower-class persons in the city's population probably does not entirely explain the increase in the rate of common crime of the last few years, however. It seems likely (the data do not allow of very confident statements on any of these matters) that upper-working- and lower-middle-class persons are considerably more crime-prone than they were a generation or more ago. If this is really the case, the reason is not that the "wage" of crime has increased relative to other (honest) work. A more plausible explanation is that these classes have come to have less respect for authority, including the authority of the law. It may be that their conventional morality has been weakened and partially destroyed by the example of the upper classes and by the efforts of these classes to "liberate" them by the process of "education." One wonders what may be the effect on boys and girls brought up to respect authority of the advice (given by an ex-nun in the magazine *Seventeen*) to "hold always the openness of questioning the president of the college, of questioning the dean of students, of questioning the policy of the United States in Vietnam, of questioning fair housing, divorce laws and birth control"[18] or of the view (attributed by the *New York Times* to a nun photographed "holding a semiofficial late evening session at Clancy's Bar on Third Avenue") that the Pope and Bishops "ought to be charismatic types who see their job as turning us on and supporting us in doing our things."[19] Conceivably, the effect of such words on working- and lower-middle-class persons may be to undermine their moral foundations rather than (as the speakers intend) to renew and strengthen them. The alternative to respect for external authority is not necessarily respect for internal authority: it may be no respect at all.

Other changes in public opinion have also made it easier for working- and lower-working-class people to commit crimes. Perhaps the most important of these changes is the wide acceptance during the 1960's of the view that individuals belonging to groups that have suffered injustice or are severely disadvantaged (for example, Negroes and the poor) have a kind of quasi right to have their offenses against the law extenuated or even to have them regarded as political acts reflecting a morality "higher" than obedience to law. Even crimes that were formerly regarded as wholly unpolitical and immoral — rape, for example — were in the 1960's invested with political and moral meaning, and hence with some justification, when committed by one who (whether this meaning was in his mind or not when he committed the crime) belonged to a group that possessed this special license to have its violations of law extenuated or even approved. Eldridge Cleaver, for example, in his autobiographical *Soul on Ice* explains the apparently numerous rapes that he committed, some of them against black women, on the grounds that racial injustice had created in him a powerful attraction-repulsion to white women.[20] Presumably many of his hundreds of thousands of readers accept the view that a rape that can be interpreted as a gesture of social protest is not wholly without justification and may even be in some way admirable.

Whether for these reasons or others, there seems to have been a marked increase since the civil rights revolution began in the amount of crime by Negroes. It is doubtful whether, prior to 1960, there was any such thing as Negro crime. There were, of course, many crimes committed by Negroes; the Census Negro (to return to the terminology used in Chapter 4) always had a high crime rate; but the crime rate of the Statistical Negro — that is, the Negro when income, class, region of origin, and other relevant variables are controlled for — may have been (there is no real evidence one way or the other) about the same as that of the white. Since about 1960, however, the Statistical Negro's crime rate seems to have increased. Presumably, the climate of opinion that caused Eldridge Cleaver to "discover his social status" and to "turn from America with horror, disgust and outrage" to become a rapist influenced many others in more or less the same way.[21] It is interesting that in Oakland, California (one of the few cities whose police department keeps sophisticated records), a sharp increase in assaults with deadly weapons by blacks against whites occurred between 1962 and 1968.[22]

In the next chapter it will be argued that this feeling that victims of oppression have a kind of license to break the law was one of the conditions that made possible the major riots of 1964 and thereafter. For the purposes of the present chapter, what is important is that the riots and the public discussion that followed them (especially the Kerner Commission's verdict, endorsed by the sale of 1.3 million copies of its report, that "white racism" was mainly to blame) almost certainly made it easier for many Negroes to commit crimes that they would not otherwise have committed. According to Walter B. Miller, thefts of all sorts became much more frequent in Negro districts of Boston in the months following the riot of April 1967; in some of these the crime rate for the first time surpassed that of certain white districts, a fact that suggests that Negroes who had not previously committed crimes were now doing so.[23]

Miller also noticed changes in youth gang behavior. Before the riots, Negro and white gangs behaved very much alike. After them, the amount and intensity of Negro gang activity increased. The Negro gangs were not more political than before, but they were more likely to participate in the usual forms of delinquent activities. For example, in preriot days, setting fires, stoning cars, and vandalizing property were more common among younger (ten to thirteen) than older (fourteen to eighteen) adolescents; after the riots, these kinds of offenses appeared to become increasingly common among the older adolescents. Negro gangs also began to innovate. In Boston and in other cities they developed a new pattern of activity out of their riot experience. It consisted of various mixtures of the following:

> Breaking store windows (sometimes to steal merchandise, sometimes merely to set off alarms)
> Turning in false fire alarms
> Setting fires
> Stoning firemen when they answer alarms
> Stoning passing cars and trains
> Setting fire to cars
> Stoning policemen

Miller remarks that the new pattern — the "mini-riot," he calls it — "combines the elements of gain, excitement, and risk of 'normal' theft and assault, with the added element of direct challenge to law-enforcement agencies which characterizes the larger riots."

Although, as this suggests, policymakers have probably increased the propensity of certain groups to crime (without, of course, intending to do so or even being aware of having done so), it does not follow that by pursuing a more enlightened policy they could significantly reduce it. Certainly in the short run, and probably in the long run as well, the main factors influencing both the propensity of various groups to crime and the size of these groups — in short, the city's potential for crime — must be taken as given. As a later chapter will contend, it is very doubtful whether in a free country, or indeed in *any* country, either the size or the culture of the lower class can be changed according to plan. With respect to the other factors that are most significant for crime — sex and age — the constraints are at least as great. The policymaker must take both the number of boys in the city and the fact that "boys will be boys" as given. Conceivably, he might in effect reduce their numbers by shortening the period of their sociological and psychological (as opposed to biological) adolescence and youth — for example, by reducing the school-leaving age and by improving their opportunities to work — but even this would not change the situation fundamentally.

What the policymaker *can* do (in principle, at least) is reduce incentives to crime. These, it will be recalled, are the benefits and costs entering into the individual's calculus in consequence of the situation in which he is placed. Even though his propensity toward crime is great, he will not commit a crime if situational factors make some noncriminal action appear more profitable. Similarly, even if his propensity is very small, he will commit a crime if the situational benefits of doing so are sufficiently great.

The implication is, of course, that efforts to deter crime should concentrate on increasing the incentives to noncriminal behavior, especially those offered to persons who are near the margin between crime and noncrime — that is, who do not need to be moved very far one way or the other. In principle, this may be done either by raising the costs of crime or by raising the benefits of noncrime.

One way to raise the benefits of noncrime is to introduce the individual to new and preferred action possibilities. Parachute jumping, skiing on fast slopes, and "golden gloves" boxing, for example, may offer slum boys better opportunities to display "heart" than does stealing cars. The practical difficulty is, however, that some of the preferred alternatives may be more costly in life and limb or in money than the actions for which substitutes are needed. Juvenile delinquency is not as destructive as most people think. The number of boys and girls who are seriously injured in gang fights is small, and the stealing that the young do is not of enormous economic importance (about 90 percent of all stolen cars are recovered). Moreover, there are some offenses for which no socially acceptable substitutes can be found. If a boy must defy authority, he obviously must do so in a way that the authorities do not approve.

Another possibility is to increase the net benefits of some existing action possibility. For example, in order to reduce the amount of stealing, one might raise the wage rate for honest work, thus causing some people to move from one occupation to the other. According to economist Belton Fleisher (who, it must be said, worked with data that were far from satisfactory), a 10 percent rise in income may be expected to reduce juvenile delinquency rates by between 10 and 15 percent when the income change occurs in highly delinquent areas and is of the type that will reduce the number of broken families as well.[24] Impressionistic evidence from social anthropologist Elliot Liebow in his book *Tally's Corner* supports the view that in the lower class the choice between stealing and work depends largely upon situational incentives.

In a recent year the crime rate in Washington for the month of August jumped 18 percent over the preceding month. A veteran police officer explained the increase . . . "It's quite simple. . . . You see, August was a very wet month. . . . These people wait on the street corner each morning around 6:00 or 6:30 for a truck to pick them up and take them to a construction site. If it's raining, that truck doesn't come, and the men are going to be idle that day. If the bad weather keeps up for three days . . . we know we are going to have trouble on our hands — and sure enough, there invariably follows a rash of purse-snatchings, house-breakings and the like. . . . These people have to eat like the rest of us, you know."[25]

Most stealing is done by persons who want small amounts *now*. For them a job that must be worked at regularly and that pays *only at the end of the week* is not a real alternative to stealing. Even if the wage rate is high, such a job is of no interest to one who wants only a few dollars — enough, say, to buy a couple of six-packs of beer and a carton of cigarettes — but wants them now — this very day, perhaps this very hour. What is needed to reduce stealing, then, is not so much high employment and rising incomes as it is greater opportunity for people who live in the present to get small sums when they want them. Paying unskilled workers by the day instead of the week would help matters some. So would paying them for days that they are prevented from working by weather, the illness of a family member, or some other good reason. So far as employment levels are concerned, the need is not so much for more "good" jobs as it is for more casual ones — jobs that, although not high paying, are readily available to persons who want to "make a few bucks" when, and only when, the spirit moves them. Boys, especially, need such job opportunities; perhaps there is no more economical way of reducing juvenile delinquency, and thus crime in general, than by repealing the minimum wage and relaxing the child-labor and school-attendance laws. The main effect of these laws, it is probably safe to say, is to make stealing the boy's easiest, if not his only, way of getting the money and other things he thinks he needs.

If making it easier to earn money is one way of influencing the outcome of the individual's calculus of profit and loss when he contemplates crime, increasing the probability both of his being caught and of his being severely punished is another. Obviously, one way of doing the former with respect to the kinds of crimes that occur in public places is to put more policemen on patrol. From the standpoint of the calculating individual, the greater probability of a policeman's appearing represents a cost; the higher this cost is, the less likely (other things being equal) the individual is to commit a crime. "Operation 25," an experiment tried all too briefly by the New York Police Department in 1954, gave indications that rather dramatic results can be obtained by "saturating" an area with patrolmen.[26] For a four-month period the force in a high-crime district of Manhattan was doubled. Muggings fell from 69 to 7, auto thefts from 78 to 24, and assaults from 185 to 132. Murders, however, increased from 6 to 8. (Since it generally takes place in private, murder is not likely to be deterred by the presence on the street of any number of policemen.) To what extent the drop in crime reflected not deterrence from crime altogether but rather deterrence from crime *in that particular precinct* (that is, its displacement to a less heavily patrolled one) there is, of course, no way of knowing.

Attaching a stiffer penalty to an offense sometimes, but by no means always, raises the cost of the action significantly. When the penalty for prostitution was drastically reduced in New York City, the number of prostitutes in the city increased very quickly, some coming from cities hundreds of miles away in order to take advantage of the lower costs of doing business there.[27] As a rule, however, the opportunities to deter crime by threatening severe penalties are very limited. One reason for this is that judges and juries will not enforce laws that carry penalties they consider "out of line." Another is that if the probability of being caught is negligible, it makes practically no difference to the calculating individual what the penalty is. In fact, the probability of being caught *is* very often negligible. (For a Negro youth gang member, a study estimated, the probability of arrest for involvement in an instance of potential violence was about .04 if he was of average skill and about half that if he was very skillful.)[28] According to a recent study, certainty of punishment has a greater effect than severity on most crime rates. For all offenses except homicide, the rate of crime decreases as the level of certainty increases, regardless of the level of severity. Curiously, the association between certainty of punishment and a low crime rate is weakest in more highly urbanized states.[29]

It will be seen that the threat of even very stiff future penalties will not have a deterrent effect upon radically present-oriented individuals. It is likely that even to a normal person a punishment appears smaller the farther off in the future it lies. With the radically present-oriented, this distortion of perspective is much greater: a punishment that is far enough off to appear small to a normal person appears tiny, or is quite invisible, to a present-oriented one. His calculus of benefits and costs is defective, since benefits are in the present where he can see them while costs are in the future where he cannot. Accordingly, even if he knows that the probability of his being caught is high and that the penalty for the act is severe, he may commit the crime nevertheless; no matter how severe, a penalty that lies weeks or months away is not a part of reality for him.

The implication is that in order to deter juveniles and lower-class persons (the present-oriented classes of offenders), penalties must follow very closely upon the commission of crimes. Speeding up court processes so that fines will be imposed or jail sentences begin hours or days, rather than weeks or months, after arrest would probably reduce somewhat the rate of common crimes even if the probability of arrest and conviction remained as low as it now is.

As a practical matter, it is probably impossible to arrange a court procedure that would bring punishment within the time horizon of the most present-oriented. In order to deter these, the judge and jury would have to be on the scene, or just offstage, at the time the action was being contemplated. This suggests that "curbstone justice" — punishment meted out on the spot by a policeman — is what is needed. This does not necessarily imply that the policeman should also *administer* the punishment. (The prospect of being "roughed up" would probably not deter many lower-class persons; among boys and young men, especially, this sort of punishment might actually increase crime by making it a surer way to display "heart.") The prospect of punishment would probably be brought within the time horizon of present-oriented persons if a policeman could issue a ticket that was tantamount to a fine. He can do this, of course, with traffic offenses. But with the common nontraffic offenses of present-oriented people, especially stealing and assault, he must go to court (often on his own time) to testify, and the disposition of the case is entirely in the hands of the judge or magistrate. Because in these cases the policeman is not the *defacto* judge, as he is in the traffic ones, penalties lie in the future rather than in the present.

There are, of course, reasons why policemen have *de facto* authority to set punishments in one kind of case but not the other. One is that the policeman *witnesses* a traffic violation but only *suspects* a theft. Another is that traffic offenses are morally neutral, whereas other offenses usually are not. One who values his good name has vastly more at stake if accused of stealing than if accused of speeding. With traffic offenses, then, there is an inherent safeguard against any very damaging error from the exercise of police discretion, whereas with other offenses there is no such safeguard. This may well be a decisive consideration against giving policemen *de facto* authority to punish the kinds of crimes that present-oriented people typically commit. If so, it should be noted in passing that it is the present-oriented who suffer from this. They have little need to be protected against any moral onus (the distinction between offenses against law and offenses against morality being unknown to them), and they are the ones who would most surely benefit by arrangements that brought deterrents within their time horizon.

One form of deterrence that *does* work with present-oriented people (in fact no less well with them than with others) has been called "hardening the target." The individual is deterred by measures that make it difficult or impossible for him to commit the crime. For example, robbers are deterred from molesting the 10,000 prosperous people who live in the eight-building Lincoln Towers complex in Manhattan by brick and mortar that seal the complex off from the surrounding slum: only persons passing the scrutiny of a private police force can enter. This, of course, is the extreme. Often simple devices — good streetlights, well-made locks, burglar alarms — suffice to make the criminal action more troublesome, inconvenient, or risky (i.e., costly) and therefore to turn it from profitable to unprofitable.

Unfortunately, this form of deterrence is inherently less amenable to use by law enforcement agencies than by the ordinary citizens who are potential victims of crime. Motorists, for example, can do more to reduce car theft simply by locking their cars than the police can do by any amount of patrol. (More than two-fifths of all cars stolen have keys in the ignition.) Similarly, householders, by putting proper locks on their doors, can do more than the police to reduce burglary. (In 657 of 3,441 burglaries in Boston in 1964, doors or windows had been left unlocked.) By displaying his goods in one way rather than another, the merchant can do more than the police to reduce shoplifting — and so on.

If the potential criminal responds rationally to deterrents, why does not the potential victim act rationally by offering them? The answer is that the potential victim usually *does* act rationally, but the structure of the situation in which he is placed is such that he seldom has much incentive to take preventive measures even when they are simple in their nature and effective in their application. Locking one's car is a nuisance, and the probability of its being stolen on any one occasion is small. If the motorist counts the nuisance of having to lock the car at no more than a fraction of a cent, it may very well be cheaper for him to run the risk of his car being stolen than to take the trouble to lock it.

In the case of shoplifting, the appropriate deterrent measures — displaying goods differently and making less use of self-service — although simple and effective may be costly in terms of profit. From a business standpoint, measures to deter theft are likely to be inefficient.

One large chain of bookdealers reported less than .5 percent loss. Instead of regarding this minuscule loss as a cause for rejoicing, it was regarded as the result of "old fashioned" merchandising methods including much personal service by a large staff of sales clerks. "Certainly," said the security representative, "we have a small inventory shortage, but our payroll for sales personnel cuts our profit to almost nothing. We could be ahead by accepting the inevitability of shoplifting. Self-service plus all the losses it will bring will net us more profit in the long run than individualized service with almost no loss at all."[30]

One thing that prevents wider use of this form of deterrence, then, is that the price to a potential victim of reducing his risk may be larger than the probable gain to him of doing so. This may be so even if it would be highly profitable for all potential victims to incur these costs collectively, for the profitability of anyone's doing it may depend upon almost everyone's doing it. One way of getting around this is to organize entities so large that it will pay them to invest in preventive measures whether others do or not — so large, that is, that the gain to them from the preventive measures, even though not the whole gain (that is, even though others "ride free") is nevertheless large enough to make the investment profitable. This is what economists call "internalizing the externalities." The Lincoln Towers complex that was mentioned above is an example of how large-scale organizations, by making it possible for potential victims to recapture a considerable part of the security that they produce, offers them an incentive to produce more of it than they otherwise would.

Another reason why a potential victim does not go to more trouble and expense to deter crime is that he often knows that if the worst happens and he becomes a victim, he can shift most — perhaps all — of his loss to an insurance company or to some other institution. If the motorist were not insured against theft, he would be more likely to lock his car. And if in addition the police charged a proper fee for recovering stolen cars, he would be still more likely to lock it.

There is much to be said for reducing the many disincentives to preventive action that the potential victim now has. Insurance companies could be forbidden to reimburse motorists for the loss of cars not equipped with automatic locking devices. Shoplifters could be arrested by the police, rather than by store detectives, and the cost of their arrest, detention, and trial charged against the merchant in whose store they were caught. The bad-check collecting services that the police perform could be charged to the storekeepers who accept bad checks. A strong argument for doing these things is that the cost to the individual of deterring crime is trifling as compared to the cost to the public of dealing with it after it has been committed. A California study showed that the average "career cost" of a forgery and check offender is $16,900, as compared to $5,800 for an adult homicide offender.[31] ("Career cost" is what the authorities spend on an average offender over his entire lifetime.)

One must take into account, however, that the present arrangements entail benefits as well as costs to the public. Millions of people are convenienced by the ease with which checks can be cashed, and millions are served by having the goods in department stores and supermarkets displayed so that close inspection of them is possible. These benefits to the consumer are worth something; possibly they are worth all the billions that they cost in the higher prices that must be charged to cover losses by theft, in the taxes that are required to support police forces, courts, and jails, and in the welfare payments to the dependents of persons who are in jail. On the other hand, one may contend that in these matters consumers' preferences should count for very little. The consumer, it may be argued, has no right to have his convenience served when the serving of it entails, even indirectly, giving people incentives to do things that are against the law.

Even if legal penalties were brought much closer to the present, and even if potential victims took all reasonable precautions, it is safe to say that some people — mostly young, lower-class males — would continue to commit a great many serious crimes. These are individuals whose propensity to crime is so high that no set of incentives that it is feasible to offer to the whole population would influence their behavior. They may be compelled, but they cannot be deterred. (Narcotics addicts present the same problem when they are unable to get drugs. In their case, however, there are the alternatives of curing them, finding a substitute drug such as methadone, or making the drug freely available so that they will not have to rob and kill to get it.)

The only entirely effective way of compelling someone not to commit crimes is to lock him up — in the most extreme case, in solitary confinement. Society does this even if the individual has not committed a crime when it is considered almost certain that he cannot be prevented in any other way from committing very serious crimes. No one would doubt the wisdom or justice of confining indefinitely a madman who, if released, would rush to attack anyone he saw — and this even if he had not as yet seriously injured anyone. The case is very different, however, if — as may be with most of those who might be found undeterrable (say, those who are very present-oriented and have little ego-strength and a preconventional conception of morality) — the probability of their committing serious crimes is, although high, by no means a certainty. Even if one could be sure — which, of course, one cannot — that a particular boy now aged sixteen has a .5 probability of committing several robberies over the next ten years, one would not lock him up for that period as a preventive measure.

If there is any acceptable way of dealing with this problem — and there may not be — it would appear to be by abridging the individual's freedom in a degree that corresponds to the expected costs in crime to society of his being free (that is, to the probability of his committing crimes times a measure of their seriousness).

Thus, for example, the boy with a .5 probability of committing several robberies might be kept under the surveillance of a parole officer, whereas one with a .9 probability of committing murder would be confined.

The principle implies, of course, that the law provide a gradation of abridgments of freedom, more or less onerous ones to be imposed upon the individual as his behavior raises or lowers the probability of his committing serious crimes. The knowledge that his freedom would be further abridged if he misbehaved would doubtless have some deterrent effect in many cases, but it must not be forgotten that the reason for the abridgments of freedom is not deterrence (it being *undeterrables* who are here under discussion) but the reduction of the individual's opportunities to commit crimes. In other words, he is not threatened with some partial loss of freedom in order to make the criminal action relatively unattractive; rather, he is deprived of some freedom in order to prevent him from taking the criminal action that he prefers.

Such a scheme might employ succesive levels of abridgment, as follows:

1. The individual would be required to keep in touch weekly with a probation officer, to observe a 10 P.M. curfew, to post a "peace" bond; he might not possess firearms or ride in private automobiles, and he would be liable to search at any time.

2. In addition to the above, he would be sequestered in a small town.

3. He would be confined to a penal village or work camp where he might receive visitors and support a family but from which he might not leave.

It goes without saying that many undeterrables could not be deterred from breaking the rules of such a system, and that they would force the authorities to abridge their freedom wholly — by imprisoning them — in order to abridge it at all. If this effect were general, the scheme would not work: it would lead to the imprisonment of all the undeterrables, including, of course, those who would never have been imprisoned but for the scheme itself. It may be doubted, too, whether the least onerous abridgments (Level 1) would be very effective in preventing crime. Conceivably, their chief effect would be to sort out rather quickly those who required more stringent abridgments.

The scheme is, of course, open to objection on the ground that *any* abridgment of an individual's freedom on the ground that he *may* commit a crime is incompatible with the essential principles of a free society.[32] But, of course, unless it is for retribution, the imprisonment of persons who have been convicted of crimes is on the assumption that they *may* commit more; the grounds of this probability judgment, although different, are not necessarily any better and under certain conditions might even be worse than those of judgments with regard to persons who so far as is known have not committed any crimes. In any event, if abridging the freedom of persons who have not committed crimes is incompatible with the principles of free society, so, also, is the presence in such society of persons who, if their freedom is not abridged, would use it to inflict serious injuries on others. There is, therefore, a painful dilemma. If some people's freedom is not abridged by law-enforcement agencies, that of others will be abridged by law breakers. The question, therefore, is not whether abridging the freedom of those who may commit serious crimes is an evil — it is — but whether it is a lesser or a greater one than the alternative.

CHAPTER NINE

Rioting Mainly for Fun and Profit

"Picketing and marching ain't getting us anywhere, man," said Byron Washington, a 16-year-old 11th-grader who was arrested during this week's riots for having a rock in his hand.

"The whites got to face it, man, this is a new generation. We aren't going to stand for the stuff our mamas and fathers stood for.

"Look at me, I've got a B average, but I can't get a summer job. And if you don't work, you can't afford to go to college."

— *New York Times* report from
Waterloo, Iowa, July 14, 1967

I N the law of most states a riot is a lawless act engaged in by three or more persons and accompanied by violence or breach of the public peace. If the rioters are Negroes it is usually taken for granted that the riot is in some sense racial. Probably the most widespread view is that Negroes riot because they can no longer contain their pent-up fury at the mistreatment they receive from whites. The Watts riot, we are told "was a manifestation of a general sense of deep outrage, outrage at every aspect of the lives Negroes are forced to live, outrage at every element of the white community for forcing (or permitting) Negroes to live such lives."[1]

On this view it follows that the way to end rioting — the *only* way to end it — is to stop mistreating the Negro and, so far as possible, to repair the damage already done him. "Doing such things as punishing police misconduct, providing decent housing and schooling, ending job discrimination and so forth are essential, but the problem goes deeper than that. The ghetto itself, with all the shameful economic, social, political, and psychological deprivation it causes, must be done away with once and for all. The riots have 'let America know' that this is what must be done. Now America must do it."[2]

This is not the view that will be taken here. The assumption that if Negroes riot it must be *because* they are Negroes is naïve. If one rejects this as a starting place and looks at the facts instead, one sees that race (and, incidentally, poverty as well) was not *the* cause of any of the Negro riots and that it had very little to do with many of the lesser ones. Indeed, it is probably not too much to say that some of the riots would have occurred even if (other things being the same) the people in the riot areas had all been white and even if they had all had incomes above the poverty line. The implication of this view is, of course, that punishing police misconduct, providing decent housing, and so on will not significantly affect the amount of Negro rioting. The causes of rioting, it will be argued, will continue to operate for another twenty years or so no matter what is done. But although more and possibly worse riots are to be expected, rioting will not destroy the cities. Dr. Kenneth B. Clark's warning that "The dark ghettoes now represent a nuclear stock-pile which can annihilate the very foundations of America,"[3] need not be taken very seriously if his metaphors refer to rioting of the sort that has occurred in recent years.

(1) Two thousand juveniles break windows after an amusement park closes early, leaving them without transportation.
(2) A gang of hoodlums robs a clothing store and smashes the display windows of three other stores, stealing watches, cameras, and rings.
(3) A young man has been shot and killed by the police during a burglary, and a crowd, shouting "This is for Willie," pelts the police with rocks, bottles, and fire bombs.
(4) Following an inflammatory speech by a racist politician, a mob overturns automobiles and assaults motorists.

To that strict behaviorist, the man on the moon, all four of these events probably look alike: all are "riots" and, if the rioters are

Negro, presumably "racial." But to an observer able and willing to take motives into account (that is, to take note of the meaning of an act to the actor) the events are very different and some are not in any sense racial. The first is a rampage by frustrated teen-agers who happen to be black. The second is a foray for pillage by young toughs who find "taking" things the easiest way of getting them. In this case, too, race is not a motive and is in fact irrelevant to behavior: the toughs are Negro, but they could as well be white. The third event is an outburst of righteous indignation on the part of people who have witnessed what they think is an act of gross injustice. The young man who was killed was black and the policeman who killed him was white, but it is possible that the indignation the crowd feels is mainly or even entirely against the police rather than against whites as such. (In September 1962, Negroes in the all-Negro village of Kinlock, Missouri, rioted when a Negro policeman shot a Negro youth.) Indeed, some members of the crowd may be indignant at whites, others at the police, and still others at both whites and the police, and so it might be impossible to say whether or not the riot was "mainly racial," even if one had full knowledge of the subjective states of all rioters. In the final case, the event is a demonstration carried on for the express purpose of calling attention to a political position; since the position is a racist one, the riot can easily be called racial.

Each of these four motivations implies a corresponding type of riot. (This is not to say that a certain type of riot is *caused* by a certain type of motive; as will be explained later, it is more useful to look elsewhere for causes.) The four types are as follows:

The rampage. This is an outbreak of animal — usually young, male animal — spirits. Young men are naturally restless, in search of excitement, thrills, "action." Also, as David Matza has explained, they are apt to feel "pushed around"; one who is caught in this mood of fatalism (as Matza calls it) wants dramatic reassurance that he can "make things happen," and breaking the law is one of the few actions open to him that immediately and demonstrably makes things happen.[4] Rioting (which Matza does not mention) is a way of making them happen on a wholesale scale. "These young people, to whom a voter registration campaign, a picket line, or an economic boycott mean very little, have found that they can stun an entire community by engaging in rioting. They can mobilize entire police forces and National Guard companies, keep mayors at their desks through the night, and bring representatives of the news media from all over the country."[5]

A rampage may start either with an incident — for example, an argument or an arrest — or "out of the blue." If it starts with an incident, the incident is more in the nature of a pretext than (as in a riot of the outburst of indignation type) a provocation; that is, the rampage begins not because the incident made the rampagers angry (although they may pretend that) but because they were looking for an excuse (signal?) to rampage. There is no pattern to the violence once it starts: it involves destruction for the sake of destruction and fighting for the sake of fighting. The police are frequently attacked by rampagers; this is not because they are hated (although they may be) but because they are at hand and will put up a good fight. Rampaging by teen-agers has always been a problem in the cities. From the very earliest times, harassing the watch, vandalism, and arson have been favorite pastimes of the young.[6] In Pittsburgh in 1809 an editor proposed satirically that the city establish a "conflagration fund" from which to buy twelve houses, one to be burned each month in a civil celebration.[7] Until the middle of the last century fire companies in the large cities were manned by volunteers, mostly boys and young men, and were in many cases what today would be called conflict gangs. Whether they put out more fires than they started is a question. In Philadelphia, for example, firemen used to riot almost every Sunday, using bricks, stones, and firearms, apparently with intent to kill.[8] In the slums of the large cities there were also street gangs, some claiming more than a thousand members, which fought each other and the police almost constantly.[9] Usually the authorities did not try very hard to interfere with these activities, which were regarded as in the nature of sporting events.[10]

Youth rampages occur today not only in the slums but elsewhere. Thousands of college boys rioted at Hampton Beach, New Hampshire, and at Seaside, Oregon, in 1964, the year the inner-city riots began, and there have been large rampages of white boys on the Sunset Strip of Los Angeles, in Atlantic City, and elsewhere since. It is not only American boys who behave this way, but boys almost everywhere. In Stockholm, for example, hordes of teen-agers hang around the subway stations committing acts of vandalism and harassing the police. "The police say that if a constable has to arrest a drunk who is disturbing the peace, the youngsters will often set upon the policeman, and a major riot looms before reinforcements can be called."[11] Probably many of the student "political demonstrations" reported in this and other countries are actually rampages.

In the upper classes the norms of culture tend to restrain the restlessness of youth and to encourage its sublimation. In the lower classes, on the other hand, cultural norms reinforce feelings of restlessness and the "mood of fatalism." Accordingly, lower-class youths are more apt than others to be caught up in frenzies of mob activity, and even adults of the lower class are, by comparison with those of the other classes, highly susceptible to the same influences.

The foray for pillage. Here the motive is theft, and here also boys and young adults of the lower class are the principal offenders. Stealing is ordinarily most conveniently done in private, of course, but when disasters — earthquakes, fires, floods, power failures, blizzards, enemy invasions, police strikes — interrupt law enforcement it may be done as well or better in public. On these occasions, when "Everyone is doing it" and "If I don't take the stuff it will just go to waste," upper-working- and middle-class adults who, under normal circumstances, would not steal, are likely to join the looters. (In 1711 the selectmen of Boston passed an act to punish persons "taking advantage of such confusion and calamities [as fire] to rob, plunder, embezzle, convey away and conceal the goods and effects of their distressed neighbours."[12]) From the standpoint of the youth or of the lower-class adult who makes a practice of stealing, it would be convenient to have a riot every day. Riots are seldom started by thieves merely to facilitate stealing, however. One reason is that the culture of the lower class renders it incapable of the planning and organization that would ordinarily be necessary to start a riot by design. Another and perhaps more important one is that although all thieves would benefit from a riot, no one thief would benefit enough from it to justify his taking the trouble and running the risks of starting it. (As an economist would put it, the riot is, from the standpoint of the thieves, a "collective good.")[13] But if thieves rarely start riots, they are always quick to join ones that are under way, and their presence in sufficient number may transform one from, say, a rampage to a foray for pillage. "I really know of no instance of a riot occurring in New York, or in any other large city, during which robbery did not play a prominent part," New York's Police Chief Walling wrote toward the end of the last century.[14]

The outburst of righteous indignation. Here the rioters are moved by indignation at what they regard, rightly or wrongly, as injustice or violation of the mores that is likely to go unpunished. Their indignation is partly at the wrongfulness of the act and partly at the wrongfulness of its going unpunished. A riot of this type is always spontaneous — people do not become indignant according to plan. Indignation is aroused by an incident of some sort (which may, of course, have been contrived by someone for the purpose), and in the nature of the case, the indignant people are without leaders. The incident itself may help to make up for this lack by serving a coordinating function; as Thomas C. Schelling has pointed out, "Without something like an incident, it may be difficult to get action at all, since immunity requires that all know when to act together."[15]

A righteously indignant mob usually consists mainly of working-class people. The lower-class individual is too alienated to be capable of much indignation, especially in a matter that he thinks does not affect him personally and directly; middle- and upper-class people are usually confident of their ability to get wrongs righted by making appeals through proper channels, and, besides, they abhor violence. The working class is not under any of these limitations: it has a capacity for righteous indignation, distrusts lawyers, public relations people, and "channels" generally, and does not greatly mind — indeed, sometimes very much enjoys — a good brawl and the spilling of some blood.

Under favorable circumstances, that is, where the working class is large and consists of people who have enough in common so that they will respond with indignation to the same provocation, an outburst of righteous indignation may involve a great many people — far more, certainly, than a rampage or a foray, both of which by their nature ordinarily draw upon relatively small "constituencies." All the large riots of the nineteenth century were mainly outbursts of righteous indignation. Some of them were very large indeed. For example, the Boston riot of 1837 (a native-American working-class attack on Irish immigrants) is supposed to have involved more than 15,000 persons, roughly one-sixth of the city's population.

In an outburst of righteous indignation the pattern of violence and destruction reflects the mob's wish to end, and also to redress or avenge, the wrong that aroused its indignation. As Rudé says in his account of popular disturbances in preindustrial France and England, the mob imposes a conception of "natural justice": "Strikers tended to destroy machinery or 'pull down' their employers' houses; food rioters to invade markets and bakers' shops and enforce a popular price control or *taxation populaire;* rural rioters to destroy fences and turnpikes or threshing machines and workhouses, or to set fire to the farmer's or landlord's stacks; and city rioters to 'pull down' dissenters' meeting houses and chapels, to destroy their victims' houses and property, and to burn their political enemies in effigy."[16]

The demonstration. Here the motive is to advance a political principle or ideology or to contribute to the maintenance of an organization. The riot is not a spontaneous, angry response to an incident. Rather, it is the result of prearrangement by persons who are organized, have leaders, and who see it as a means to some end. The word "demonstration" is descriptive, for the event is a kind of show staged to influence opinion. Those who put it on are usually middle or upper class, these being the classes from which the people who run organizations and espouse political causes are mostly drawn. Demonstrations characteristically involve breach of the public peace rather than violence (if they involve neither they are by definition not riots); the middle- and upper-class cultural style favors the use of mock violence (for example, the spraying of slogans with paint and the throwing of steer's blood), "happenings" (for example, halting traffic with police whistles), and behavior calculated to make the demonstrator the object, or the apparent object, of violence inflicted either by himself (as when he chains himself to something) or by the authorities (as when he "goes limp"). The middle and upper classes' abhorrence of violence is so great that techniques like these, which trade upon it without requiring the demonstrator to hurt anyone but himself (and usually not himself either), are often effective as a means of putting "the other side" at a moral disadvantage in the eyes of the middle- and upper-class television viewers for whose benefit the demonstration is staged.

These four types of riots are presented as analytical models. Some concrete riots very closely approximate a "pure" type, but most riots — and probably all large ones — are compounds of two or more of the types. The New York Draft Riot of 1863, for example, was a compound of at least three. It was a rampage of young toughs from the slums (three-fourths of those actively engaged in violence were boys and men under twenty years of age who were not subject to the draft, a *Times* writer estimated; it was a foray for pillage (houses and places of business were ransacked all along Eleventh Avenue); and it was also — and perhaps mainly — an outburst of righteous indignation on the part of the Irish working class at the prospect of having to compete with freed Negroes for jobs and against the alleged injustices of the draft law.[17] Large riots tend to be compound, if for no other reason, simply because they attract looters. But it is likely that the fact of their being compound also tends to make them larger: that is, that interaction among types of rioters tends to reinforce the motives and heighten the activity of each type. For example, the looters and rampagers in the Draft Riot no doubt got some moral support from having all about them rioters motivated by righteous indignation; at the same time, the presence of the looters and rampagers, most of whom were not clearly identifiable as such, must have added to the general sense of confusion and frenzy and by so doing must have helped sustain the fury of the righteously indignant. That these latter had *two* objects of indignation — Negroes and the draft law — must also have increased the interaction. One may conjecture that the greater the variety of motivational elements appealed to, the larger the number of rioters who will be recruited and — what is more important — the more interaction tending to sustain and escalate the riot there will be among the rioters.

Looking from this perspective at the recent series of inner-city riots, one is struck by the fact that for twenty years prior to July 18, 1964, there had been very few riots by Negroes, and that these few, with only one exception, had been protests against racial injustice. In 1961, for example, white mobs in six cities attacked Negroes, but there were no riots by Negroes. In 1962 there were four Negro riots — one was a demonstration by Black Muslims, two seem to have been outbursts of righteous indignation provoked by incidents of alleged police brutality, and the fourth, the exception, was a rampage by high school students after a football game in the District of Columbia stadium. In 1963 and the first half of 1964 there were eleven Negro riots, all apparently outbursts of righteous indignation and all but three occurring in the South. In none of these years was there a major Negro riot — one involving several hundred rioters and lasting more than a day.[18]

On July 18, 1964, a riot began in Harlem that proved to be a turning point. Two days before, an off-duty white police lieutenant had shot and killed a fifteen-year-old Negro youth whom he said had attacked him with a knife. The incident created widespread anger, and there was a protest march on the precinct police station the next day. The following evening (July 18) a second group of marchers refused to disperse; instead, it began throwing bottles and stones at the police station and was soon joined in this by a band of black nationalists who had been meeting nearby. The riot, which lasted in Harlem for three days, spread to the Bedford-Stuyvesant district of Brooklyn and six days later, for no apparent reason, to Rochester.[19] (The incident — an attempt by a policeman to arrest a drunk and disorderly adolescent at a street dance — seems to have been a pretext rather than a provocation.) A few days later the rioting spread, also for no apparent reason, to three New Jersey cities, an industrial suburb of Chicago, and Philadelphia.

In Harlem, when it first broke out, the rioting was mainly an outburst of righteous indignation at the police. There was little looting; the mob was chiefly occupied in bitter fighting with the police. As the rioting continued and moved to other cities, however, its nature changed. Looting and rock throwing became the mob's principal activities, with attacks on the police sporadic and incidental. In Rochester, the city manager said later, the riot had "racial overtones" but was not actually a race riot.[20] In Philadelphia, the first policeman attacked was a Negro. Nowhere did a Negro mob invade a white neighborhood or assault whites as such.

Opinion leaders and publicists did not at this time see the riots as manifestations of deep unrest or anger on the part of Negroes. At the end of the summer, J. Edgar Hoover, whose views were probably close to one end of the spectrum, reported to the President that although racial tensions had been a factor, none of the disorders — not even the Harlem one — was a race riot in the accepted meaning of the term (that is, race against race); they were, he said, "purposeless attacks" in which youths were responsible for most of the violence, and he classed them with the college-boy riots that occurred about the same time.[21] Others made similar assessments. Most civil rights leaders dismissed the idea that the riots were conscious protests; that was not merely an after-the-fact rationalization, Kenneth B. Clark said, it was an "independent of the fact" one.[22] Bayard Rustin was applauded by an audience of New York planners when he explained that the violence was caused by "merely a few confused Negro boys throwing stones in windows or a Molotov cocktail at a cop who was perfectly capable of ducking."[23] The police commissioner of New York said in effect that they were rampages and forays. "They riot either out of sheer cussedness or for criminal reasons, and in some instances because mob action seems to be taking on the aspects of a fad. . . . Bedevil the police, strip stores, shout and yell, crush anyone who opposes you . . . and if the police try to stop it, just yell 'brutality.' This is the pattern. . . ."[24]

The view that riots did not manifest feelings of outrage widespread among Negroes was consistent with the findings of an elaborate survey of Negro opinion made late in 1964 by Gary T. Marx. It showed that most Negroes were neither sunk in hopelessness nor consumed with anger. Only about a third were in any sense militant, and the proportion of Negroes who were strongly antiwhite was much smaller. Most thought that things were getting better for the Negro (81 percent of a sample in non-Southern metropolitan areas thought this), that America was worth fighting for (87 percent), that a day would come when whites would fully accept Negroes (70 percent), and that the police treated Negroes either fairly well or very well (59 percent). "The overwhelming majority of those questioned," Marx concluded, "felt that progress is being made and that integration is being pushed by the government at the right speed and were optimistic about the future."[25] That most Negroes held these opinions does not necessarily mean that the rioters held them, of course; in fact, however, there is some reason to suppose that most of them did.[26]

The 1964 riot pattern was repeated the following August in the Watts district of Los Angeles. This area was not a slum in the usual sense (it was an area of single-family, detached houses, most of which were in good condition), and Los Angeles was a city in which the Negro fared better than in most places (the Urban League rated it first among sixty-eight cities on the basis of a "statistical portrait" drawn in 1964). In this case, too, the incident that supposedly set off the riot could hardly have aroused a great deal of righteous indignation (a drunken Negro motorist had been arrested in what seems to have been a proper manner). Apparently, the incident was mainly important as a pretext for a rampage by teen-age Negro boys and young men who began throwing whiskey and beer bottles and pieces of asphalt and cement at motorists on Avalon Boulevard.[27] Two hours after the incident the mob, which then numbered about fifteen hundred, consisted mostly of these boys and young men. There was nothing "racial" about what they were doing. "One thing that impressed me was that these Negroes who were hurling stones were throwing them right into their own people. That's why I believe this didn't start out to be a race riot. These were just young hoodlums working off their frustrations. They were out to do destruction. They just wanted to hurt anybody, black or white."[28]

The statistics on arrests at Watts provide some slight basis for inferences about the motives of the rioters. About 15 percent of those arrested were juveniles. (The percentage would have been much higher, it has been suggested, were it not for the fact that the police, being short-handed, arrested the people who were easiest to catch.) Of the 3,438 adults arrested, nearly one-third had been convicted of major crimes (that is, crimes for which they had received sentences of more than ninety days) and fully one-third had minor records (that is, arrest or conviction with a sentence of ninety days or less).[29] Since the police may be quicker to arrest Negroes than whites, it is hard to say what significance should be attached to the proportion having minor records. It is more noteworthy that one-third had never been arrested.

Although the Watts riot followed the pattern that had been set the year before, Negro spokesmen at once proclaimed that it was politically motivated — it was, they insisted, a revolt, not a riot. Bayard Rustin wrote that it was carried on for an "express purpose" and was "the first major rebellion."[30] No one gave a very clear or convincing account of what the rioters were revolting against, however. The facts did not support the view that they were expressing hatred for the white man; even Rustin said the rebellion was against the Negro's "own masochism." Nor did the facts support very well the view that the rioters were asserting that (in Rustin's words) they "would no longer quietly submit to the deprivation of slum life"; after all, most Watts people lived comfortably in fairly good housing. It was somewhat more plausible to claim that they were angry about mistreatment by the police, but even this view did not fit the facts entirely, for the rioters had shown themselves more interested in burning and looting than in fighting the police.

However unjustifiably, Watts was regarded by many Negroes as something to be proud of — a kind of black Bunker Hill. This definition tended to make the rioting of the year before appear in retrospect as a kind of black Concord and Lexington and to establish a moral basis for any battles that might yet be fought in a black revolution. As one would expect, the frequency of rioting increased after Watts. In 1966, there were eleven major (that is, two-day or more) and thirty-two minor riots, and in 1967 there were twenty-five major and thirty minor riots. In most instances, the rioting began either without any precipitating incident, boys and young men simply smashing windows, starting fires, and assaulting passers-by for no apparent reason, or with an incident that was a pretext rather than a provocation. Only two of the major riots in 1966 (those in

Jacksonville, Florida, and San Francisco) seem to have started from a provocation and only eight (six of which were in Southern cities) of those in 1967 seem to have started from provocations.

The Detroit riot of 1967, although vastly more destructive, was in many ways typical. Like Los Angeles, Detroit was a city of relative prosperity and opportunity for the Negro; it had no real "ghetto" and its police had for several years been under very enlightened and determined leadership. The incident with which the riot started seems to have been a pretext rather than a provocation: when the police raided a speakeasy early one Sunday morning, a crowd began pelting the policemen with stones. This might not have led to a riot were it not for the fact that at that particular time very few policemen could be mustered. (Early Sunday morning was a "low crime" period and the stronger daytime shift was not scheduled to report for duty at precinct stations until 8 A.M.) For several critical hours the police were conspicuous by their absence. It was well known, too, that the police would not use their guns except in the most extreme circumstances. For five or six hours after the speakeasy raid Negroes and whites mingled on the streets and looted amicably side by side. On the second day of the riot Governor Romney said that it was "not primarily a civil rights disturbance but rather lawlessness and hoodlumism by Negroes and whites," an opinion with which Mayor Cavanagh agreed.[31] Almost all the arrests made were for looting, and of those arrested nearly half were aged nineteen through twenty-four. The pattern of destruction was what one would expect in a foray for pillage. Stores having things that could be consumed directly — liquor, cigarettes, drugs, clothing, television sets, appliances, furniture — were looted no matter who owned them. Stores having things that would have to be "fenced" — jewelry — were usually left untouched, as were all buildings symbolic of the "white power structure" — banks, public offices, and schools. As one of the rioters, a child, explained, "There was nothing to steal in the school. Who wants a book or a desk?"[32]

It would appear, then, that what requires explanation is not so much rebellion by Negroes (whether against the whites, the slum, their "own masochism," the police, or something else) as it is outbreaks of animal spirits and of stealing by slum dwellers, mostly boys and young men and mostly Negro. (A few non-Negroes participated, mostly as looters, in the Detroit riot and possibly in some of the others, and one major riot, a rampage-foray for which there seems to have been no precipitating incident, was carried on entirely by Puerto Rican youths in Perth Amboy, New Jersey, at the end of July 1966.) That racial injustice may have had less to do with the riots than is generally supposed is strongly suggested by the fact that a major riot (two men were killed and scores injured, and an estimated $5 million in damage was done by looting, vandalism, and arson to some 175 stores, hotels, and office buildings) occurred in Montreal in October 1969 during a sixteen-hour wildcat strike of policemen.

In framing an explanation, it will be useful to begin by listing certain events ("accelerating causes"), each of which independently increased the probability of such riots occurring. This listing will be followed by a description of a set of states ("background causes"), the concurrent existence of which established *some* probability of their occurring.[33]

Accelerating Causes. Without attempting to pass on their relative importance, several such causes may be listed.

1. Sensational television coverage of the riots recruited rampagers and pillagers. As the mayor of Plainfield, New Jersey, explained, "The sensational coverage of the Newark riot showed persons looting stores while the police took no action to halt them. This view of looting appealed directly to the criminal and susceptible element."[34] Prior to the advent of television, it would have been very difficult for the authorities to have brought the possibilities for fun and profit in rioting to the attention of the lower class even if they had wanted to do so. Lower-class people do not read newspapers, but nearly all of them have at least one television set.

2. By carrying vivid accounts of rioting to cities all over the country, television not only eliminated the necessity that would otherwise have existed for the independent discovery of certain techniques of rioting (for example, the use of fire bombs) but also, and especially, it established the *possibility* of it. That by throwing

rocks, smashing windows, and setting fires one can throw a great city into turmoil is something that the ordinary person does not recognize until it happens. Once the possibility of an action has been established, the probability of someone's taking it is very much increased. "Some cats come in the bar and talk about how they are going to start burning again next month — down about Broadway. Mostly, it is just talk, but they know that they could do it."[35] The main point here is that, thanks to television, knowledge that "they could do it" was widely disseminated to people who otherwise would have been slow to discover it for themselves. In 1935 and 1943 Harlem had riots, but for lack of television coverage these did not provide a model that was known and imitated in cities all over the United States.

3. The rioters knew that they had little or nothing to fear from the police and the courts. Under the pressure of the civil rights movement and of court decisions and as the result of the growing "professionalism" of police administrators (these developments, in turn, being consequences of "middle-class-ification" of the population), the patrolman's discretion in the use of force declined rapidly after the war. At the same time courts were lenient with juvenile offenders. "Tough kids" had always attacked policemen when they got the chance, but by the 1960's the amount of toughness required was not very great, for in most cities it became more and more apparent that a policeman who shot a boy would be in serious trouble. Not being able to use force, the police could not effectively use the *threat* of it. It was not uncommon for a gang of boys to disarm and beat a policeman who, following orders, would not use his gun against them. During a riot, the police were especially ineffective — because their offenses were not very serious, most rioters could not be successfully threatened; the only thing that could be done with them was to take them into custody, and this was something the police were seldom numerous enough to do. Sometimes the police had to stand by and allow looting to go on before their eyes. This, of course, increased the tempo of the rioting.

"Those first hours, when the cops pulled out, were just like a holiday," recalls one young man who joined in the looting of shops on 12th Street that morning. "All the kids wandered around sayin', real amazed like, 'The fuzz is scared; they ain't goin' to do nothin'.' I remember one day me and another kid, we was locked in the school and there wasn't any teachers around and we had a ball, we did all the things we'd been wantin' to do for a long time. We set some fires in the baskets and we emptied the teachers' desks and we stuck a whole mess of toiletpaper in the principal's mailbox. Well, that's what it was like out on the Street."[36]

4. The probability of rioting was increased by several factors that tended to give it legitimacy in the eyes of potential rioters. One was an outpouring of vivid television and newspaper portrayals of outrages against Negroes and civil rights workers in the South; perhaps Sheriff "Bull" Connor of Alabama created much of the indignation that was discharged in Harlem against the officer who shot the boy in July 1964. Another was a barrage of statements by leaders of both races that represented the Negro's problems as entirely, or almost entirely, the result of racial injustice, implying that only white racism stood between the Negro and affluence. Another was the discovery that rioting was possible; as David Matza points out with reference to juveniles, learning through experience that an infraction *can* be done leads, by an illogic characteristic of childish thought, to the conclusion that it *may* be done.[37] Another factor was the spread of the rioting to several cities; the knowledge that "everybody is doing it" tended, by more childish illogic, to the conclusion that doing it could not be very wrong. "If they can do it in Detroit, we can do it here," Milwaukee teen-agers cried as they began smashing store windows. But what probably did most to make rioting seem legitimate was acceptance of the claim that the Watts riot was a "revolt" and that the rioting everywhere had some political purpose. Byron Washington, the Waterloo, Iowa, youth whose words appear at the head of this chapter, doubtless threw his stone with the strength of ten because he knew (having heard it over television perhaps) that he was not a boy out raising hell but a victim of injustice fighting for a college education. Whether correct or not, explanations that find the cause of rioting in the rioters' environment are bound to be taken as justifications, or at any rate extenuations, of their behavior and therefore tend to reinforce the irresponsibility that is characteristic of the age and class culture

from which rioters are largely drawn.[38] Rustin may have been right in saying that the looters were "members of a deprived group who seized a chance to possess things that all the dinning affluence of Los Angeles has never given them."[39] But, right or wrong, the effect of such statements is to make it easier for the potential rioter to justify his behavior, and therefore the statements are themselves a contributing cause of rioting. One can see this process clearly enough in something a twenty-year-old Watts rioter said to a reporter: "The white power structure looks on us as hoodlums when actually we are deprived people."[40]

If explaining the riots tended to justify them, so did predicting them. One who said that if drastic measures were not taken to end injustice riots could be expected might be correct, but correct or not his words would help form an impression in the public mind that rioting is a natural and perhaps even laudable response to the continuance of an injustice. From the very beginning of the civil rights movement its leaders have been wont to predict that violence will occur if reforms are not accepted at a faster pace; the riots, of course, made these predictions much more credible and therefore gave the civil rights leaders more incentive than ever to make them.[41] At the end of 1966, Dr. Martin Luther King, Jr., after acknowledging that "a prediction of violence can sometimes be an invitation to it," went on to predict that "failure to pursue justice" would result in more riots.[42] Rustin, at about the same time, told a Senate subcommittee that if the President asked for only a small increase in funds for the poverty program, the Negro leadership "can no longer be responsible for what happens"; and Senator Robert Kennedy said that unless "major steps" were taken "we will reap a whirlwind that will be completely uncontrollable."[43] Even if these predictions had been based on actual knowledge, and even if by making them — and *only* by making them — it had been possible to secure the needed reforms, one would have to say that making the predictions increased the probability of there being riots; obviously, it was impossible for the reforms to achieve their effect in time to prevent what was being predicted. Realistically, however, those who made the predictions could not be at all sure that the measures they were proposing, some of which — for example, "pursue justice" — were so vague as to be almost meaningless, would have any tendency to prevent rioting; moreover, they had little or no reason to believe that their making the prediction would bring about the adoption of the measures they advocated. Rustin, for example, could not have supposed that his words to the Senate subcommittee would cause the President to ask for a larger increase in the poverty program. The one thing the predictions *were* likely to do was to make rioting appear more natural, normal, and hence justifiable.[44]

Background Causes. For there to be *any* probability of rioting of the kind here under discussion, several conditions had to exist concurrently.

1. Without a large supply of boys and young men of the lower classes to draw on, major rampages and forays would be impossible. In the 1920's and 1930's (as was explained in Chapter 2) the number of such people in the inner cities was very much reduced from what it had been in the previous century because of the aging of the immigrant population and the movement of the relatively well-off to outlying neighborhoods and suburbs. During the Depression it looked for a while as if the inner-city slums and semislums might be permanently depopulated. During and after the war, however, these districts were filled or nearly filled once again by a new migration, this one from the rural South (and, in New York, from Puerto Rico). Being a young population with a very high birthrate, the newcomers quickly put more boys and young men on the streets than had been there before. The new (black) generation of inner-city youth may be somewhat more prone to violence than the earlier (white) ones. (Southerners, both white and black, tend to be violent as compared to other Americans.) But if so, the difference is not great. Lower-class youth in every generation and in every ethnic and racial group are extremely violent as compared to middle- and upper-middle-class adults.

2. The lower- and lower-working-class people who now comprise much of the inner-city residential population are largely cut off from participation in institutions that in times past regulated and restrained the behavior of people whose class culture and situation were similar to theirs. Racial discrimination, although obviously a

factor, is not the main thing that cuts them off from these institutions; rather, what cuts them off is the changes that have occurred in the nature of the institutions because of the "middle-class-ification" of the population of this country. In the last century, for example, the volunteer fire company gave boys and young men of the lower classes opportunities to express animal spirits under conditions that were to some degree controlled: the firemen fought *each other,* usually for the "honor" of their companies. Today, of course, fire departments are run on a professional basis and are open only to mature men who have placed well in an examination. More or less the same thing has happened in politics. Not so long ago party machines labored to establish claims on even the lowest of the low; the trading of jobs and favors in return for loyalty tended to create some sort of bond between the individual and the government. Now that the machine, precinct captain, and corner saloon have been replaced by the welfare bureaucracy, the nonpartisan election, and the candidate who makes his appeal on educational television, the lower classes no longer participate in politics at all and are therefore no longer held by any of the old ties. Even in criminal activities there has been the same trend. Like fire-fighting and politics, the money-making kinds of crime (as opposed to "kid stuff") are organized in such a way as to exclude — and therefore to exert no discipline upon — the unskilled and incapable.

This exclusion from institutions of those who are not able or willing to participate on the terms set by the now predominant middle class has the effect of reducing the influence within the lower classes of those persons who, although not able to perform according to the standard set by the middle class, could nevertheless lead and set an example for — and thus place some restraint upon — less able members of their class. The situation is strikingly like that which, when it occurs in prisons, is said to cause riots. "It is the cohesively-oriented prisoner committed to the values of inmate loyalty, generosity, endurance, and the curbing of frictions who does much to maintain the prison's equilibrium. When the custodians strip him of his power — when the custodians destroy the system of illicit privileges, of preferential treatment and laxity which has functioned to increase the influence of the cohesively-oriented prisoner who stands for the value of keeping things quiet — the unstable elements in the inmate population have an opportunity to capitalize on the tensions of prison life and to rise into dominance. The stage has been set for insurrection"[45]

3. A considerable number of upper-working-class, middle-class, and upper-class people who have made large income and status gains in recent years and are impatient to make even larger gains live in the inner city in close physical proximity to the lower classes. Upwardly mobile members of earlier slum populations very quickly left not only the slum but the inner city as well, and usually the neighborhoods they vacated were occupied by some different newly arrived ethnic group. In the case of the Negro, the outward movement has been rather slow, partly because of job and housing discrimination and partly because of a preference Negroes have for living near other Negroes; moreover, in the case of the Negro, the places of those who *have* moved away have usually been taken by newly arriving Negroes. Upwardly mobile Negroes who for one reason or another live in or near the slum tend, of course, to be very sensitive to the dangers and unpleasantnesses of slum life and to blame them not on conditions common to the white and the Negro (for example, lower-class culture, low income, and so on) but on racial injustice past and present, real and imaginary. If, like the upwardly mobile members of earlier groups, these Negroes lived in suburbs far from the inner-city slums, they would not be available physically (and perhaps psychologically) for participation in riots. As it is they do not participate in them actively in large numbers. They do provide enough politically motivated rioters, however, to make possible the interaction effect that, it was argued earlier, tends to escalate a rampage-foray into a major riot. Even those who do not participate in the rioting tend to help legitimate it in the eyes of potential rioters by putting forward or concurring in the claim that it has a political purpose.

Several conclusions bearing on policy may be drawn from this analysis. One is that there is likely to be more rioting for many years to come, and this no matter what is done to prevent it. So long as there are large concentrations of boys and young men of the lower classes on the streets, rampages and forays are to be expected. Without some support from righteously indignant members of the working class and from politically minded members of the middle and upper classes, such outbreaks probably will not reach the scale that was reached in Los Angeles, Newark, and Detroit, but even so some of them will probably be well beyond the ability of local police forces to deal with. Eventually, much of the inner-city population will move to the suburbs; this change, which is already under way, will reduce the potential for very large riots by physically separating the lower class from the working class and the working class from the middle and upper classes and thus (1) curtailing the number of persons available in any one place as recruits for a riot and (2) making interaction between rioters of different motivational types (for example, rampagers and demonstrators) less likely. For at least another twenty years, however, there will be enough potential rioters of all types in the inner cities to produce frequent rampage-forays and some major riots.

It is naïve to think that efforts to end racial injustice and to eliminate poverty, slums, and unemployment will have an appreciable effect upon the amount of rioting that will be done in the next decade or two. These efforts are not likely to be very serious or, if they are, very successful. But even if they are both serious and successful they will not significantly affect the factors that produce riots. Boys and young men of the lower classes will not cease to "raise hell" once they have adequate job opportunities, housing, schools, and so on. Indeed, by the standards of any former time, they have these things now. It may be that in the very long run good opportunities and a high standard of living will bring about the assimilation of the lower classes into the middle and by so doing will make them less violent. But this will happen over the long run — say, from one generation to the next — if it happens at all, and, besides, even middle- and upper-class boys riot sometimes. As for the upwardly mobile and politically minded Negro who has a potential for outbursts of righteous indignation and for demonstrations, even serious and successful efforts at reform are likely to leave him more rather than less angry. The faster and farther the Negro rises the more impatient he is likely to be with whatever he thinks prevents his rising still faster and still farther. As the HARYOU manual, "Youth in the Ghetto," remarks: "The closer the Negro community gets to the attainment of its goals — the closer it gets to the removal of the determinants and manifestations of racial exploitation and powerlessness — the more impatient individual Negroes will become for total equality."[46]

It is not only the Negro who will become more disaffected as his situation improves. The process of "middle-" and "upper-class-ification" is making the whole society more sensitive to departures, both real and imaginary, from the ideal, inherently unrealizable, of how things ought to be. As the economy becomes more productive and social arrangements more decent, the well-off — and among them youth especially — become more restless and more intolerant of the continued failure to achieve social perfection. Demonstrations, confrontations, protests, dialogues, and so forth, are bound to be more frequent as the middle and upper classes grow and more and more people have the leisure to act upon what the Judeo-Puritan tradition tells them is a positive obligation to make society over. Paul Goodman, who, it seems likely, is a portent of things to come, says that he looks forward to a "conflictual community" that will "combat the emptiness of technological life."[47] No doubt most of the blood spilled by the middle and upper classes will be steer's blood carried for the purpose in plastic containers. The effect on the lower classes of this sort of behavior by the upper classes may be serious, however.

Although the underlying factors making for riots will not change for quite some time, there may be changes in accelerating factors. Television coverage of riots may be less provocative; if so, one force feeding the growth and spread of riots will be reduced. (This will not, however, undo the main damage already done: the discovery that burning and looting on a wholesale scale is possible will not be forgotten.) The ability of the police to bring incipient riots under control may be improved by the introduction of better methods and equipment; of importance, perhaps, is the chemical Mace, which, if it proves to be both effective and acceptable to public opinion, may change the situation significantly by giving police the upper hand in dealing with juveniles and other offenders whom it would be wrong to shoot. On the other hand, one accelerating factor will doubtless gain in strength. This is the opinion that rioting is a way of protesting injustice and is therefore in large degree justified. As was remarked earlier, the spread of this opinion has made each successive wave of rioting somewhat more ideological than the last. Now that the rationale of rioting has been well worked out, future riots may be mainly for protest rather than for fun and profit.

Insofar as the motives of the past few years predominate in the future, however, it is safe to say that none of the following will make riots less likely: the election of Negro mayors, a mayor's courageous strolling in the slums, the elimination of police brutality and the improvement of police manners, efforts to placate, co-opt, or restrain Negro extremist leaders, the measurement of the "grievance level" of the Negro community, and the provision of jobs for the "hard-core" unemployed. Politically motivated persons may perhaps be influenced by such things, but looters and youthful rampagers will not be.

There is no intention here to extenuate the crime of rioting. It is easy, however, to exaggerate the harm that riots of the kind that have occurred since 1964 have done and are likely to do. In the first place, not many people were killed or seriously injured by the rioters; in all of the more than one hundred riots from 1964 through 1967, apparently no more than about twenty persons were killed by rioters.[48] It is angry or panicky policemen who do most of the killing and maiming, and when the police are equipped with nonlethal weapons there will probably be much less of this. Because "routine" crime sometimes ceases or is much reduced during a major riot, there may even be some net saving of life and limb by virtue of riots.

The property losses are not as staggering as may be supposed either. In the majority of the recent riots the damage consisted mainly of smashed windows, the theft of liquor, and the burning of some not very valuable buildings. It would not take a very heavy snowfall to cost a city and its people more than an average-sized riot costs them. Major riots are another story, of course, but even they do not cause destruction very different in kind or amount from what would be caused by a sizable urban renewal program. Wasteful as it is to destroy useful structures in either way, the costs of doing so are well within the ability of a very affluent society to bear. In the course of time, too, property losses will be cut as people adapt to the likelihood of rioting by changing the location of structures or the design of them. In Europe, heavy metal shutters are used to protect store windows; doubtless the same thing will be done here (in the worst slums it long has been, of course) when the danger to windows becomes great enough. (On the other hand, if, as seems likely, the government compels insurance companies to insure properties in high-risk areas at normal premium rates, incentives to make such adaptations will be removed.)

The danger that a riot will so disrupt essential services — sewage disposal and water supply, for example — as to create a major public health hazard is very small. To inflict serious damage of this kind would require a considerable degree of expertise and organization. If anything of this sort is to be feared, it is to be feared from a highly disciplined band of political zealots, not from a mob — least of all from a mob of rampagers and looters.

There are those who think that up to now, at least, the riots have been a good thing on the whole because (the Negro view) they have impressed white society with the necessity of drastic action to improve the Negro's conditions of life or (the white view) because they have helped to instill in the Negro a sense of pride. According to the executive secretary of the Milwaukee Teachers Education Association, "There is a certain amount of Negro pride which resulted from the riot. The pride factor is evident when you walk or drive down the street. Caucasians are sensitized to Negroes; they are aware that they exist. Before, they could psychologically dismiss them as inferior. . . . The Negroes feel this focus on them. And when they are in school, they are going to expect something to happen. Frankly, I think it's great."[49]

Such claims are impossible to evaluate and yet they cannot be ignored.[50] Very probably, the immediate effects of the burning, looting, and killing are of little importance as compared to the enduring changes in attitudes, feelings, and opinions that have been brought about by the rioting. No one now can have the least idea of the nature of these changes, however, and even in retrospect the cause-and-effect relations will remain unclear. The rioting may have given Negroes a new pride (that the facts do not justify it is of course beside the point), and this may do more for the lower-class Negro than all the compensatory education, public housing, job training, and community organization that could be provided with a dozen Freedom Budgets. It may also have impressed whites as nothing else would with the need for immediate and far-reaching reforms, and this may — although there is no reason for confidence — lead to much good and little or no harm. If one could be certain that these effects were indeed produced by the rioting, one would be tempted to conclude that it was a good thing in spite of its cost in life and property. But one cannot be certain. Moreover, even if these effects were produced, others that are disastrous may also have been. A racial myth may be very helpful to the Negro lower class and very harmful to the society as a whole. It may be that the principal effect of the rioting has been on white opinion, that it has checked a growing disposition on the part of the working and lower-middle classes to accept reforms, and that it has established as something beyond question for everyone the mistaken notion that the "problem" is mainly one of race rather than, as has been maintained here, of class. Explaining as "racial" behavior what can as well or better be explained in other terms would seem to be a dangerous game even when played with the best of motives.

CHAPTER TEN

The Future of the Lower Class

If the children of the degraded classes could be taken in infancy, before their bad habits have had time to form, and trained to earn a livelihood, a certain proportion of them would be redeemed. If those who could not be so trained were allowed to starve, the number to grow up a burden on society would be diminished. The greatest difficulty in the way of such a policy is to organize charitable effort in such a way that it shall be intelligently directed to this end. The natural tendency of such effort is the very opposite of that here pointed out.

— Simon Newcomb, 1886

Let us take the little child in the future from its possibly ignorant, filthy, careless mother, as soon as it can walk . . . and give it three hours daily in the kindergarten, where during that time it will be made clean, will enjoy light, color, order, music and the sweet influence of a loving and self-controlled voice.

— Annie Adams (Mrs. James T.) Fields, 1886

So long as the city contains a sizable lower class, nothing basic can be done about its most serious problems. Good jobs may be offered to all, but some will remain chronically unemployed. Slums may be demolished, but if the housing that replaces them is occupied by the lower class it will shortly be turned into new slums. Welfare payments may be doubled or tripled and a negative income tax instituted, but some persons will continue to live in squalor and misery. New schools may be built, new curricula devised, and the teacher-pupil ratio cut in half, but if the children who attend these schools come from lower-class homes, they will be turned into black-board jungles, and those who graduate or drop out from them will, in most cases, be functionally illiterate. The streets may be filled with armies of policemen, but violent crime and civil disorder will decrease very little. If, however, the lower class were to disappear — if, say, its members were overnight to acquire the attitudes, motivations, and habits of the working class — the most serious and intractable problems of the city would all disappear with it.

As the last several chapters have contended, the serious problems of the city all exist in two forms — a normal-class and a lower-class form — which are fundamentally different from each other. In its normal-class form, the employment problem, for example, consists mainly of young people who are just entering the labor market and who must make a certain number of trials and errors before finding suitable jobs; in its lower-class form, it consists of people who prefer the "action" of the street to any steady job. The poverty problem in its normal-class form consists of people (especially the aged, the physically handicapped, and mothers with dependent children) whose only need in order to live decently is money; in its lower-class form it consists of people who would live in squalor and misery even if their incomes were doubled or tripled. The same is true with the other problems — slum housing, schools, crime, rioting; each is really two quite different problems.

The lower-class forms of all problems are at bottom a single problem: the existence of an outlook and style of life which is radically present-oriented and which therefore attaches no value to work, sacrifice, self-improvement, or service to family, friends, or community. Social workers, teachers, and law-enforcement officials — all those whom Gans calls "caretakers" — cannot achieve their goals because they can neither change nor circumvent this cultural obstacle.

Despite all that was said to the contrary in the earlier chapters of this book, some readers may suspect that when the author uses the words "lower class" what he has in the back of his mind is "Negro." They may suspect, too, that the "real" purpose of the rather pessimistic account of the possibilities of reducing the size of the lower class that follows is to lay the basis for the conclusion that nothing should be done about any of the city's serious problems. There is, of course, no arguing with a reader who is determined to mistake one's meaning. All the author can do is to repeat once more that there are lower-class people, as defined here, in *all* ethnic groups, including the Anglo-Saxon white Protestant one, and to point to the obvious fact that most Negroes are not improvident, do not live in squalor and violence, and therefore are plainly *not* lower class. As for the suspicion that the argument of this chapter will be used to justify a program of inaction, the reader is advised to wait and see.

It cannot be taken for granted that eventually the process of middle-class-ification will eliminate the lower class.[1] That many millions of the poor, the unschooled, and the low-status have risen dramatically on the class-cultural scale from one generation to another does not necessarily mean that the lower class has risen. It may be that those who rose were all at least somewhat future-oriented; on *a priori* grounds, a present-oriented person could not be expected to take even a first step toward self-improvement. On empirical grounds, too, this proposition is somewhat plausible. With the exception of the autobiographical accounts of a few very gifted individuals — Frederick Douglass, Malcolm X, and Claude Brown, for example — there is no direct evidence of there ever having been any upward mobility from the lower class.

There is, perhaps, some *indirect* evidence of such mobility in the past. Most lower-class persons in the city now are not descendants of the lower-class persons who lived in them fifty or one-hundred years ago. This is evident from the fact that the present lower class is mostly black, whereas the former one was mostly white. It may be that the descendants of the old lower class have been assimilated into the other classes.

It is possible, however, that the old lower class produced very few descendants. It may even have died off without reproducing itself. Since it probably had a high birthrate, the number of its descendants could have been small — and thus the amount of assimilation small — only if its deathrate was phenomenal.[2]

No data exist on the deathrate in the lower class as defined here. However, such data as do exist suggest that, in the last century and in the early decades of this one, it may have been high enough nearly to offset the birthrate (which also can only be guessed at). In 1864, Boston's crusading Unitarian minister, Theodore Parker, exclaimed in horror that three-fifths of the children born there to Catholic parents "die before the sun of their fifth year shines on their luckless heads."[3] The infant and child mortality rates among *lower-class* Catholics were no doubt even higher, which means that the sun could have shone on very few lower-class heads indeed. Although death took its heaviest toll in infancy and childhood, adult deathrates among the poor were also high (and among the *lower-class* poor they were certainly highest of all). Probably the lower-class poor died from want more often than did the other poor; certainly they died more often from syphilis, excessive drinking, accidents, and homicide. It is probably indicative of differences in class culture that, at the turn of the century, the life expectancy at age ten of the Irish immigrant was only thirty-eight years, whereas for the Russian Jew (who did not brawl or drink and whose religious observances probably had some hygienic value), it was a little more than fifty.[4]

Fifty or more years ago, the Malthusian checks of poverty and vice may have been operating so strongly on the lower class of the largest cities as to cause it nearly to die out every generation or two. There is no "hard" evidence to support this proposition, however. Moreover, even if the lower class did fall far short of replenishing itself, *some* of those born into it probably entered the higher classes.

Whatever was the case half a century or more ago, the lower class is probably growing now. Poverty is no longer a major cause of death in the cities. Improvements in public sanitation and in medical and hospital care for the indigent, together with the development of antibiotics and other miracle drugs, keep many lower-class people alive, often in spite of themselves, as it were. Since 1940 infant mortality among the poor has dropped sharply. For instance, in that year the mortality among Negro males under one year of age was 101.2 per 1,000, which was about what it had been among slum dwellers in general for several decades. By 1950 it was down to 59.9 and by 1963 to 44.8. This rate was still twice that of the population as a whole, but the decrease meant (to quote a writer who neglected to point out the class basis of Negro crime) "that fifty more Negro infants of every 1,000 now born can reach an age where they have a chance of contributing to statistics on crime and delinquency."[5]

The lower-class deathrate is still high relative to that of the other classes, and will no doubt remain so. Studying a sample of young urban Negro men, Lee N. Robins and her associates found that 27 percent had one or more medical problems resulting from drinking. Of the middle-class men in the sample, 40 percent were or had been heavy drinkers; of the lower-class men, 84 percent were or had been.[6] Narcotics addiction, too, takes its toll: "Diseases related to narcotics addiction," the *New York Times* reports, "cause more deaths among New Yorkers fifteen to thirty-five years old than murder, suicide, accidents or natural causes."[7] Homicide is the second leading cause of death among male Negroes aged fifteen to twenty-five and the third leading cause among those aged twenty-five to forty-four. These causes of death, along with infant mortality, are all especially frequent among the lower class. However, public agencies can do little to eliminate them: large reductions in deaths from these causes can occur only as a result of changes in life-style, which is to say, from the lower class's ceasing to be lower class.[8] Despite its high deathrate, it is nevertheless likely that the lower class is now more than reproducing itself. Its deathrate is probably no longer high *relative to its birthrate,* although the latter has probably fallen too.

If the lower-class birthrate falls far enough, the decline in the deathrate may be offset, so that the lower class will again fail to replenish itself. There is reason to believe that, in general, the poor *want* to limit the size of their families and also that they have the necessary information about contraceptive techniques. A study of mothers on welfare in New York City found that among those under thirty years of age and with fewer than three children, 60 percent did not want more children, and a large majority knew about "the pill."[9] It by no means follows that there will be a dramatic decline in the birthrate, however; as Lee Rainwater points out in his book *Family Design,* among lower-class women, in particular, knowledge about birth-control techniques is often "not integrated into either their own sense of available technology or their world's."[10] (It is interesting that although 60 percent of the welfare mothers in the study cited did not want more children, 63 percent expected to have more.) In most sizable cities public clinics have recently been established to make birth-control information and devices available to all women who request them, and in some cities volunteer workers are energetically trying to persuade the poor to have fewer children. Whether because of these efforts or for other reasons, the birthrate of the poor in the cities has been dropping; probably it would drop a good deal faster if the clinics were in a position to give more intensive care and supervision, but probably, too, a substantial proportion of the *lower class* could not or would not limit the size of their families no matter what the clinics did. These conclusions are suggested by the results of an experimental effort in Britain to provide contraceptive care on an intensive basis to 150 casual laborers and their wives. In the course of five years it reduced the number of pregnancies to one-fifth of what might have been expected. Since "failure" was found to be correlated with "personal and social grade," a considerable proportion of those in the lowest grade must have been impervious even to intensive care.[11]

Two things appear to be necessary before a substantial reduction in the lower-class birthrate can take place. One is the development of a technique of contraception that even the most present-oriented can use without difficulty. The other is the discovery of a way to motivate lower-class people to begin birth control before unwanted children have arrived and to use it regularly. The first of these problems will very likely be solved in the laboratory before long. The other will be hard to solve, however — it may even turn out to be insoluble. Failure to make early and regular use of birth-control methods may reflect features of lower-class culture that cannot be changed short of changing — that is, eliminating — lower-class culture itself. Rainwater mentions three such features: lack of communication between husband and wife, knowledge on their part that the cooperation required for family limitation is not possible within their kind of marital relationship, and lack of sexual interest on the wife's part.[12] The present-orientedness of lower-class culture is also of importance in this connection. Rainwater does not discuss this explicitly, but he presents some data that may be pertinent. The accompanying table is reproduced from *Family Design*.[13] His "Upper-Lower" class is probably roughly equivalent to the working class of this book and his "Lower-Lower" to its lower class.

ATTITUDE TOWARD LIKELIHOOD OF SUCCESS
IN LIMITING FAMILY TO DESIRED SIZE

(in percent)

	Planful and Self-Assured	Hopeful but Unsure	Passive and Fatalistic
Middle-class Protestants (60)*	63	37	—
Middle-class Catholics (51)	23	63	14
Upper-lower class (whites and Negroes) (126)	18	58	24
Lower-lower class (whites and Negroes) (152)	5	32	63

* Numbers in parentheses represent number interviewed.

Evidently, it cannot be taken for granted that the lower-class birthrate will fall very much. Despite its high deathrate, the lower class may more than maintain itself in the future even if it gains no recruits from immigration from rural America or from abroad. In fact, some immigration — perhaps a considerable amount of it — is to be expected. Therefore, unless lower-class persons display an unprecedented amount of upward mobility, the lower-class population of the city may grow, perhaps rather rapidly. The question of what, if anything, may be done to hasten the assimilation of the lower class into normal culture is for this reason of added importance.

It will be convenient to enter upon this question by making some conceptual distinctions that have not been needed until now. Three analytical types of present-orientedness will be described. An individual of one type acts very much like one of another: all are improvident, irresponsible, without strong attachments to family, friends, or community, and unable or unwilling either to control impulses or to put forth any effort at self-improvement. The types differ according to the *cause* of the individual's present-orientedness.

Type 1: Cognitive. An individual of this type is *psychologically incapable* either of taking account of the future or of controlling impulses — that is, of what will here be called "investing": exchanging present for future satisfaction. The future simply does not enter into the world as the cognitively present-oriented individual perceives it. In the case of small children, whose inability to take the future into account or to control impulses is notorious, such present-orientedness presumably has a physiological basis. Adults who were brought up in a group or society whose culture does not provide concepts by which to think about the future are cognitively present-oriented by virtue of their culture. Other adults may be cognitively present-oriented despite having been socialized into a culture that is not present-oriented; with them, present-orientedness is a personality disturbance.

Type 2: Situational. A representative of this type is psychologically capable both of taking the future into account and of controlling his impulses. He lives from moment to moment because he believes his *situation* to be such that investment in the future is either impossible or unprofitable. For example, an individual whose resources barely suffice to keep body and soul together would be foolish to give much thought to the future — especially to a future the essential features of which he knows he cannot change. ("Hopeless poverty," Reverend Theodore Parker remarked a century ago, "tempts a man to squander.")[14] Since his present-orientedness is a rational adaptation to reality as he perceives it, an individual of this type becomes future-oriented whenever he perceives changes in the situation that make providing for the future profitable.

Type 3: Volitional. This type of individual, despite being psychologically capable of providing for the future and despite being in a situation which (as he perceives it) may afford excellent opportunities for investing, nevertheless lives from moment to moment simply because he *prefers* that style of life. It may be that for him the "good things in life" are "good" precisely because they require no planning, or he may strongly prefer present over future satisfaction merely because it is present. In either case he is present-oriented by choice. ("One suspects," writes economist Kenneth Boulding, "that a certain amount of the poverty of the hillbilly or the subsistence farmer, and even perhaps of the urban slumdweller and of the bum, involves the rejection of the whole middle-class way of life rather than the inability to find opportunities.")[15]

The three types being analytical, there is no reason why the "real-life" individual's present-orientedness should not be a mixture of types. For example, the individual might (as the quotation from Boulding suggests) be at once volitionally and situationally present-oriented.

In Chapter 3 the lower-class individual was said to be present-oriented by virtue of having been socialized into the present-oriented culture of the lower class. This proposition by no means precludes his being present-oriented for other reasons as well (indeed, there is a strong presumption that both his tastes and his situation as he perceives it will tend to make him so). It will be seen, too, that while one cannot be lower class without being present-oriented, the reverse is not true: class culture is only one of several possible causes of present-orientedness.

Perhaps from fear of saying things that might be used politically against efforts at reform, social scientists tend to stress the situational causes of present-orientedness and to ignore or play down the others. Miller, Riessman, and Seagul, for example, "feel that many lower-income people have a shorter time perspective than do many middle-income persons," but they caution against theories that explain behavior on psychodynamic rather than on situational grounds, because emphasis on the former "leads to social policies which emphasize 'rehabilitation' rather than expanding opportunity."[16] It is not surprising that economists view the individual's time horizon as a function of his opportunities; most economic theory assumes that the individual is rational in the sense that he acts so as to maximize utility. The economist, therefore, naturally assumes that an individual will invest more (that is, in the terms used here, become more future-oriented) when his situation changes so as to make doing so more profitable. It *is* surprising, however, that sociologists and anthropologists, who for the most part consider the economist's model of *homo economicus* to be ludicrously unreal, are equally willing to assume that one who lives from moment to moment will change his ways once he is given good incentives to provide for the future.[17] For example, anthropologist Elliot Liebow (from whom, incidentally, the terms *cognitive* and *situational* were borrowed) in his book about Negro streetcorner men, *Tally's Corner,* claims that the men live from moment to moment not because a present-oriented style of life has been culturally transmitted to them, but because each has discovered, from his own experience, that trying to provide for the future is futile and hopeless.[18] When, and only when (Liebow says), the men's experience of life convinces them that they have a real chance of gaining something important by providing for the future will they do so. Because they have the same goals in life as other people, he says, they will respond much as others would to improvements in their job, educational, and other opportunities.

The assumption that individuals, and for that matter cultures, adapt rationally to the incentives and disincentives offered to them is highly congenial to the present writer. Although it is metaphorical to speak of a culture's "rationality," much empirical evidence suggests that people *by and large* tend to act rationally in the sense of making choices that promise to give them more rather than less of whatever it is that they want, even without engaging in conscious calculation and indeed even when they are intellectually incapable of making the required calculations.[19] Consider, for example, a sociologist's finding that a reformatory inmate's sense of control over his environment affects the amount of attention and effort he devotes to acquiring information relevant to his prison career.[20] This finding is consistent with the proposition that even a present-oriented individual (it can probably be assumed that most prison inmates are more than normally present-oriented) will take account of the future *when he has reason to think that it will "pay" him to do so.*

Some general implications for policy follow from this analysis. One is that present-oriented people ought to be given genuine opportunities to make large gains in both material and nonmaterial income, and ought also to be persuaded of the reality of these opportunities. A related implication is that the present-oriented person should be helped to see the world as a less chaotic, risky, and unpredictable place than it now appears to him to be: a rational person does not exchange present for future satisfaction if the world appears so full of uncertainty as to make a return on the investment most unlikely. A third implication, related to the others, is that the present-oriented individual should be helped to acquire confidence in his ability to influence the future in matters of importance to him; being able to make things happen does, after all, reduce uncertainty. Of course, the individual's confidence in his ability to influence the future cannot be increased except as his actual ability to influence it is increased.

It is, however, much easier to formulate these very general guides to policy than it is to specify particular measures that will prove effective in particular circumstances. How, for example, is it possible to give a "really good job" to someone who has no skills and perhaps cannot or will not acquire any? Even if he is capable of learning skills, a vicious circle may have to be broken somewhere; perhaps only giving him a "really good job" will convince him that it is worthwhile to prepare himself for one. Similarly, how is one to make rewards "contingent upon the individual's own behavior" (a recommendation that James S. Coleman bases upon the finding that reformatory inmates acquire information when they think they can use it to their advantage)?[21] This principle implies that the individual should be allowed to suffer penalties (loss of the reward at the very least) if he does not behave as he should. Herbert Spencer was prepared to follow this principle to its logical conclusion, allowing those who failed to provide for the future to starve in their old age in order that others might see from their example the advantage of saving. Few people today, however, would consider the issue settled by the principle that a cruel deterrent may in the long run be less cruel than the consequences of not deterring. Indeed, few people recognize that there sometimes *is* a problem of choice between these alternatives. The almost universal opinion today is that, both for his own sake and for that of his society, an individual must not be left to suffer the consequences of his actions. If, for example, he has chosen a life of improvidence, he cannot for that reason be allowed to remain below the poverty line. To give him money, however, is to give him an incentive to persist in his ways. Indeed, there is perhaps no better way to make converts to present-orientedness than to give a generous welfare check to everyone.[22] Between giving "the poor" strong material incentives to exchange present for future satisfactions and giving them equally strong ones to do the opposite, it may as a practical matter be possible to draw only a very faint and fine line.

Moreover, the assumption that individuals tend to respond rationally to incentives and disincentives does not imply that *all* individuals respond to the *same* incentives or that they respond to any *particular* incentives with equal sensitivity. It is to be expected that the situationally present-oriented individual will adapt more readily to improvements in his opportunities than will other present-oriented persons, but even he may adapt slowly and incompletely. He may think it not worth his while to change his style of life even slightly if the advantage of doing so would be small and transitory (as an economist might put it, he may place a "reservation price" on adapting). It is also possible that over a long period of time he may have become habituated to a style of life; the more deeply rooted his habits, the larger (it may be conjectured) the incentives necessary to bring about a change in his behavior. One whose present-orientedness is volitional may be expected to be about as resistant to incentives as the habitually present-oriented individual; indeed, incentives are not evaluated as such by him (and therefore, strictly speaking, are not incentives at all) except as they are compatible with his value system. It is possible, too, that an individual may more or less deliberately choose a present-oriented style of life even when he recognizes that there exists for him an alternative that *measured by another set of values* is very good. Pondering why welfare workers have not had more success in luring men "away from a life of irresponsibility, sensuality, and free-wheeling aggression," Alvin Gouldner, a sociologist, concludes that many men may simply judge that the bargain offered them — " 'give up promiscuous sex, give up freely expressed aggression and wild spontaneity . . . and you, or your children, may be admitted to the world of three square meals a day, to a high school or perhaps even a college education, to the world of charge accounts, of secure jobs and respectability' " — is not a very attractive one.[23] In short, it is not enough that the "market basket" of incentives be well filled: if it does not contain things that the individual wants, he will not "buy" it even though it is filled to overflowing.

Cognitive present-orientedness (it would seem) must be the slowest of the three types to respond to incentives to change. Over the short run, it may be that the best that can be done is to insure that cognitive present-orientedness is not reinforced by situational or volitional constraints. If an individual's cognitive incapacity is culturally given, as it is in the case of the lower class, his adaptation to new opportunities may be extremely slow — slower, probably, than that of an individual whose present-orientedness is habitual (or "overlearned"). The crucial difference between culture and deeply rooted habit is that the former consists of traits that are mutually supportive and hence harder to change piecemeal. It is not at all unlikely that cultures (as opposed to individuals) change their time horizons so as to adapt to changes in environment, but any such change must occur very slowly: a certain stability over time is a defining characteristic of culture.

Since the potential for inducing change differs from one type or mix of present-orientedness to another, it is important that the policymaker know which type or types he is dealing with in particular circumstances. It may be, for example, that *some* streetcorner men are cognitively present-oriented, whereas others are not. How is one to tell which is which? That an individual sometimes uses words that, when used by people of other classes, refer to the future does not necessarily mean that he has real awareness of the future: people sometimes parrot words — that is, use them without content.

The most convincing test is to give the individual powerful incentives to provide for the future; if he then begins to provide for it, one can safely say that his previous present-orientedness was *not* cognitive. However, it is seldom practical to provide incentives that are powerful ("really good jobs," for example) or that one can be confident are powerful *enough* (if one knew this, the test would be unnecessary). A more practicable method, but one which yields results of uncertain value, involves the use of psychological tests; a number of researchers have made promising attempts at measuring individuals' time horizons, and reasonably reliable indicators for this purpose can no doubt be developed.[24] A third important method is that of the cultural anthropologist; if examination of "the entire way of life of a people" reveals that way to be present-oriented, it is safe to conclude that the present-orientedness of persons socialized into that way of life will be cognitive, whatever else it may also be.

Until such tests as these have been extensively made and carefully analyzed, statements about the relative importance of one or another type of present-orientedness in the city should be regarded as highly provisional. It may turn out that the lower class that has figured so largely in this book does not exist (that whatever present-orientedness exists is neither cultural in origin nor cognitive in nature) or that it exists among so few persons as to be inconsequential. Moreover, no matter what tests show, time may tell a different story. Powerful opportunities and incentives may over two or three generations produce changes that theory and observation now declare to be impossible. Before concluding too hastily that habit and culture cannot be offset, except perhaps in the very long run, by the opportunities and incentives that American urban society provides, one should consider the words of a very well-informed observer of the last century — Jane Addams, of Chicago's Hull House:

The theory that wealth brings responsibility, that possession entails at length education and refinement, in these cases fails utterly. The children of an Italian immigrant owner do not go to school and are no improvement on their parents. His wife picks rags from the street gutter and laboriously sorts them in a dingy court. Wealth may do something for her self-complacency and feeling of consequence; it certainly does nothing for her comfort or her children's improvement nor for the cleanliness of anyone concerned.[25]

It is reasonable to suppose, however, that no matter how successful improvement of opportunity proves to be as a general method of dealing with present-orientedness, there will be some persons, if only a few, whose present-orientedness will remain almost un-affected. Also, even if provision of good opportunities were sure to eliminate all present-orientedness within two or three generations, there would be good reason to look for ways by which this outcome might be secured more quickly. Without prejudice to the idea that making it in some sense profitable for people to take account of the future is in general a necessary and possibly a sufficient condition of getting them to do so, the remainder of this chapter will discuss the uses and limitations of some quite different approaches.

Psychotherapy holds almost no promise as a means of changing the lower class. It possesses no techniques for changing personality; even if it did, there would be obstacles — perhaps insuperable ones — in the way of wholesale application of them to the lower class.[26] One problem is that the nature of lower-class culture makes its bearers bad subjects. Lower-class people, write Hollingshead and Redlich,

> are not able to understand how thinking and talking can help them. They have not learned to verbalize and symbolize in the same way higher class persons have. Neither have they learned to sublimate present needs for the realization of future goals.[27]

In any case, there are not nearly enough therapists to treat the insane, let alone the present-oriented.

Two different lines of experiment and analysis in the field of child development are of special interest. Adherents of neither approach expect to be able to derive a formula for turning present-oriented children into future-oriented adults, but both approaches have clear implications, albeit perhaps mainly negative ones, for policy.

Language and class culture. In the last half-century, philosophers, anthropologists, and psychologists have all become increasingly interested in the way language shapes thoughts and feelings. A psychologist at the University of London, Basil Bernstein, has taken the lead in applying this line of analysis to problems of child development.[28] His thesis is that linguistic codes ("fashions of speaking") are shaped by social structure (by the nature of family, work, and community groups, for example) and in turn shape class culture. The lower classes (that is, semiskilled and unskilled), for example, are oriented toward the communal rather than the individual, toward the concrete rather than the abstract, and toward the here and now rather than the future. Linguistic codes thus set certain limits on what a child learns and on how it will learn it. The lower classes use only a "restricted" code, which is a language of largely implicit meanings; the speaker relies heavily upon gestures, intonation, and other nonverbal cues; his meaning is never abstract or complicated. He calls attention to features of the situation that his listener will perceive and evaluate as he does. The middle and upper classes, by contrast, use "elaborated" as well as restricted codes. Communication by means of an elaborated code employs more varied and complicated syntactic elements; the message is relatively individualized rather than conventionalized, explicit rather than implicit, and abstract rather than concrete. Bernstein illustrates these codes with two imaginary conversations, each between a mother and a child who sits on her lap in a bus.

MOTHER: Hold on tight.
CHILD: Why?
MOTHER: Hold on tight.
CHILD: Why?
MOTHER: You'll fall.
CHILD: Why?
MOTHER: I told you to hold on tight, didn't I?

MOTHER: Hold on tightly, darling.
CHILD: Why?
MOTHER: If you don't you will be thrown forward and then you'll fall.
CHILD: Why?
MOTHER: Because if the bus suddenly stops you'll jerk forward onto the seat in front.
CHILD: Why?
MOTHER: Now hold on tightly darling and don't make such a fuss.[29]

The low level of conceptualization in the lower-class mother's communication code influences, Bernstein thinks, the child's basic model of thinking and feeling as well as his desire and ability to learn. This low level of conceptualization constrains, among other things, the intensity and extent of his curiosity, his attitude toward authority (as opposed to power), and his ability to identify with the aims and principles of a society (as opposed to a local group), to verbalize feelings and to express them in socially approved ways, and to take an instrumental (which is to say a future-oriented) attitude toward people and things.

It seems likely that linguistic limitations are a cause, although not necessarily the only one, of present-orientedness. Without language one could have no sense of a future — one could not hope, much less plan.[30] The more limited one's linguistic (and, therefore, conceptual) equipment, it seems reasonable to suggest, the less able one will be either to take account of the future or to control impulses.[31] There is much evidence to support this view.[32]

Relation to a mother-figure in childhood. Another line of theory and experiment that appears to be particularly relevant in this context stresses the importance for normal personality development of a close and satisfying relation in the early years of life with a mother or mother substitute. The infant and young child, Bruno Bettelheim writes, "must have a star to steer by."[33] Erik H. Erikson explains that a "regular and mutual affirmation and certification" between the infant and one who cares for it will in later life reassert itself in strong emotional ties to others — family, friends, and political leaders. Failure to form such bonds "can harm an infant radically, by diminishing or extinguishing his search for impressions."[34]

The supportive function need not necessarily be performed by a single person, however. As Bettelheim puts it: "a constellation can replace the individual star provided what is lost in intensity is made up for in the definiteness of the direction by which to navigate."

Typically, the lower-class child does not get from its mother or from anyone else the support and stimulation that it needs. This is not to say that lower-class mothers do not love their children. It may be, as Rainwater asserts, that they find fulfillment in motherhood in a way that middle-class mothers, who are taught the value of outside interests for establishing their validity as persons, do not.[35] However this may be, the lower-class mother or mother substitute is not ordinarily a "star to steer by," especially after the child has passed babyhood. Consider the following report on child-rearing among 250 urban (Negro) women "who all belong to the lowest social class":

[The child] was permitted to grow at his own speed. If he was unable to perform, he did not meet with criticism and pressure to do better. He learned how to work. He was encouraged to fight for his rights. On the other hand, there was confusion as to who had authority over him and what behavior was acceptable, since many persons with different expectations had a parental role. He was accustomed to extremes of adult authority, being very controlled at times, and not at all controlled in others. He early became used to corporal punishment. He was treated with relative coldness and he was not praised for achievement. The stimuli which are supplied by books, toys, and cultural experiences were often missing. There was little opportunity for a boy to identify with a male figure. There was lack of interest in the personality characteristics which differentiate one individual from the other and which contribute to a strong feeling of self-identification.[36]

How much difference having a star (or constellation) to steer by may make in a child's development and later life is dramatically suggested by an Iowa study in which two groups of children, all considered mentally retarded at the outset, were followed for about thirty years.[37] The experimental group, consisting of thirteen children under the age of three, was taken from an orphanage in which the children received "depersonalized and affectionless but otherwise adequate" care and was placed in an institution for the retarded. There the attendants and older girl inmates treated the children as guests, and each child found some one girl who was particularly interested in him or her. The contrast group included twelve children who were much like the others except for having a higher mean IQ — 86.7 as compared to 64.3. The children in this group remained in the orphanage, where they continued to get the kind of care that both they and the others had been getting before the study began.

After only two years, it was found that the experimental group had made striking gains in IQ, whereas the other group had made equally striking losses. The mean IQ's were now 91.8 and 60.5, *with the experimental group in the lead.* With one exception the members of the experimental group were then placed in adoptive homes. After another two and one-half years their mean IQ had risen from 91.8 to 101.4; in the same period, that of the contrast group had risen also, but very slightly, from 60.5 to 66.1.

Twenty years later a follow-up study was made. All those in the experimental group were found to be self-supporting, and their average education and occupational achievement compared favorably with that of the population at large. Eleven of the thirteen had married, and the mean IQ of their children was 104. The members of the contrast group had not fared nearly so well. One had died in adolescence and four were still in institutions. Only two had married. Those who were not in institutions had low-paying jobs.

While either of the factors just discussed — namely, language patterns and the support of a mother or mother-substitute — may by itself profoundly influence the child's development, the *interaction* of the two factors would seem likely to produce the most marked effects. In the lower class, language deficiencies and lack of support, stimulation, and direction from a mother or mother-substitute are found together. So, at the upper end of the class-cultural scale, are the opposites — verbal facility and a close relation to mother. It is noteworthy that in one of the most upwardly mobile and presumably future-oriented of all ethnic groups, the Jewish, the pattern of child-rearing in the last generation emphasized both of these elements to an extraordinary degree. The Jewish mother, as described by Zena Smith Blau, was in this respect the exact opposite of the lower-class Negro mother, as described earlier. The Jewish mother held her son in bonds of love and mutual dependence beyond his childhood and even his youth, all the while subjecting him to intense and constant verbal stimulation.

Whatever Yiddishe Mamehs did for their children . . . was accompanied by a flow of language, consisting of rich, colorful, expressive words and phrases. Their vocabulary of endearments alone can fill a modest-sized paperback, but they also had a superb store of admonishments, curses, imprecations, explanations, songs, and folk-sayings that they effortlessly invoked as they went about ministering to the needs of their children and their husbands. The freedom that they exhibited with the spoken word invited a similar response from their children and it carried over into school. . . .[38]

It would seem that the problems posed by the lower class can be solved fundamentally only if the children of that class are removed from their parents' culture. As a matter of policy, the implication is that efforts to change the culture of the lower-class child should concentrate, whenever possible, on the early, formative years — when the child most needs "a star to steer by." Anecdotal evidence suggests that damage done to the child's personality may occasionally be repaired as late as adolescence. However, it is probably safe to say that the earliest possible exposure of the child to the culture of the larger society will increase the chance of successful adaptation while lowering costs, both emotional and material, to all concerned.

A second implication is that in many cases helping the mother or mother-substitute will be a prerequisite to helping the child. How the father relates to the child apparently matters less.[39] His effect on the child's development in its early years is indirect for the most part, making itself felt through the mother's attitudes. Although there seems to be no clinical or experimental evidence on the subject, one suspects that it is better for a child not to have a father present at all than to have one who keeps the mother upset and distracted.

A third implication may seem to be that the child should be taken from its lower-class parents at a very early age and brought up by people whose culture is normal. It will do little good to explain to a lower-class mother wherein her child-rearing practices are wrong: she is not really interested in improving her practices, perhaps because she cannot see anything wrong with them. In this and in other areas as well, her class culture sets sharp limits on what it is possible for her to do. It may seem, therefore, that the only thing to do is to take the child from her and put it in the care of a substitute who will bring it up properly.

However, the case is not as clear as it may at first appear. It is not certain that taking the child from its mother may not cause even greater injury to it than would leaving it with her. (It should be remembered that the Iowa children whose IQ improved so remarkably were transferred from an *institution*.) After a comprehensive review of the scientific literature, psychologist Leon J. Yarrow concludes that keeping a child with "grossly inadequate parents in a depriving and hostile environment" does not seem warranted by what is known of the dangers in separating a child from its mother; he stresses, however, that before a child is removed, strong efforts should be made to improve family conditions.[40]

Presumably, the danger to the child in taking it from its mother is a function not only of the mother's incompetence but also of the ability of the mother-substitute to give it the support and stimulation that it needs. Even supposing (as it seems plausible to do) that at present the average substitute provides a much better environment for the child than does the average mother from whom children are taken, one still cannot conclude that *all* lower-class children should be taken from their mothers. For as the number of such removals increased, the quality of the average substitute would surely fall and that of the average mother would probably increase. It is one thing to provide proper adoptive homes and institutions for a few thousand children a year and an altogether different one to provide them for several hundred thousand. With respect to institutions, at least, it is likely that "depersonalized and affectionless but otherwise adequate" care is the best that can be expected on a large scale.

Finally, it is questionable whether the state has a right to take a child from its parents in order to prevent an injury as impalpable and contingent as its socialization into lower-class culture. Even if it were certain (and of course it is not) that a child brought up in the lower class would turn out to be a "social problem" of some sort, it would not automatically follow that society has a right to interfere so drastically in people's lives. If failure to provide a child with adequate linguistic equipment is considered sufficient grounds for removing a child from its parents, so in consistency ought failure to provide it with "a star to steer by." This latter criterion would probably find almost as much application in the upper classes as in the lower. As a practical matter there is, of course, not the slightest possibility of a rule being adopted that might be applied to the rich as well as to the poor; this appears from the practice of the courts at the present time. "Neglect" and "abuse," the grounds for child removal in the law of most states, are everywhere interpreted narrowly to mean abandonment of the child, failing to supply it with food, clothing, shelter, and medical care, grossly mistreating it (as, for example, beating it or locking it in a closet for a long time), or outrageously endangering its moral welfare (as, for example, by carrying on the trade of prostitution in its presence.)[41] "Emotional neglect seems the most obvious type to social workers," one of them writes, "but it is the most obscure to the courts in our experience."[42] The inability of psychiatrists to specify precisely what "emotional neglect" consists of is one reason why the courts do not take note of it.[43] One suspects, however, that if the condition were found only among the poor, it would prove no more difficult to define for legal purposes than, say, loitering.

In fact, even laws with respect to gross physical neglect and abuse are not enforced stringently or uniformly. Most cases of neglect and abuse never come to the attention of the authorities. Neighbors are reluctant to "interfere," teachers rarely report it when a pupil comes to school with cuts and bruises, and physicians frequently either fail to recognize the "child abuse syndrome" or decline to take the risk of being sued for damages if the parents are acquitted. Even when a case is reported and the facts are beyond dispute, the court may be unwilling to take custody of the child.[44]

As a matter of logic, the simplest way to deal with the problem — and one which would not involve any infringement of parents' rights — would be to permit the sale of infants and children to qualified bidders both private and public. (Public bidding might be needed to insure a price high enough to induce a sufficient number of lower-class parents to sell their children.) This assumes, of course, both that a parent who would sell a child would probably abuse or neglect it, and also that one who would buy it (especially if the price were high) would want it enough to take good care of it. The trouble with the idea, of course, is, first, that it is wrong to represent human beings as commodities to be bought and sold; and, second, that if it worked (i.e., if the price were high enough to secure the effect desired) it would almost certainly have the unintended effect of encouraging some people to bring children into the world for the purpose of selling them. This second objection might possibly be got around by making sterilization of the vendor a condition of sale, but the first one would be decisive nevertheless.

Another possibility would be to offer "scholarships" to lower-class infants in amounts sufficient to induce their parents to place them in approved boarding schools on a year-round basis. These schools could be located in or near the children's neighborhoods and could be staffed by working-class women and girls from those neighborhoods. These arrangements would enable parents to see their children without having any responsibility for their care. This, of course, is the basic principle of *kibbutzim* in Israel. The teaching of the children could not be done entirely on a classroom basis, however. In the early stages of the acquisition of a new subject matter like reading or arithmetic, a tutorial arrangement (which is what the middle-class child gets from his parents at home) may be necessary; in effect, substitute mothers would have to be provided at least part of the time.[45]

If it is not feasible to establish boarding schools, day nurseries may be the next best thing. They are, however, a poor substitute. Even under the best of circumstances, they are not likely to succeed in bringing children out of lower-class culture. In an experimental project in Boston, twenty-one children, aged two and one half to six, from disorganized, lower-class families spent two to three mornings a week in a nursery school generously staffed with highly trained personnel. The school was intended to help the child "gain a sense of mastery over his immediate surroundings."

Trips were followed up with related stories and play activities and we usually saw to it that there was something to carry home. By encouraging the children to tell details about these trips to parents (standing by to make sure they would be listened to and adding facts of interest specifically for the parents), we assisted communication between parents and child and gave emphasis to the importance of the experience for the child.[46]

After attendance of from one to three years, there was noticeable improvement in the children's appearance, body use, and self-esteem, and many had "learned to express their thoughts, feelings, and experiences with accuracy sufficient for communication." These gains certainly justified all the effort that was put forth, but the lives of the children did not change drastically. Language problems, for example, continued to hamper the children's ability to learn even after three years, and the experimenters doubted that these problems would ever be overcome. Reports that filtered back to them after the experiment had ended were not at all encouraging.

Many of the children were placed in situations where more demands were made on them than they were mature enough to fulfill. At least five of them repeated one of the early grades.

It is our impression that as failures began to follow one another, the inevitable regression to more discouraged, impatient, frightened, passive behavior occurred.[47]

Lower-class children could probably benefit a great deal more than they do from day nurseries were it not for the fact that they are at once confused and stultified by what they are (and are not) exposed to at home. When the influence of the nursery has made conditions for changing the child's outlook and life style feasible, even small improvements in home life might have large effects. As a rule, it is on the mother, or mother-substitute, that efforts to improve the home environment should concentrate. She is best able to give the child the support and stimulation it needs, and, fortunately, she is likely to be less — perhaps much less — improvident, irresponsible, and violent than her mate. As was noted in Chapter 3, it is the male, especially the young one, to whom lower-class culture comes most "naturally." For some reason — perhaps because extreme present-orientedness is incompatible with the childbearing function, perhaps because lower-class sex is sometimes too much like rape to be very enjoyable to women, or perhaps because "toughness" (one of Walter B. Miller's foci of lower-class culture) is usually regarded as a male attribute — women born and brought up in the lower class very often behave in ways that are not characteristic of that class. The lower-class mother — but not the father — is often very much concerned about the children's welfare: she may try to keep them in school and out of trouble; sometimes she struggles to buy a house. Usually, her efforts are futile. Her mate and, as soon as they are old enough, her sons are at best noncontributors to any "family" project and at worst active opponents. If she manages to save anything, they soon lay hands on it and squander it. "Getting ahead" is her idea, not theirs.

It would seem, then, that the aim of policy should be to encourage the mother's aspirations and to strengthen her hand as much as possible. This is easier said than done, however. One suggested innovation is the "peace bond," an arrangement by which a man incurs an agreed-upon penalty, usually the forfeiture of a small sum, if he does what he has agreed not to do. It is unlikely that the lower-class male will be deterred by such a penalty, nor even perhaps by the prospect of jail. Another proposal is that police powers be redefined to allow arrests for misdemeanors on probable cause (in most states a police officer who did not see a misdemeanor committed cannot make an arrest without a signed complaint). This suggestion is open to several objections. One is that such a redefinition of police powers might lead to greater embarrassment and inconvenience for those persons who (because of color, low income, or whatever) are taken to be lower class when in fact they are not. Moreover, the lower-class woman may be just as unwilling to offer the police a verbal complaint as she is to offer them a signed one. There is still another reason why workable ways of protecting the woman from her mate are unlikely to be found: the lower-class woman will often tolerate considerable abuse rather than lose the companionship of a man. Rather than risk being abandoned, she may deny that she and her children were beaten, that the welfare money was spent on a drunken spree, and all the rest. (In Illinois, the police *can* arrest for probable cause on many misdemeanors but they almost never do, partly for these reasons, partly because they do not want to create additional frictions within families, and partly because they want to avoid assaults by angry mates.)[48] Against her own unwisdom (if this is what it really is) the police, the courts, and the whole power of government cannot protect her. And so it appears that it will be very difficult if not impossible to realize even the minimum goal of policy — namely, to protect the lower-class woman and her children against the violence of her mate.

The conclusion is unavoidable that for at least several decades there will be a lower class which, while small both in absolute numbers and as a percentage of the whole population, will nevertheless be large enough to constitute a serious problem — or, rather, a set of serious problems — in the city. The question arises, therefore, as to what policies might minimize the difficulties that must inevitably exist when a lower-class minority lives in the midst of an increasingly middle- and upper-class society.

When the lower class lived on farms and in small cities like Elmtown (the population of which, it will be recalled, was about 25 percent lower class), its members were to some extent both held in check and protected by being physically isolated from each other. Also, there were few, if any, opportunities for easy money, and without money the lower-class person was effectively tied down. An even greater constraint on him, perhaps, was his visibility. In the slums of a big city, it is easy to drop out of sight. In a town or small city, on the other hand, there is no place to hide. The individual is known personally by the landlord, corner merchant, and policeman; he cannot escape into anonymity. In the big city he need never see the same merchant, landlord, or policeman twice. As an economist might put it, one who wants to lead a lower-class style of life has the advantage of numerous "economies of scale" in the big city.

Therefore, from the standpoint of a society that wants at once to protect lower-class people from each other and to protect itself from them, there are advantages in having lower-class people live in the town or small city, or, if they must live in the large one, in having them scattered in a way such that they will not constitute a "critical mass" anywhere.[49] These considerations suggest that government programs (subsidies to large farmers, for example) that tend to push unskilled people off the land and out of rural areas ought to be stopped, that welfare programs should aim at making life in towns and small cities much more advantageous to the chronically poor than it is now (thereby reducing one of their incentives to come to the city), and that, within the large cities, there should be an end to that kind of urban renewal (almost the only kind, in fact) the tendency of which is to dislodge lower-class families who live in or near neighborhoods that are largely middle class.

It might be argued that the hardest cases among the lower class ought to be treated as semicompetent (incompetents being those — for example, children, the insane, the feeble-minded — who are incapable of knowing where their own interest, not to mention the social interest, lies). Such persons could be cared for in what may be called semi-institutions, which would consist of small enclaves of lower-class people who, either because they wanted help in "staying out of trouble" or because they desired certain material benefits (extragenerous allowances for housing, food, clothing and health care) would agree to accept certain limitations on their freedom. For example, they might agree to receive most of their income in kind rather than in cash, to forego ownership of automobiles, to have no more than two or three children, and to accept a certain amount of surveillance and supervision from a semi-social worker–semi-policeman.

Several considerations, however, argue against semi-institutional care for the lower class. As a practical matter, it is unlikely that many of the hardest cases — those from whom society most needs protection — would choose semiaffluence in a semi-institution in preference to the life of the slum. If these hardest cases are to be controlled at all, they must be controlled totally — that is, put into prison. This approach is obviously out of the question, since "being lower class" is not a crime or commitable condition and is not at all likely to be made one. The tendency, in fact, is in the opposite direction: to confine fewer and fewer of those who have been convicted of crimes or have been judged to be mentally incompetent.

A very important danger in such efforts to restrain the lower class is that they might be applied also to people who are *not* lower class, thus abridging the freedom of these others without justification. This danger exists in part because euphemisms — e.g., "the poor" — have collapsed necessary distinctions between the competent and the semi-competent. (The blind, for example, are often lumped together in welfare programs with the lower-class poor.)[50] It exists also because prejudice or convenience sometimes causes caretakers to treat externals — skin color, speech ways, and so forth — as indicators of lower-class culture.

Another objection arises from the fact that at the present time (fifty or more years ago it was otherwise) most lower-class people in the large cities are black. Putting them in semi-institutions would inevitably appear to be a reflection of racial inferiority or an expression of racial prejudice. What is even more important, perhaps, is that taking the lower-class black out of the slum of the great city would tend to cut him off psychologically from the black community. It is by no means inconceivable that the "black pride" movement may engender morale in the mass of black people — morale that the lower class may in some degree share if it is in close physical contact with the main body of blacks. To be sure, one could argue this the other way, contending, first, that nothing would do more for the morale of the black community than to have the worst of the lower class removed from its midst and, second, that lower-class people are by the nature of their culture immune to any moral influence from the surrounding society.

Finally, there is clearly a tension if not an out-and-out incompatibility between the goal of restraining the lower-class individual and that of stimulating him. The first calls for reducing his freedom, the second for enlarging it. If it were possible to identify persons who are irremediably lower class and to place them and them alone under restraints, this objection would not apply. In fact, there is no way of knowing which individuals would respond significantly to incentives and which would not. The danger of perpetuating and increasing present-orientedness while endeavoring to restrain it makes the whole enterprise of restraint suspect. Despite the high costs to society and to the lower-class individual himself that follow from increasing his freedom, doing so may well be the best course of action in the long run.

CHAPTER ELEVEN

What Can Be Done?

> Often travelers, technical advisers, or "old hands" from
> a given country return with tales of how disorganized, dis-
> honest, or untrustworthy the people are; but once the tales
> have been told, everyone settles down to a theoretical de-
> scription of, or plan for, the economy of that country which
> does not take into account in any formal way the psycholog-
> ical characteristics of the people just described.
> — David McClelland

I T will be convenient to approach the question that forms the title
of this chapter by distinguishing the feasible from the acceptable.
A measure is *feasible* if (and only if) government (local, state, or
national) could constitutionally implement it and if its implementation would result in the achievement of some specified goal or level
of output at a cost that is not obviously prohibitive. For example,
it is not feasible for every city dweller to have a one-acre lot (physical reality prevents), for every child to get a high school education
as distinguished from a high school diploma (social and perhaps
even biological reality prevent), to prohibit the movement of the
poor from one city to another (this would be unconstitutional), or to
replace the present cities with new ones in the space of a few years
(the cost would be wildly out of relation to the benefits). The ac-
ceptability of a measure does not depend upon its feasibility: a
measure is *acceptable* if those who have authority in government
(elected or appointed officials or sometimes voters) are willing to
try to carry it into effect. Thus, a measure could be entirely feasible
but quite unacceptable or entirely acceptable and quite infeasible.

It goes without saying that it is often impossible to know in advance whether a particular measure is either feasible or acceptable. One can rarely be sure that the knowledge needed to make the measure "work" is at hand or within reach; its constitutionality may be in doubt; and there is always some possibility that unanticipated consequences will make its cost prohibitively high. ("Cost" in this context means any undesired effect or foregone advantage, not just an outlay of money or material resources.) These practical difficulties do not affect the validity of the distinction, however, or destroy its usefulness for purposes of analysis.

This chapter tries to show, first, that the range of feasible measures for dealing with the serious problems of the cities is much narrower than one might think, and second, that within this range hardly any of the measures are acceptable. If what is, in general, feasible is not acceptable, the reverse is also true: what is acceptable is not, in general, feasible. Government seems to have a perverse tendency to choose measures that are the very opposites of those which would be recommended on the basis of the analysis in the preceding chapters. The reasons for this perversity may be found in the nature of American political institutions and, especially, in the influence on public opinion of the upper-class cultural ideal of "service" and "responsibility to the community."

Clearly, a measure is infeasible if aimed at the simultaneous attainment of mutually exclusive ends. Two persons cannot both be satisfied if one's satisfaction is *constituted* of the other's nonsatisfaction. Insofar as the poverty problem, for example, has this relational character (that is, insofar as it is one of "relative deprivation"), it is insoluble. In Hollywood, Leo C. Rosten writes, "it is natural for the actress who earns $20,000 a year to envy the actress who earns $50,000 who envies the actress making $100,000. In a community where one can make $350,000 a year, $75,000 a year is not especially impressive — either to the group or the self."[1] The same problem arises, of course, even in the least glamorous places and with people of very ordinary income. That objective differences in income can be reduced to almost nothing does not necessarily mean that the problem of relative deprivation can be solved, for the smaller objective difference in income may come to have a greater subjective importance. The same problem arises with the distribution of things other than income. It is in the nature of deference, for example, that some persons receive more than others. There is really no way to prevent those who receive relatively little from perceiving that fact and being made unhappy or suffering a loss of self-respect because of it. As Frank H. Knight has written, "The real scarcity which seriously afflicts individualistic civilization is the scarcity of such things as distinction, spectacular achievements, honor, victory, and power."[2] Since there can never be enough of these things to go around, the problem of poverty with respect to them is logically insoluble.

Another class of "solutions" must be considered infeasible because in the absence of an adequate specification of the means by which they are to be brought about it must be presumed that no one knows how and that they represent mere wishful thinking. Doubtless a "change in the heart and minds of men" would solve a great many problems. But how is such a change to be brought about? Until the means are specified, this "solution" must be dismissed as utopian.

Those who use the terminology of social science may talk of changing "culture," rather than "hearts and minds." The fact is, however, that no one knows how to change the culture of any part of the population — the lower class or the upper, whites or Negroes, pupils or teachers, policemen or criminals. Moreover, even if one *did* know how, there is good reason to suppose that doing so would be infeasible on other grounds; for example, it might require unconstitutional methods, such as taking infants from their parents at birth, or entail other disadvantages that more than offset its advantages.

Some "solutions" are infeasible because (1) there is no reason to expect people to do the things that would constitute a solution unless government motivates them to do them, and (2) government for one reason or another cannot so motivate them. If, as Lee Rainwater asserts, "only effective protest can change endemic patterns of police harassment and brutality, or teachers' indifference and insults, or butchers' heavy thumbs, or indifferent street cleaning and garbage disposal,"[3] then (assuming that effective protest must be carried on from *outside* the government) measures to correct these abuses lie beyond the bounds of feasibility. In other words, if there *are* solutions to these problems they are not *governmental* ones, which is to say that one cannot implement them by calling into play the state's ultimate monopoly on the use of force.

Repeal of the minimum-wage laws is certainly feasible, but elimination of the *informal* minimum wage, which would reduce unemployment among the low-skilled even more, is not. Government cannot prevent the formation of a social definition of what is a "decent" wage, and (what amounts to the same thing) it cannot prevent workers from feeling some loss of self-respect in working for "peanuts." From the standpoint of the policymaker, then, the informal minimum wage presents an insoluble problem.

In the nature of the case, it is impossible to have a very clear idea of what government can and cannot do in the way of forming public opinion. Nothing except the elimination of lower-class culture would contribute as much to a general solution of the urban problem as would certain changes in public opinion — for example, greater awareness of the importance of class-cultural and other nonracial factors in the Negro's situation and a more realistic sense of what levels of performance it is reasonable to expect from such institutions as schools and police forces and from the economy as a whole. However, it is very questionable to what extent, if at all, government can bring these changes about. It is a question also whether *if* it can bring them about it *ought* to — that is, whether the unintended and long-run effects of a strenuous exercise of its opinion-forming capacities would not be likely to change American society for the worse rather than for the better.

People often respond to government measures by making adaptations the aggregate effect of which is to render the measures ineffective or even injurious. As was pointed out in Chapter 5, some economists believe that it is impossible for government to keep unemployment permanently below 3 percent by fiscal policy devices, the reason being that investors respond to the price outlook in such a way as to check any policy except the impossible one of a continuous and accelerating inflation. Other examples of the same phenomenon are easy to find. Subsidies to induce employers to hire "hard-core" workers achieve very little because the employers tend to make adjustments (which may be perfectly legitimate) that enable them to take the subsidies while employing workers who are not significantly different from those whom they would have employed anyway. Similarly, efforts to reduce unemployment, poverty, or slum housing in a particular city may be counterproductive in that they attract more poor workers to the city. Thus, the *Wall Street Journal* reports from Detroit:

> A massive industry effort to help avert future riots in Detroit appears to be backfiring as hundreds — possibly thousands — of unemployed persons from out of state come to the city seeking work.
>
> The result: Some out-of-staters have failed to get a job, swelling the unemployment that many believe contributed to last July's riot.
>
> Others have snapped up jobs that might have gone to the city's own so-called hard-core unemployed.[4]

There is much to be said for the idea of giving small sums at any hour of day or night to persons, mostly youths, who might otherwise steal or kill to get the price of a few drinks or a "fix" of heroin. It would not be feasible to do this, however, because of the adaptive behavior that it would evoke. Once it became known that money was being given away (and of course the scheme would not work unless it *was* known), the demand would become too great to satisfy.

Essentially the same problem will exist with any welfare program that offers generous support to all who can be considered poor. Such a program will encourage people to adapt either by reducing their incomes (the wife leaving her job, for example) or by lying, thus increasing the number of the "poor" and, if the inducement is strong enough, eventually swamping the system.[5]

Some "solutions" are infeasible because the very feature(s) of social reality that constitute the problem make them impracticable. Training programs do not as a rule offer any solution to the problem of hard-core unemployment because the same qualities that make a worker hard-core also make him unable or unwilling to accept training. More generally, giving lower-class persons "really good" jobs is not a feasible way of inducing them to change their style of life, because that very style of life makes it impossible to give them "really good" jobs.

"Solutions" that deal with minor, as opposed to key or strategic, factors in a situation are also infeasible. To put the matter in another way, it does not help to create a necessary condition when there is no way of creating the sufficient conditions; similarly, in situations of multiple causation, it is of little use to set in motion a cause that contributes a trivial amount to the total effect desired when there is no way to set in motion those that would contribute a significant amount to it. It is less than likely that the McCone Commission, in its report on the background of the Watts riot, was correct in asserting that "an adequate mid-day meal is essential to a meaningful educational experience"[6] (it may be a contributing factor, but it is certainly not *essential*). Even assuming for the sake of argument that the Commission *was* correct, the conclusion does not follow that a school lunch program would have an appreciable effect on the problem of preventing riots of the sort that occurred in Watts. The school lunch program "solution," however desirable it might be on other grounds, would not touch a great many much more important causes that would make riots just as likely as ever.

The assumption of the McCone Commission that an improvement in material welfare is bound to make a major contribution to the solution of almost any social problem is a pervasive one: better nutrition, better housing, better transportation, better street cleaning and refuse removal — all such things are commonly seen as ways of reducing crime, of preventing the break-up of the family, of encouraging upward social mobility, and so on. Although one cannot demonstrate it rigorously, such measures probably do have some effects of this kind.[7] However, even if this is the case, the policymaker needs to ask the same question about them as about adequate mid-day meals: Is the contribution that this one cause makes to the total effect that is desired (i.e., what would constitute the solution of the problem) more than trivial?

Even if it is feasible in all other respects, a measure lies outside the bounds of feasibility if its implementation would entail costs that more than offset its benefits. The proponents of a particular measure are usually blessed with tunnel vision: they can see only their objective; all peripheral and background values are invisible. The policymaker, however, should take *all* relevant values into account, and however great the gain in terms of his objective, he must discard a measure as infeasible if the losses in terms of peripheral and background values would be even greater. Stopping immigration of the unskilled from present-oriented cultures would reduce the size of the lower class from what it would otherwise be, and involuntary sterilization of chronic delinquents and heads of "problem families" would before long eliminate it entirely. To make invidious distinctions among cultures on the basis of their orientation toward the future would create ill will for the United States abroad, however, and the violation of human rights involved in involuntary sterilization would be an intolerably high price to pay even for the many benefits that would follow from the elimination of the lower class. A generous welfare program would put an immediate end to poverty (defined otherwise than as relative deprivation), but by causing the break-up of a great many families, by reducing motivation to work and to save and in general to take some account of the future, and by discouraging migration from areas of poor opportunity to areas of good opportunity it might in the long run do more harm than good on the whole. Making heroin and other addictive drugs readily available on prescription would reduce violent crime in New York and some other large cities by relieving the addict of the necessity of stealing — and therefore of sometimes killing — in order to support his habit. But the effect would also be to increase the number of addicts (unless the demand for a commodity is inelastic, the amount sold tends to increase as the price goes down), and it is likely that the resulting harm would be greater than the benefit from the reduction in violent crime.

There follows a list of measures that might well be regarded as feasible by one who accepts the analysis of the previous chapters. It will be seen that the list is rather short; that many of the items on it are not "constructive" — that is, they call for *not* doing something; and that far from being a comprehensive program for making the city into what one would like, it hardly begins to solve any of the problems that have been under discussion. Even if all the recommendations were carried out to the full, the urban situation would not be fundamentally improved. Feasible measures are few and unsatisfactory as compared to what it would be nice to have happen or what one would do if one were dictator. What is more to the present point, however, *hardly any of the feasible measures are acceptable.* The list is as follows:

Feasible but unacceptable solution

1. Avoid rhetoric tending to raise expectations to unreasonable and unrealizable levels, to encourage the individual to think that "society" (e.g. "white racism"), not he, is responsible for his ills, and to exaggerate both the seriousness of social problems and the possibility of finding solutions.

2. If it is feasible to do so (the disagreement among economists has been noted earlier), use fiscal policy to keep the general unemployment level below 3 percent. In any case, remove impediments to the employment of the unskilled, the unschooled, the young, Negroes, women, and others by (a) repealing the minimum-wage and occupational licensure laws and laws that enable labor unions to exercise monopolistic powers, (b) ceasing to overpay for low-skilled public employment, and (c) ceasing to harass private employers who offer low wages and unattractive (but not unsafe) working conditions to workers whose alternative is unemployment.

3. Revise elementary and secondary school curricula so as to cover in nine grades what is now covered in twelve. Reduce the school-leaving age to fourteen (grade 9), and encourage (or perhaps even require) boys and girls who are unable or unwilling to go to college to take a full-time job or else enter military service or a civilian youth corps. Guarantee loans for higher education to all who require them. Assure the availability of serious on-the-job training for all boys and girls who choose to go to work rather than to go to college.

4. Define poverty in terms of the nearly fixed standard of "hardship," rather than in terms of the elastic one of "relative deprivation," and bring all incomes above the poverty line. Distinguish categorically between those of the poor who are competent to manage their affairs and those of them who are not, the latter category consisting of the insane, the severely retarded, the senile, the lower class (inveterate "problem families"), and unprotected children. Make cash income transfers to the first category by means

of a negative income tax, the rate structure of which gives the recipient a strong incentive to work. Whenever possible, assist the incompetent poor with goods and services rather than with cash; depending upon the degree of their incompetence, encourage (or require) them to reside in an institution or semi-institution (for example, a closely supervised public housing project).

5. Give intensive birth-control guidance to the incompetent poor.

6. Pay "problem families" to send infants and children to day nurseries and preschools, the programs of which are designed to bring the children into normal culture.

7. Regulate insurance and police practices so as to give potential victims of crime greater incentive to take reasonable precautions to prevent it.

8. Intensify police patrol in high-crime areas; permit the police to "stop and frisk" and to make misdemeanor arrests on probable cause; institute a system of "negative bail" — that is, an arrangement whereby a suspect who is held in jail and is later found innocent is paid compensation for each day of confinement.

9. Reduce drastically the time elapsing between arrest, trial, and imposition of punishment.

10. Abridge to an appropriate degree the freedom of those who in the opinion of a court are extremely likely to commit violent crimes. Confine and treat drug addicts.

11. Make it clear in advance that those who incite to riot will be severely punished.

12. Prohibit "live" television coverage of riots and of incidents likely to provoke them.

There can be little doubt that with one or two possible exceptions these recommendations are unacceptable. A politician with a heterogeneous constituency would strenuously oppose almost all of them. In most matters, the actual course of policy is likely to be the very opposite of the one recommended, whichever party is in power. Government is likely to raise expectations rather than to lower them; to emphasize "white racism" as *the* continuing cause of the Negro's handicaps rather than to de-emphasize it; to increase the minimum wage rather than to decrease or repeal it; to keep children who cannot or will not learn in school a longer rather than a shorter time; to define poverty in terms of relative deprivation rather than in terms of hardship; to deny the existence of class-cultural differences rather than to try to distinguish the competent from the incompetent poor on this basis; to reduce the potential victim's incentives to take precautions against crime rather than to increase them; to give the police less discretionary authority rather than more; to increase the time between arrest, trial, and punishment rather than to decrease it; and to enlarge the freedom of those who have shown themselves to be very likely to commit violent crimes rather than to restrict it.

One reason why these recommendations are politically out of the question is that there exist well-armed and strategically placed veto groups (as David Riesman calls them in *The Lonely Crowd*) which can prevent them from being seriously discussed, much less adopted. The recommendation of the Moynihan Report, that government try to strengthen the Negro family, is a case in point: official consideration of this idea had to stop abruptly when the civil rights organizations and their allies objected.[8] What these organizations did with this proposal organized labor could do with one to free up the labor market, organized teachers could do with one to reduce the school-leaving age, organized social workers could do with one to define poverty in terms of hardship, and so on.

That interest groups have such power does not represent a malfunctioning of the political system. When they designed the system, the Founding Fathers took great pains to distribute power widely so that "factions" would check one another, thus preventing the rise of any sort of tyranny. The arrangement has worked remarkably well, but there is no denying that it has the defects of its virtues. One of these defects is that a small minority can often veto measures that would benefit a large majority.

Obviously, proposals are frequently adopted despite the opposition of such groups. Why does this not happen in the case of the measures recommended above? There are more prospective gainers than losers from each measure (if this were not thought to be so, the measures would not have been recommended); why, then, do not the prospective gainers organize themselves to overcome the opposition of the veto groups? At the very least, why do they not themselves function as veto groups when the opposites of the measures that would serve their interests are proposed? For example, if they cannot get the minimum-wage law repealed, why do they not at least prevent the rate from being raised?

Part of the answer to these questions is that in most instances the benefits from the recommended measures would be what economists call "public goods" — that is, goods such that if *anyone* benefited *everyone* would benefit. This being the case, the prospective gainers can "ride free" and therefore have little or no incentive to contribute to the support of an organization to fight for the benefits.[9] Another part of the answer is that the voter must usually accept or reject *combinations* of measures (what the candidate or the party stands for); he cannot pick and choose, he must cast his vote one way or the other. His choice therefore turns upon his evaluation of the one or two items in the "package" that touch his primary (which in many cases means his bread-and-butter) interests most closely; if he thinks that his primary interests are well served by these one or two items, he will vote in favor of the "package" even though it contains many other items that are undesirable from the standpoint of his subsidiary interests. Thus, even if the measures recommended above would benefit every voter without exception, there would nevertheless be a unanimous vote against them if they were presented in combinations such that each voter could serve one of his primary interests only by voting against them. In their effort to bring together winning coalitions of interests, candidates and parties tend to be very much aware of such considerations.[10]

Public opinion consists largely of opinions on subjects that do *not* touch the primary interests of the one holding the opinion, and if political choices were made *only* in the light of primary interests, public opinion would matter very little. In fact, of course, it matters a good deal. And there can be no doubt that it supports practically none of the recommendations on the list above.[11] Indeed, in many matters it favors the opposite. In part, then, the perversity that government exhibits in its choice of measures reflects a corresponding perversity in public opinion.

It is pertinent to inquire, therefore, why *public opinion* is perverse. An answer sometimes given is that in matters such as these it is generally dominated by the opinion of the well-educated and well-off. These people (so the argument runs) are indifferent to or downright hostile to the interest of the less well-off and the poor. In short, the "masses" are against the recommended measures because they have been misled by an elite that is looking after its own interests.

The trouble with this theory is that with respect to most measures it runs counter to the facts.[12] The well-off are not benefited by an increase in the minimum wage or by any other measures that price low-value labor out of the market and onto the welfare rolls. They are not benefited by laws that keep children who cannot or will not learn in schools that they (the well-off) must support. They are not benefited by the making of sweeping charges about "white racism" or by crisis-mongering of any kind.

Public opinion is indeed decisively influenced in many matters by the opinion of the well-educated and well-off. But this opinion, which reflects the "service" ideal of the upper class, tends to be altruistic. And it is precisely this altruistic bias that accounts for its perversity.

The American political style was formed largely in the upper classes and, within those classes, mainly by people of dissenting-Protestant and Jewish traditions. Accordingly, it is oriented toward the future and toward moral and material progress, for the individual and for the society as a whole. The American is confident that with a sufficient effort all difficulties can be overcome and all problems solved, and he feels a strong obligation to try to improve not only himself but everything else: his community, his society, the whole world. Ever since the days of Cotton Mather, whose *Bonifacius* was a how-to-do-it book on the doing of good, service has been the American motto. To be sure, practice has seldom entirely corresponded to principles. The principles, however, have always been influential and they have sometimes been decisive. They can be summarized in two very simple rules: first, DON'T JUST SIT THERE. DO SOMETHING! and second, DO GOOD!

These two rules contribute to the perversity that characterizes the choice of measures for dealing with the urban "crisis." Believing that any problem can be solved if only we try hard enough, we do not hesitate to attempt what we do not have the least idea of how to do and what, in some instances, reason and experience both tell us cannot be done. Not recognizing any bounds to what is feasible, we are not reconciled to — indeed, we do not even perceive — the necessity, so frequently arising, of choosing the least objectionable among courses of action that are all very unsatisfactory. That some children simply cannot be taught much in school is one example of a fact that the American mind will not entertain. Our cultural ideal requires that we give every child a good education whether he wants it or not and whether he is capable of receiving it or not. If at first we don't succeed, we must try, try again. And if in the end we don't succeed, we must feel guilty for our failure. To lower the school-leaving age would be, in the terms of this secular religion, a shirking of the task for which we were chosen.

The recommendations listed earlier are mostly unacceptable, even repellent, to public opinion because what they call for does not appear to be and (although this is beside the point) may in fact not be morally improving either to the doer or to the object of his doing. It does not appear to be improving to a youth to send him to work rather than to school, especially as this is what it is in one's interest as a taxpayer to do. It does not appear to be improving to a recidivist to keep him in jail pending trial, especially as this is what accords with one's feelings of hostility toward him. It does not appear to be improving to a slum dweller to say that if he has an adequate income but prefers to spend it for things other than housing he must not expect the public to intervene, especially as it is in one's "selfish" interest that the public not intervene. In reality, the doing of good is not so much for the benefit of those to whom the good is done as it is for that of the *doers,* whose moral faculties are activated and invigorated by the doing of it, and for that of the community, the shared values of which are ritually asserted and vindicated by the doing of it. For this reason, good done otherwise than by intention, especially good done in pursuance of ends that are selfish or even "nontuistic" is not really "good" at all. For this reason, too, actions taken from good motives count as good even when in fact they do harm. By far the most effective way of helping the poor is to keep profit-seekers competing vigorously for their trade as consumers and for their services as workers; this, however, is not a way of helping that affords members of the upper classes the chance to flex their moral muscles or the community the chance to dramatize its commitment to the values that hold it together. The way to do these things is with a War on Poverty; even if the War should turn out to have precious little effect on the incomes of the poor — indeed, even if it should *lower* their incomes — the undertaking would nevertheless represent a sort of secular religious revival that affords the altruistic classes opportunities to bear witness to the cultural ideal and, by doing so, to strengthen society's adherence to it. One recalls Macaulay's remark about the attitude of the English Puritans toward bear-baiting: that they opposed it not for the suffering that it caused the bear but for the pleasure that it gave the spectators. Perhaps it is not far-fetched to say that the present-day outlook is similar: the reformer wants to improve the situation of the poor, the black, the slum dweller, and so on, not so much to make them better off materially as to make himself and the whole society better off morally.

There is something to be said for this attitude. The Puritans were surely right in thinking it worse that people should enjoy the sufferings of animals than that animals should suffer. And the present-day reformers are surely right in thinking it more important that society display a concern for what is right and just than that the material level of the poor, which is already above the level of hardship in most cases, be raised somewhat higher. There are problems here, however. One is to keep the impulse for doing good from gushing incontinently into mass extravaganzas — domestic Marshall Plans, Freedom Budgets, and the like — into which billions are poured for no one knows what or how; surely, if it is to be morally significant, good cannot be done from motives that are contrived for the individual by people who have large organizations to maintain or foisted upon him by the mass media. Another problem is to find ways of doing good that are relatively harmless — that do not greatly injure those to whom the good is done (as, for example, children who cannot or will not learn are injured by too-long confinement in school), that are not grossly unfair to third parties (taxpayers, for example), and that do not tend to damage the consensual basis, and thus eventually the political freedom, of the society (as headline-catching official declarations about "white racism" do). Still another problem is to retain, as an element of the cultural ideal itself, what Lionel Trilling has termed moral realism — "the perception of the dangers of the moral life itself."[13]

If the process of middle- and upper-class-ification tends to make public opinion more perverse, it also tends to make it more important. Half a century or more ago, the basis of city and state political power — and therefore, to a large extent, of national political power as well — was the machine. The bosses who ran it kept themselves in power by dispensing patronage and by trading in ethnic, sectional, and party loyalties, and therefore could pretty well disregard public opinion when it suited them to do so.[14] Middle- and upper-class-ification rendered this system obsolete and brought into being one in which the politician, in order to compete successfully for office, has to combine offers of benefits to *classes* of voters (homeowners, taxpayers, and so on) with appeals to general ideas and conceptions of the public interest. Whereas the old system had promised personal rewards, the new one promises social reforms. Accordingly, the smoke-filled room was replaced by the talk-filled one. "The amount of talk which is now expended on all subjects of human interest is something of which a previous age has had not the smallest conception," E. L. Godkin remarked at the end of the last century, adding that "the affairs of nations and of men will be more and more regulated by talk."[15] But even Godkin, since he did not anticipate television, had not the smallest conception of the extent to which affairs would be regulated by talk in our day.

The politician, like the TV news commentator, must always have something to say even when nothing urgently needs to be said. If he lived in a society without problems, he would have to invent some (and of course "solutions" along with them) in order to attract attention and to kindle the interest and enthusiasm needed to carry him into office and enable him, once there, to levy taxes and do the other unpopular things of which governing largely consists. Although in the society that actually exists there are many problems, there are still not enough — enough about which anyone can say or do anything very helpful — to meet his constant need for program material. Moreover, the real and important problems are not necessarily the ones that people want to hear about; a politician may be able to attract more attention and create more enthusiasm — and thus better serve his purpose, which is to generate power with which to take office and govern — by putting real problems in an unreal light or by presenting illusory ones as if they were real. The politician (again like the TV news commentator) can never publicly discuss an important matter with the seriousness that it deserves; time is short, if's, and's, and but's make tedious listening, and there are always some in the audience who will be confused or offended by what is said and others who will try to twist it into a weapon that they can use against the speaker. Besides, the deeper a discussion goes, the less likelihood of reaching an outcome that the politician can use to generate support.

The changes brought about in the political system by the process of middle- and upper-class-ification have greatly reduced its effectiveness in finding the terms on which people will act together or even live together in peace. The upper-class ideal recommends participation as intrinsically good, but unfortunately, the more participants there are, the larger the number of issues that must be dealt with and the greater the disagreements about each. The ideal also requires that issues be settled on their merits, not by logrolling, and that their merits be conceived of in terms of general moral principles that may not, under any circumstances, be compromised.[16] In the smoke-filled room, it was party loyalty and private interest that moved men; these motives always permitted "doing business." In the talk-filled room, righteous indignation is the motive, and therefore the longer the talk continues, the clearer it becomes to each side that the other must either be shouted down or knocked down.

Looking toward the future, it is impossible not to be apprehensive. The frightening fact is that large numbers of persons are being rapidly assimilated to the upper classes and are coming to have incomes — time as well as money — that permit them to indulge their taste for "service" and doing good in political action. Television, even more than the newspapers, tends to turn the discussion of public policy issues into a branch of the mass entertainment industry. Doing good is becoming — has already become — a growth industry, like the other forms of mass entertainment, while righteous indignation and uncompromising allegiance to principle are becoming *the* motives of political commitment. This is the way it is in the affluent, middle-class society. How will it be in the super-affluent, upper-middle-class one?

CHAPTER TWELVE

The Prospect

It is probable that at this time we are about to make great changes in our social system. The world is ripe for such changes and if they are not made in the direction of greater social liberality, the direction forward, they will almost of necessity be made in the direction backward, of a terrible social niggardliness. We all know which of those directions we want. But it is not enough to want it, not even enough to work for it — we must want it and work for it with intelligence. Which means that we must be aware of the dangers which lie in our most generous wishes.

— Lionel Trilling

I T is impossible to avoid the conclusion that the serious problems of the cities will continue to exist in something like their present form for another twenty years at least. Even on the most favorable assumptions we shall have large concentrations of the poor and the unskilled, and — what, to repeat, is by no means the same thing — the lower class in the central cities and the larger, older suburbs. The outward movement of industry and commerce is bound to continue, leaving ever-larger parts of the inner city blighted or semi-abandoned. Even if we could afford to throw the existing cities away and build new ones from scratch, matters would not be essentially different, for the people who moved into the new cities would take the same old problems with them. Eventually, the present problems of the cities will disappear or dwindle into relative unimportance; they will not, however, be "solved" by programs of the sort now being undertaken or contemplated. On the contrary, the tendency of these programs will be to prolong the problems and perhaps even make them worse.

For the most part, the problems in question have arisen from and are inseparably connected with developments that almost everyone welcomes: the growth and spread of affluence has enabled millions of people to move from congested cities to new and more spacious homes in the suburbs; the availability of a large stock of relatively good housing in the central cities and older suburbs has enabled the Negro to escape the semislavery of the rural South and, a century late, to move into industrial society; better public health measures and facilities have cut the deathrate of the lower class; the war and postwar baby boom has left the city with more adolescents and youths than ever before; and a widespread and general movement upward on the class-cultural scale has made poverty, squalor, ignorance, and brutality — conditions that have always and everywhere been regarded as inevitable in the nature of things — appear as anomalies that should be removed entirely and at once.

What stands in the way of dealing effectively with these problems (insofar as their nature admits of their being dealt with) is mainly the virtues of the American political system and of the American character. It is because governmental power is widely distributed that organized interests are so often able to veto measures that would benefit large numbers of people. It is the generous and public-regarding impulses of voters and taxpayers that impel them to support measures — for example, the minimum wage and compulsory high school attendance — the ultimate effect of which is to make the poor poorer and more demoralized. Our devotion to the doctrine that all men are created equal discourages any explicit recognition of class-cultural differences and leads to "democratic" — and often misleading — formulations of problems: for example, poverty as lack of income and material resources (something external to the individual) rather than as inability or unwillingness to take account of the future or to control impulses (something internal). Sympathy for the oppressed, indignation at the oppressor, and a wish to make amends for wrongs done by one's ancestors lead to a misrepresentation of the Negro as the near-helpless victim of "white racism." Faith in the perfectibility of man and confidence that good intentions together with strenuous exertions will hasten his progress onward and upward lead to bold programs that promise to do what no one knows how to do and what perhaps cannot be done, and therefore ends in frustration, loss of mutual respect and trust, anger, and even coercion.

Even granting that in general the effect of government programs is to exacerbate the problems of the cities, it might perhaps be argued that they have a symbolic value that is more than redeeming. What economist Kenneth Boulding has said of national parks — that we seem to need them "as we seem to need a useless dome on the capitol, as a symbol of national identity and of that mutuality of concern and interest without which government would be naked coercion"[1] — may possibly apply as well to Freedom Budgets, domestic Marshall Plans, and other such concoctions. That government programs do not succeed in reducing welfare dependency, preventing crime, and so on, is a rather minor objection to them if in fact without them the feeling that the society is "not worth saving" would be widespread. One would hope, however, that other and better means — a useless dome on the capitol, for example — would serve the symbolic need well enough. Moreover, there is an evident danger that the failure of urban programs to contribute to the attainment of our objectives will make them symbols not of national identity and mutual concern, but rather of national divisiveness, confusion, and unwisdom.

That government cannot solve the problems of the cities and is likely to make them worse by trying does not necessarily mean that calamity impends. Powerful accidental (by which is meant, nongovernmental and, more generally, nonorganizational) forces are at work that tend to alleviate and even to eliminate the problems. Hard as it may be for a nation of inveterate problem-solvers to believe, social problems sometimes disappear in the normal course of events.

One powerful accidental force at work is economic growth. Because capital tends to increase by geometric progression, a rich country becomes exceedingly rich in the space of a few years. If Americans in the future take no more of their income in the form of leisure than they do now, the national income should increase from

$713 billion in 1968 to $2,628 billion in the year 2000. If there has meanwhile been no great amount of immigration by people who are slow to adapt to the ways of industrial society, the end of urban poverty, in the sense of hardship, will be at hand even if the pattern of income distribution remains substantially unchanged.

A second such force is demographic change. The presence of large numbers of adolescent boys is (along with the presence of a large lower class) mainly responsible for school, job, crime, and disorder problems. This troublesome part of the population is now increasing at an extraordinarily rapid rate (in the ten years ending in 1975 the number of males aged 15 to 24 will increase from 15,540,000 to an estimated 20,296,000). The increase will almost stop before long, however (in 1985 there will be about 21,107,000 males in this age group), and the proportion of boys and young men in the population will be smaller than it is now. A decline in the relative importance of the young male part of the population will do more to relieve strain on city institutions, it is safe to say, than even the most "massive" of government programs.

A third such force — perhaps the most important of all — is the process of middle- and upper-class-ification. For the reasons that were given in Chapter 10, it does not seem likely that the lower class will be absorbed into the culture of the larger society. With this important exception, however, there will no doubt continue to be a general upward movement all along the class-cultural scale. This will mean a softening of manners, better performance in schools, less violence (but not necessarily less nonviolent crime and disorder), and a reduction in racial prejudice and discrimination.

The decline of prejudice and discrimination should proceed with gathering momentum because of the operation of what Gunnar Myrdal, in *An American Dilemma,* called "the principle of cumulation."

White prejudice and discrimination keep the Negro low in standards of living, health, education, manners and morals. This, in turn, gives support to white prejudice. White prejudice and Negro standards thus mutually "cause" each other. . . . Such a static "accommodation" is, however, entirely accidental. If either of the factors changes, this will cause a change in the other factor, too, and start a process of interaction where the change in one factor will continuously be supported by the reaction of the other factor.[2]

It is impossible to judge how much effect these accidental forces will have on the lower class. As was pointed out in Chapter 10, it makes a great deal of difference how much of the present-orientedness of that class is cognitive, how much situational, and how much volitional, but this is a question for which answers do not exist at present. If, as many social scientists want to believe, present-orientedness is mainly or even entirely situational, rapid economic growth may before long offer the lower class the incentives — especially job opportunities — needed to bring its members into normal culture. On the other hand, increasing affluence may have a contrary effect: overgenerous welfare programs may destroy more incentives to look ahead and provide for the future than improved job and other opportunities can provide. For this and other reasons that have already been discussed, an increase in the absolute (if not the relative) size of the lower class is by no means out of the question. Unless the increase were very large, however, it would not necessarily lead to a radical worsening of the situation or precipitate a crisis in the life of the nation.

Although the *objective* situation does not warrant the alarmist tone of much that is said and written about the city, the *subjective* one may. However much the accidental forces may reduce the *real* importance of the problems that have been under discussion, they may have no impact on their *seeming* importance. Indeed, this is likely to grow, for some of the very same factors that improve the objective situation also raise people's standards and expectations, thus leaving the subjective situation no better — and perhaps even worse — than it was to begin with. What people *think* a situation is may (as sociologist Robert K. Merton has pointed out) become an integral part of that situation, and therefore a factor in its subsequent development. A false public definition of the situation may, as Merton says, evoke new behavior that makes the originally false definition come true, thus perpetuating a "reign of error."[3] In short, wrong public definitions of urban problems may lead to behavior that will make matters worse despite the ameliorating influence of the accidental forces.

This possibility is most painfully apparent in the case of the Negro. That racial prejudice has long been declining and may be expected to continue to decline at an accelerating rate counts for little if the Negro *thinks* that white racism is as pervasive as ever; that his opportunities to improve his position by acquiring skills are at last fairly good counts for little if he *thinks* that "massive" government welfare, housing, and other programs — and *only* these — can help him. If he misperceives the situation in these ways, he is likely to do things that are counterproductive (for example, to cut himself off from "white" schools, jobs, and politics and to enter the fantasy world of black separatism). Such a course, if carried far enough, may validate his original (false) hypothesis — that is, he may become in fact as dependent upon government programs as he (wrongly) supposed himself to be and may revive the fact of white prejudice by giving it some objective grounds to feed upon.

Nothing could be so tragic and ironic as the acceptance of a false public definition of the situation that proves to be a self-fulfilling prophecy of racial hatred. Even if nonracial factors had not in recent years superseded the racial ones as the Negro's main handicap, it would be well to pretend that they had, for a self-fulfilling prophecy of the unimportance of racial factors would be as great a blessing as its opposite would be a curse.

Except as they create, or reinforce, counterproductive public definitions of problems and thereby encourage a "reign of error," wrong governmental measures are not likely to lead to catastrophe or even to any very significant worsening of the situation. Most wrong measures will lead to nothing worse than some additional waste and delay, usually a trivial amount. (One gets a sense of how unimportant even "important" governmental actions may be from one economist's estimate that the elimination of monopoly in the United States in 1929 would have raised income by no more than 1/13 of 1 percent, and from the estimate of another that benefits attributable to better resource allocation by virtue of the Common Market would also be much less than 1 percent.)[4] The governmental measures having the largest effect upon the city since the turn of the century are probably subsidization of truck and automobile transportation and subsidization of home ownership for the well-off;

these measures certainly hastened the departure of the white middle class from the central city and, *a fortiori,* the entry of the poor — especially the black poor — on a large scale, but they did not significantly change the pattern of metropolitan growth; this was determined by accidental forces — the demographic, technological, economic, and class-cultural imperatives described in Chapters 2 and 3.

Although it is easy to exaggerate the importance, either for good or ill, of the measures that government has adopted or might adopt, there does appear to be a danger to the good health of the society in the tendency of the public to define so many situations as "critical problems" — a definition that implies (1) that "solutions" exist or can be found and (2) that unless they are found and applied at once, disaster will befall. The import of what has been said in this book is that although there are many difficulties to be coped with, dilemmas to be faced, and afflictions to be endured, there are very few problems that can be solved; it is also that although much is seriously wrong with the city, no disaster impends unless it be one that results from public misconceptions that are in the nature of self-fulfilling prophecies.

Insofar as delusory and counterproductive public definitions of the situation arise from biases that lie deep within the culture (for example, from the impulse to DO SOMETHING! and to DO GOOD!), they are likely to persist in the face of all experience. To exhort the upper classes to display more of the quality that Trilling calls moral realism would be to offer a problem-begging "solution," since the very want of moral realism that constitutes the problem would prevent their recognizing the need of it.

The biases of the culture limit the range of possibilities, but they do not determine fully how the public will define the situation. This definition is in large part the result of a process of opinion formation that goes on within a relatively small world of officials, leaders of civic associations and other interest groups, journalists, and social scientists, especially economists; from this small world opinion is passed on to the public-at-large through the mass media, books, classroom instruction, campaign oratory, after-dinner speeches, and so on. Needless to say, a vast amount of misinformation, prejudice, and illogic enters into the process of opinion formation. (The agony of the cities, someone has remarked, is what the network executive and his fellow-commuters on the Long Island Railroad see out the window as they make their agonized way to and from their offices in Manhattan.) Within the past decade or two, developments have occurred that could make for a more realistic view of the urban situation — for example, the number of technically trained persons working on urban problems has increased greatly, their resources for gathering and manipulating data and the analytical apparatus that they can bring to bear upon policy questions are much improved, and what they have to say is taken much more seriously by politicians and administrators and therefore also by journalists. It would not be surprising if the conventional wisdom were to be very much revised in the next decade or two as a consequence of these developments. Turnover within the small world of opinion-makers is rapid, and the young newcomers in that world tend to be open to new ideas and even in search of them. Because communication within the small world and between it and the public-at-large is excellent, a new definition of the situation, once formulated, could catch on very quickly.

It would be pleasant to be able to end this discussion on that relatively optimistic note. Unfortunately, another side to the matter requires mention. Technically trained persons have their own characteristic biases, and if their view of the city is different from that of the commuter on the Long Island Railroad it is not necessarily more realistic. Moreover, as the technician comes to play a more important part in policy-making he is bound to come more and more under the discipline of large organizations, especially foundations and government agencies, whose maintenance and enhancement depends in some way upon the elaboration of an alarmist, or at any rate expansionist, public definition of the situation. That young newcomers to the small world of opinion-makers tend to be open to new ideas is not altogether reassuring either, for they may tend to accept new ideas *just because* they are new. To the pessimist, the prospect is that a new conventional wisdom about the problems of the city, the product of many millions of dollars' expenditure on research, cast in the language of systems analysis and the computer, will only compound the existing confusion. The optimist, however, will see reason to believe that facts, rational analysis, and deliberation about the nature of the public interest will play a somewhat larger part than hitherto in the formation of both opinion and policy.

Note on the Size of the Social Classes

D ATA do not exist from which one can make reasonably good estimates of the size of the various social classes as defined in this book. Under the circumstances, the best that can be done is to interpret data on the size of the classes *otherwise defined.* This would be a hazardous proceeding at best, but it is all the more so because the various estimates that have been made are all extremely fragmentary. Frank Riessman, in *The Culturally Deprived Child* (New York, Harper & Row, 1962), says that in 1950 approximately one child in ten in the fourteen largest cities was culturally deprived, that by 1960 this number had risen to one in three, and that it might reach one in two by 1970. He does not say how these estimates were arrived at, however, and he uses the term *culturally deprived* interchangeably with educationally deprived, deprived, underprivileged, disadvantaged, lower class, and lower socioeconomic group. The meaninglessness of his figures does not, however, prevent Patricia Cayo Sexton from using them (without citing a source) as if they were authoritative in *Education and Income* (New York, Viking, 1961), p. 246.

Less impressionistic estimates have been made for particular cities or parts of cities; there is, however, no way of knowing how representative the place studied is of all urban places or even of places of about the same size and demographic type. Pierre Martineau, using a probability area sample of 3,880 households, divided metropolitan Chicago on the basis of an index of occupation, sources of income, and housing type as follows (the terms are not his): upper 8.1, middle 28.4, working 44.0, and lower 19.5. Pierre Martineau "Social Classes and Spending Behavior," *The Journal of Marketing,* 23:2 (October 1958); reprinted in Martin M. Grossack, ed., *Understanding Consumer Behavior* (Boston, Christopher Publishing House, 1966, p. 139). Richard A. Cloward and James A. Jones constructed an index of social class on the basis of education, occupation of head of household, and total family income adjusted by number of persons in the family. ("The typical lower class person in our index has had less than an eighth grade education, is employed as an unskilled or service worker, and lives in a family whose income per person is less than the minimum wage" p. 196.) The lower East Side of New York, they found, was 44 percent lower class, 36 percent working class, and 20 percent lower-middle or above. In A. Harry Passow, ed., *Education in Depressed Areas* (New York, Columbia Teachers College, 1963). On the basis of a 5 percent sample of New Haven, Hollingshead and Redlich (*Social Class and Mental Illness,* New York, Wiley, 1958, p. 202) offer the following measures by race:

Class	White	Negro
I–II (Upper?)	11.7	1.0
III (Middle?)	20.8	4.0
IV (Working?)	50.1	36.9
V (Lower?)	17.4	58.1

Although Hollingshead and Redlich define class in terms of position in a deference hierarchy, it is noteworthy that the groups that emerge are subcultures that closely resemble the ideal types described in this book.

Lee Rainwater in *Family Design* (Chicago, Aldine, 1965, p. 24) says that the lower class (lower lower in his terminology) "represents about one-quarter of the working class and about thirteen percent of the population of a city like Chicago." This estimate was based (he writes in a personal communication) on studies using one or another form of W. Lloyd Warner's *Index of Status Character-istics,* especially a study by Social Research, Inc., of the Chicago metropolitan area. Richard P. Coleman, for Social Research, Inc., using two main indices, male occupation distribution and educational background, sometimes supplemented by two others, family income and housing conditions, has prepared the following estimates on the basis of 1960 Census data (the terminology is not his):

Class	All Urban Total	Non-whites	Whites
Upper	14	3	15
Middle	31	13	33
Working	39	43	38
Lower	16	41	14

(*Source:* Social Research Inc., "The Urban Negro: Sampling Considerations and Statistical Overview," August 1968, p. 24.)

A U.S. Bureau of the Census report, *Socioeconomic Characteristics of the Population: 1960* (Series P-23, No. 12, July 31, 1964), combines measures of occupation, income, and education in a socioeconomic status (SES) score. If persons in the lowest 20 percent of SES scores are taken to be lower class (a janitor or kitchen worker with an income slightly below the poverty line and with seven grades of schooling would have scored near the upper limit of this class on each count), 6 percent of whites and 20 percent of nonwhites in central cities of standard metropolitan statistical areas (SMSA's) of more than 250,000 population belong to that class. For the procedure by which the scores were constructed, see U. S. Bureau of the Census, *Methodology and Scores of Socioeconomic Status,* Working Paper No. 15, 1963. The following table was prepared from tabulations run by the Census Bureau under contract for Professor Basil Zimmer of Brown University and kindly made available by him.

PERCENT DISTRIBUTION OF THE POPULATION IN SOCIOECONOMIC
STATUS CATEGORIES FOR STANDARD METROPOLITAN STATISTICAL
AREAS, 250,000 AND OVER POPULATION

SES Score	CENTRAL CITY		URBAN PART OF RING	
	White	Non-white	White	Non-white
80–99 (Upper?)	15	3	24	3
50–79 (Middle?)	47	22	50	21
20–49 (Working?)	32	55	23	54
0–19 (Lower?)	6	20	3	22

Chapter Notes

CHAPTER 1

1. See Daniel J. Elazar, "Are We a Nation of Cities?," *The Public Interest*, no. 4 (Summer 1966), pp. 42–44.
2. Sloan R. Wayland, "Old Problems, New Faces, and New Standards," in A. Harry Passow, ed., *Education in Depressed Areas* (New York: Columbia University Teachers College, 1963), p. 66.
3. Hans Blumenfeld, "The Modern Metropolis," *Scientific American* 213 (September 1965): 67.
4. This was the finding of a six-year study directed by Lawrence B. Cohen of the Department of Industrial Engineering of Columbia University and reported in the *New York Times*, December 16, 1965.
5. J. R. Meyer, J. F. Kain, and M. Wohl, *The Urban Transportation Problem* (Cambridge, Mass.: Harvard University Press, 1965), p. 359.
6. *New York Times*, July 19, 1967, p. 33.
7. Kenneth B. Clark, *Dark Ghetto* (New York: Harper & Row, 1965), table, p. 25.
8. Kenneth B. Clark, "The Wonder Is There Have Been So Few Riots," *New York Times Magazine*, September 5, 1965, p. 10.
9. Alexis de Tocqueville, *Democracy in America,* trans. by Henry Reeve (New York: Knopf, 1945), 1: 289–290.
10. Cf. Robert C. Weaver, "Class, Race and Urban Renewal," *Land Economics*, 36 (August 1960): 235–251. On urban renewal in general, see James Q. Wilson, ed., *Urban Renewal: The Record and the Controversy,* (Cambridge, Mass.: M.I.T. Press, 1966).
11. Scott Greer, *Urban Renewal and American Cities* (Indianapolis: Bobbs-Merrill, 1965), p. 3.
12. Theodore W. Schultz, *Economic Crises in World Agriculture* (Ann Arbor: University of Michigan Press, 1965), p. 94.
13. Karl E. and Alma F. Taeuber, "The Negro as an Immigrant Group: Recent Trends in Racial and Ethnic Segregation in Chicago," *American Journal of Sociology* 69 (January 1964): 382.
14. William G. Grigsby, *Housing Markets and Public Policy* (Philadelphia: University of Pennsylvania Press, 1963), p. 322.
15. Gary T. Marx, *Protest and Prejudice* (New York: Harper & Row, 1967), p. 6.

16. Irving Kristol, "The Lower Fifth," *The New Leader,* February 17, 1964, pp. 9–10.
17. Robert Blauner, "Whitewash Over Watts," *Trans-action* 3 (March–April 1966): 6.
18. Burton A. Weisbrod, "Preventing High-School Drop-outs," in Robert Dorfman, ed., *Measuring Benefits of Government Investments* (Washington, D.C.: The Brookings Institution, 1965), p. 118.
19. Wayland, "Old Problems," in *Education in Depressed Areas,* p. 67.

CHAPTER 2

The quotation from F. J. Kingsbury at the head of the chapter is from an article, "The Tendency of Man to Live in Cities," *Journal of Social Science,* Vol. 33 (November 1895). The article is excerpted in Charles N. Glaab, *The American City: A Documentary History* (Homewood, Ill.: Dorsey Press, 1963).

This chapter owes more to the writings of Raymond Vernon, John F. Kain, and Bernard J. Frieden than the footnote references suggest.

1. "Report of the Select Committee Appointed to Examine into the Condition of Tenant Houses in New York and Brooklyn," transmitted to the Legislature March 9, 1857 (Albany, N.Y.), pp. 11–12. Excerpts of this report appear in Glaab, *The American City.*
2. In the Boston area, however, more than 20,000 passengers a day were being carried in and out of the city, by ferry and otherwise, as early as 1847. Oscar Handlin, *Boston's Immigrants,* rev. ed. (Cambridge, Mass.: Harvard University Press, 1959), p. 18.
3. Blake McKelvey, *The Urbanization of America* (New Brunswick, N.J.: Rutgers University Press, 1963), pp. 78–79. See also Glaab, *The American City,* p. 178; and Sam B. Warner, Jr., *Streetcar Suburbs* (Cambridge, Mass.: Harvard University Press and M.I.T. Press, 1962).
4. Richard C. Wade, *The Urban Frontier* (Chicago: University of Chicago Press, Phoenix Books, 1964), p. 307.
5. In Philadelphia the outward movement was proportionately greater between 1860 and 1910 than between 1900 and 1950 (Hans Blumenfeld, "The Modern Metropolis," *Scientific American* 213 [September 1965]: 67). For an account of Philadelphia's early pattern of growth, which was not that of the ideal type described in the text, see Sam B. Warner, Jr., *The Private City* (Philadelphia: University of Pennsylvania Press, 1968), ch. 3.
6. Edward Crapsey, *The Nether Side Of New York* (New York: Sheldon and Company, 1872), p. 9.
7. Quoted in J. Leslie Dunstan, *A Light to the City* (Boston: Beacon Press, 1966), p. 91.
8. Mabel L. Walker, *Urban Blight and Slums* (Cambridge, Mass.: Harvard University Press, 1938), pp. 18–21.
9. Constance McLaughlin Green, *The Rise of Urban America* (New York: Harper & Row, 1965), pp. 132–133.
10. Davis McEntire, *Residence and Race* (Berkeley: University of Cali-

fornia Press, 1960), pp. 300–301. FHA discriminated against Negroes until well into the Truman administration. Afterward it discriminated against them *in effect* by insisting on very low-risk loans.

11. Gilbert Osofsky, *Harlem: The Making of a Ghetto* (New York: Harper & Row, 1963), p. 128.

12. Edith Elmer Wood, *Slums and Blighted Areas in the U.S.,* Administration of Public Works, Housing Division Bulletin Number 1 (Washington, D.C.: U.S. Government Printing Office, 1935), p. 19.

13. Leo F. Schnore, *The Urban Scene* (New York: The Free Press, 1965), pp. 256–257.

14. McEntire, *Residence and Race,* ch. 3.

15. Raymond Vernon, *Metropolis 1985* (Cambridge, Mass.: Harvard University Press, 1960), p. 141.

16. On the comparability of 1950 and 1960 Census data, see Bernard J. Frieden, "Housing and National Urban Goals: Old Policies and New Realities," in James Q. Wilson, ed., *The Metropolitan Enigma* (Cambridge, Mass.: Harvard University Press, 1968), pp. 166–168.

   Substandard housing is "dilapidated" or lacks one or more plumbing facilities. *Dilapidated* housing does not provide safe and adequate shelter and endangers the health, safety, and well-being of the occupants because it has one or more "critical defects," or a combination of lesser ones, or is of inadequate original construction. *Critical defects* are those that indicate continued neglect and serious damage to the structure (p. 163).

   Frieden (p. 173) divides the Census income categories into groups representing roughly the bottom third ($0–1,999 in 1950, $0–2,999 in 1960), middle third ($2,000–3,999 in 1950, $3,000–5,999 in 1960), and upper third ($4,000 and above in 1950, $6,000 and above in 1960). The percentage of families in each third living in substandard housing was as follows:

	1950 (percent)	1960 (percent)
Upper third	12	4
Middle third	30	14
Lower third	53	36

17. The table is adapted from data presented by Bernard J. Frieden in *The Future of Old Neighborhoods* (Cambridge, Mass.: M.I.T. Press, 1964), p. 24.

18. See the chapter on technological change by Boris Yavitz in Eli Ginsburg et al., *Manpower Strategy for the Metropolis* (New York: Columbia University Press, 1968), especially pp. 49–55.

19. It will be understood that the account that has been given of metropolitan development refers to an ideal type. Concretely, the older (Eastern and Midwestern) cities conform to the type much better than do the newer (Western and Southwestern) ones. Los Angeles, which had practically no history prior to the automobile and truck, conforms

hardly at all. Chicago is fairly representative of most large metropolitan areas.

20. Between 1960 and 1968 the number of Negroes living in central cities increased from 9.7 million to 11.9 million, while the number of whites dropped by almost 2 million. Between 1960 and 1966 whites had been leaving central cities at a rate of about 150,000 per year, but the rate rose to almost 500,000 per year between 1966 and 1968. Negroes had been moving into central cities at a rate of about 400,000 per year between 1960 and 1966; this rate declined to about 100,000 per year in the 1966–1968 period. In this latter period, the Negro metropolitan population *outside* central cities increased by about one million persons— an increase of 35 percent over the number of Negroes living in those areas in 1960. As of 1968, 54 percent of the total Negro population of the United States lived in central cities and about 15 percent in suburbs. U.S. Bureau of the Census, *Current Population Reports,* Population Characteristics, Series P-20, No. 181, "Population of the United States by Metropolitan-Nonmetropolitan Residence: 1968 and 1960" (Washington, D.C.: U.S. Government Printing Office, 1969), pp. 1–3, tables A, B, and D.

21. *Economic Report of the President,* transmitted to the Congress, January 1965 (Washington, D.C.: U.S. Government Printing Office, 1965), p. 169.

22. Robert Weaver in New York City Planning Commission, "The Future by Design," (multilithed transcript of symposium, October 1964), p. 169.

23. Raymond Vernon, *The Myth and Reality of Our Urban Problems* (Cambridge, Mass.: Harvard University Press, 1962), p. 33.

24. See Yavitz, in Ginsburg et al., *Manpower Strategy,* pp. 58–61.

25. Ibid., p. 59.

26. The financial troubles of Reston, Va., are described by Monroe W. Karmin in *The Wall Street Journal,* October 13, 1967, p. 1.

27. The *New York Times* of October 18, 1966, gives an account of a couple who purchased a brownstone at 155 West Ninety-first Street, paying $30,000 for the house and investing another $55,000 in reconstruction and improvements. Presumably, this building, which had been a rooming house, was purchased from a private party.

28. Glaab, *The American City,* p. 11.

29. Ibid. Other measures proposed by the Committee were regulations to insure easy egress from tenements in case of fire, prevention of prostitution and incest by requiring a sufficient number of rooms per family and by prohibiting subletting, and prevention of drunkenness "by providing for every man a clean and comfortable home" (p. 3).

30. Code enforcement and rent control, along with apprehension about civil disorder, are held responsible for decreases in land values in Harlem in the last ten years. Because of vigorous enforcement of the building code, many buildings are vacant and have been vandalized. (*New York Times,* April 28, 1968).

31. Before the arrival of the Irish, Handlin remarks with reference to Boston, "the rigid labor supply had made industrialization impossible." (By "rigid" he presumably means one that demanded and got rela-

tively high wages.) And the Irish, he adds, could not have been housed without cellar holes. (*Boston's Immigrants,* pp. 82, 110).
32. Jacob A. Riis, in Robert A. Woods et al., *The Poor in Great Cities* (New York: Scribner's, 1895), p. 88.
33. William T. Elsing, "Life in New York Tenement Houses as Seen by a City Missionary," in *The Poor in Great Cities,* p. 76.
34. Marcus T. Reynolds, *The Housing of the Poor in American Cities* (New York: American Economic Association, March and May 1893), p. 109.
35. *Reports of the Industrial Commission, Immigration,* Vol. XV (Washington, D.C.: U.S. Government Printing Office, 1901), p. 491.
36. Morris Eagle, "The Puerto Ricans in New York City," in Nathan Glazer and Davis McEntire, eds., *Studies in Housing and Minority Groups* (Berkeley: University of California Press, 1960), p. 176.

CHAPTER 3

The quotation at the head of the chapter is from John Dollard, *Caste and Class in a Southern Town* (Garden City, N.Y.: Anchor Books, 1957), p. 433. The original edition was published in 1937.

Richard F. Muth, *Cities and Housing, The Spatial Pattern of Urban Residential Land Use* (Chicago: The University of Chicago Press, 1969), a technical treatise in economics, makes an important contribution to the subjects discussed in this chapter. Unfortunately, it was received too late to be mentioned in the text.

1. Adna F. Weber, *The Growth of Cities in the Nineteenth Century* (New York: Macmillan, 1899), p. 469.
2. This estimate assumes that to buy a house costing $12,500 without spending more than 20 percent of income one must have an income of at least $9,000.
3. The *Oxford English Dictionary* defines a slum as "a thickly populated neighborhood or district where the houses and conditions of life are of a squalid and wretched character." Squalor is defined as "a combination of misery and dirt." In *The Urban Villagers* (New York: The Free Press, 1962), p. 309, Herbert J. Gans says that slums are residential districts that "have been proven to be physically, socially, or emotionally *harmful* to their residents or to the larger community" (italics in the original). Robert Hunter, in *Poverty* (New York: Harper Torchbooks, 1965), p. 108, considers it a "great injustice" to use the word to refer "to working-class districts or to poverty-stricken districts relatively free from vice."
4. See the discussion of class in Gans, *The Urban Villagers,* chs. 2 and 11. See also Joseph A. Kahl, *American Class Structure* (Holt, Rinehart & Winston, 1959), especially ch. 7.
5. In many (but not all) particulars the account of class culture that follows depends heavily upon the work of Herbert J. Gans and Walter B. Miller. See especially *The Urban Villagers,* ch. 11, and Miller's articles, "Implications of Urban Lower-Class Culture for Social Work,"

Social Service Review, Vol. 33 (September 1959), and "Lower Class Culture as a Generating Milieu of Gang Delinquency," *Journal of Social Issues,* Vol. 14 (1958). See also A. B. Hollingshead, *Elmtown's Youth* (New York: Wiley, 1949); Allison Davis, "The Motivation of the Underprivileged Worker," in William Foote Whyte, ed., *Industry and Society* (New York: McGraw-Hill, 1946); William Foote Whyte, *Street Corner Society,* 2nd ed. (Chicago: University of Chicago Press, 1955); Mirra Komarovsky, *Blue-Collar Marriage* (New York: Vintage Books, 1967); A. B. Shostak and W. Gomberg, *Blue-Collar World: Studies of the American Worker* (Englewood Cliffs, N.J.: Prentice-Hall, 1965); D. G. McKinley, *Social Class and Family Life* (New York: The Free Press, 1964); Lee Rainwater, "The Lower Class: Health, Illness, and Medical Institutions" in Irwin Deutscher and Elizabeth J. Thompson, eds., *Among the People: Encounters With the Poor* (New York: Basic Books, 1968), and St. Clair Drake and Horace R. Cayton, *Black Metropolis* (New York: Harper & Row, 1945), in addition to the works cited below.

6. See Charles A. Valentine, *Culture and Poverty: Critique and Counter-Proposals* (Chicago: University of Chicago Press, 1968). Valentine complains of the use that writers on poverty make of the concept of culture; their conceptions, he says, prejudge empirical questions in the direction of policies he deplores.

Gans reassesses his views as presented in *The Urban Villagers* in *People and Plans: Essays on Urban Problems and Solutions* (New York: Basic Books, 1968), ch. 22.

7. For a critique of the claim that lower-class people cannot control their impulses ("probably the most frequently used element in discussion of lower class life") see S. M. Miller, Frank Riessman, and Arthur A. Seagull, "Poverty and Self-Indulgence: A Critique of the Non-Deferred Gratification Pattern," in Louis A. Ferman et al., *Poverty in America: A Book of Readings* (Ann Arbor: University of Michigan Press, 1965), pp. 285–302. Here, too, the argument turns largely on the implications of the concept for the content of policy. It should be noted in passing that the question of whether or not lower-class people are aware of the future is largely and perhaps wholly independent of the question of whether or not they can (or do) control their impulses. One may conceptualize the future and yet (for one reason or another) *not* be able to control an impulse.

8. Most of the statements about time horizons in what follows are empirical: they employ a somewhat special terminology to report facts that have been observed by social scientists and others. The main proposition, namely, that individuals and cultures have differing orientations toward the future, is of this character; so are many subsidiary propositions, such as that present-oriented persons tend to be in constant search of sensual gratifications. Some propositions, however, are *implications* of the main proposition; they are themselves deductive but they have been arrived at from premises that have been inductively established. No "data" support the statement that present-oriented persons are uncon-

cerned about the welfare of their grandchildren yet unborn; such a statement follows from the *meaning* of present-orientedness.

9. An ideal type "is a freely created mental construct . . . by means of which an attempt is made to 'order' reality by isolating, accentuating, and articulating the elements of a recurrent social phenomenon . . . into an internally consistent system of relationships." Julius Gould and William L. Kolb, eds., *UNESCO Dictionary of the Social Sciences* (New York: The Free Press, 1964), p. 312.

10. The difference is greatest with respect to the class here called upper. In ordinary usage this class would probably be called upper-middle. It it not called that here because it seemed that a scale of classes running from lower to upper-middle (there being no upper class that could be placed on the same scale as the others) would be even more likely than the present terminology to cause confusion.

11. C. Burt, "Intelligence and Social Mobility," *British Journal of Statistical Psychology*, 14 (1961): 3–24. The case for the relative importance of genetic factors is argued by Arthur R. Jensen in "How Much Can We Boost IQ and Scholastic Achievement?" *Harvard Educational Review*, 39 (Winter 1969): 1–123. Rejoinders by several other educational psychologists and by Jensen appeared in the next two issues of the *Review* (Spring and Summer 1969).

12. Melvin L. Kohn, "Social Class and Parental Values," *American Journal of Sociology*, 64 (January 1959): 340, 344, 350. See also his "Social Class and Parent-Child Relationships: An Interpretation," *American Journal of Sociology*, 68 (January 1963): 475.

13. Kenneth Keniston, *The Young Radicals* (New York: Harcourt, Brace and World, 1968), p. 265. Keniston's observation was made with respect to the upper-middle class.

14. For data on the voting behavior of various classes on local public expenditure issues, see J. Q. Wilson and E. C. Banfield, "Public-Regardingness as a Value Premise in Voting Behavior," *American Political Science Review*, 58 (December 1964): 876–887. For data on participation in organizations, see Murray Hausknecht, *The Joiners: A Sociological Description of Voluntary Association Membership* (Totowa, N.J.: Bedminster Press, 1962).

15. W. J. Cash, *The Mind of the South* (New York: Knopf, Vintage Books, 1941), p. 80.

16. Cf. Basil Bernstein's description of the British working class, "Some Sociological Determinants of Perception," *British Journal of Sociology*, Vol. 9 (1958):

> The specific character of long-term goals tends to be replaced by more general notions of the future, in which chance, a friend or a relative plays a greater part than the rigorous working out of connections. Thus present, or near present, activities have greater value than the relation of the present activity to the attainment of a distant goal. The system of expectancies, or the time-span of anticipation, is shortened and this creates different sets of preferences, goals and dissatisfactions. This environment limits the perception of the developing child of and in time. Present gratifications or pres-

ent deprivations become absolute gratifications or absolute deprivations for there exists no developed time continuum upon which
present activity can be ranged. Relative to the middle-classes, the
postponement of present pleasure for future gratifications will be
found difficult. By implication a more volatile patterning of af-
fectual and expressive behaviour will be found in the working-
classes.

17. David Riesman (in collaboration with Nathan Glazer), *Faces in the
Crowd,* abr. ed. (New Haven: Yale University Press, 1965), p. 254.
18. According to Lee Rainwater, in *Family Design: Marital Sexuality,
Family Size, and Contraception* (Chicago: Aldine, 1965), p. 55, in the
"upper-lower class" (the working class as defined here):

> Though husband and wife may not go their separate ways as
> much as in the lower-lower class, they tend to adhere to a sharper
> division of labor than is true in the lower-middle class, and though
> they may participate together in many family activities, this seems
> to be more the result of default (they are thrown together in
> the same small home) or of a desire to keep away from un-
> welcome involvements outside the home than to be dictated by
> the values of equality and togetherness that dominate the think-
> ing of lower-middle class men and women.

19. Erving Goffman, in "Where the Action Is" (*International Ritual* [Garden
City, N.Y.: Anchor Books, 1967], p. 268), says:

> Looking for where the action is, one arrives at a romatic di-
> vision of the world. On the one side are the safe and silent
> places, the home, the well-regulated role in business, industry, and
> the professions; on the other are all those activities that generate
> expression, requiring the individual to lay himself on the line
> and place himself in jeopardy during a passing moment. It is
> from this contrast that we fashion nearly all our commercial
> fantasies. It is from this contrast that delinquents, criminals, hus-
> tlers, and sportsmen draw their self-respect. . . .

20. Eleanor Pavenstedt, "A Comparison of the Child Rearing Environment
of Upper Lower and Very Low-Lower Class Families," *American
Journal of Orthopsychiatry,* 35 (1965): 89–98.
21. On this and on the "foci" of lower-class culture, see the articles by
Walter B. Miller cited earlier.
22. Jerome K. Myers and B. H. Roberts, *Family and Class Dynamics in Mental Illness* (New York: Wiley, 1959), p. 174. See also Hollingshead and
Redlich, *Social Class and Mental Illness,* p. 175, and S. Minuchin et al.,
Families of the Slums (New York: Basic Books, 1968), p. 34.
23. Gans, *The Urban Villagers,* p. 246.
24. Ralph Barton Perry in *Puritanism and Democracy* (New York: Van-
guard, 1944), p. 298, remarks of the English and colonial American
yeomen, artisans, and tradesmen: "They were neither so unfortunate as
to be imbued with a sense of helplessness, nor so privileged as to be

satisfied with their present status. They possessed just enough to whet their appetites for more and to feel confident of their power to attain it."

25. Theodore Sedgwick, *Public and Private Economy* (New York: Harper and Brothers, 1836), part 1, p. 8. See also T. C. Grattan, *Civilized America* (London, Bradbury and Evans, 1859), 2: 376.
26. Cf. Richard C. Wade, *The Urban Frontier* (Chicago: University of Chicago Press, Phoenix Books, 1964), pp. 217–220.
27. J. Leslie Dunstan, *A Light to the City* (Boston: Beacon Press, 1966), pp. 41–43.
28. Grattan, *Civilized America*, 1: 98–99.
29. Quoted by Oscar Handlin in *Boston's Immigrants* (Cambridge, Mass.: Harvard University Press, 1959), p. 51. (Italics in the original.)
30. In Robert A. Woods et al., *The Poor in Great Cities* (New York: Scribner's, 1895), pp. 102–103.
31. Stephan Thernstrom, *Poverty and Progress; Social Mobility in a Nineteenth Century City* (Cambridge, Mass.: Harvard University Press, 1964), pp. 103, 107.
32. *Reports of the Industrial Commission Immigration*, Vol. XV (Washington, D.C.: U.S. Government Printing Office, 1901), p. 480. On ethnic differences relating to mobility, see Bernard C. Rosen, "Race, Ethnicity, and the Achievement Syndrome," *American Sociological Review*, 24 (1959): 47–60.
33. James Q. Wilson, in "A Guide to Reagan Country," *Commentary*, May 1967, pp. 40–41, has described vividly the care that his generation of Los Angeles boys lavished on their cars. "After marriage," he continues, "devoting energy to the improvement of a house was simply a grown-up extension of what, as a juvenile, one had done with cars."
34. Opinion polls have shown that the higher a person's socioeconomic status is, the more likely he is to favor integration of housing, transportation, and schools, as well as other forms of integration. See Paul B. Sheatsley, "White Attitudes Toward the Negro," in Talcott Parsons and Kenneth B. Clark, eds., *The Negro American* (Boston: Houghton Mifflin, 1966), p. 315.

A study of social class and voting behavior in Little Rock found: "The higher the social class, the stronger was support for desegregation. Conversely, the lower the social class, the greater was support for segregation." Harlan Hahn, L. Michael Ross, and Thomas F. Pettigrew, unpublished paper, 1966.
35. Cf. Bennett M. Berger, *Working-Class Suburb: A Study of Auto Workers in Suburbia* (Berkeley: University of California Press, 1960), ch. 5.
36. Cf. John R. Seeley, "The Slum: Its Nature, Use and Users," *Journal of the American Institute of Planners*, 25 (February 1959): 10–13.
37. Patricia Cayo Sexton, *Spanish Harlem; Anatomy of Poverty* (New York: Harper & Row, 1965), p. 116.
38. The problem of estimating the size of the classes from these and other data is discussed in the Appendix.
39. Blake McKelvey, *The Urbanization of America* (New Brunswick, N.J.:

Rutgers University Press, 1963), p. 94; Jane Addams, "An Effort Toward Social Democracy," *The Forum,* October 1892, p. 228.

40. Mrs. Helen Campbell, *Darkness and Daylight; or, Lights and Shadows of New York Life* (Hartford, Conn.: Hartford Publishing Co., 1896), p. 170. On brutality in general, see Richard O'Connor, *Hell's Kitchen* (Philadelphia: Lippincott, 1958).

41. Patricia Cayo Sexton, *Education and Income* (New York: Viking, 1961), p. 200.

42. Consider, for example, the probable meaning to all concerned of the announcement (*New York Times,* July 13, 1966) by New York City's chief health officer, Dr. Howard J. Brown, that thousands of wooden benches would be burnt in "a public declaration of conscience" as symbols of dehumanized medical services in the city's clinics. That the service provided by the city to its poor was remarkably good by any standard except that of the more affluent middle class ("No hospital in the world has better professional talent," Dr. Brown admitted) was a fact obscured by the announcement ("disgraceful . . . patients . . . have to barter their dignity for their health"). That people sat on benches rather than in chairs and waited without appointments until a doctor could see them was not, until the rise of new class standards made it so, an affront; it is therefore factually incorrect to use the benches as symbols of mistreatment *in the past.* The effect of the announcement, however, must have been to make upper-middle- and upper-class people ashamed of a city which has long treated its poor so shabbily and also to tell the poor that if by any chance they thought they were fortunate in being cared for by professionals as good as any in the world they were being outrageously put upon and that they should be aggrieved and angry at not always having been given the deference and amenities that the middle class now gives to itself.

CHAPTER 4

The quotation at the head of the chapter is from *The Autobiography of Malcolm X* (New York: Grove, 1966), p. 344.

1. Kenneth B. Clark, *Dark Ghetto: Dilemmas of Social Power* (New York: Harper & Row, 1965), p. 11.

2. Because they are highly correlated, one cannot simply add together the separate effects of all the various factors controlled for in order to arrive at a "total effect of nonracial factors."

3. Pascal K. Whelpton, Arthur A. Campbell, and John E. Patterson, *Fertility and Family Planning in the United States* (Princeton, N.J.: Princeton University Press, 1966), pp. 342–348.

4. James S. Coleman et al., *Equality of Educational Opportunity,* Office of Education, U.S. Department of Health, Education and Welfare (Washington, D.C.: U.S. Government Printing Office, 1966), pp. 454–456.

5. Ibid., p. 274.

6. Harry J. Gilman, "Economic Discrimination and Unemployment," *American Economic Review,* 55 (December 1965): 1077–1095. The data Gilman analyzed were for 1950 and 1957–1961.

7. See Morton Zeman, "A Quantitative Analysis of White-Nonwhite Income Differentials in the United States," Unpublished Ph.D. dissertation, Department of Economics, University of Chicago, September 1955, especially ch. 3. See also Lowell E. Gallaway, "The Negro and Poverty," *The Journal of Business,* 40 (January 1967): 27–35; and Lester C. Thurow, *The Economics of Poverty and Discrimination* (Washington, D.C.: The Brookings Institution, 1969).

8. Richard F. Muth, "Urban Residential Land and Housing Markets," Institute for Urban and Regional Studies, Washington University. Paper prepared for Conference on Urban Economics, January 1967, pp. 29–30. Professor Muth has since published a book, *Cities and Housing* (Chicago: University of Chicago Press, 1969), that deals with the subject elaborately.

9. Martin J. Bailey, "Effects of Race and of Other Demographic Factors on the Value of Single-Family Homes," *Land Economics,* 42 (May 1966): 218–219.

10. Katherine Anthony, "Mothers Who Must Earn," in *West Side Studies,* Russell Sage Foundation (New York: Survey Associates, 1914), p. 20.

11. Otho G. Cartwright, "Boyhood and Lawlessness," in *West Side Studies,* Russell Sage Foundation (New York: Survey Associates, 1914), pp. 156, 55.

12. Charles Loring Brace, *The Dangerous Classes of New York and Twenty Years Work Among Them,* 3rd ed. (New York: Wynkoop and Hallenbeck, 1880), p. 27.

13. Belton M. Fleisher, *The Economics of Delinquency* (Chicago: Quadrangle Books, 1966), pp. 89–92.

14. See Thomas F. Pettigrew, "Negro American Personality: Why Isn't More Known?" *The Journal of Social Issues,* 20 (April 1964): 4–23.

Rohrer and Edmonson "find reason to doubt that such a thing as '*a* Negro personality' exists at all. Despite the unquestioned fact that differences of a statistical order between whites as a group and Negroes as a group are well established in a variety of connections, there is no basis for assuming that durable patterns of behavior are related to racial status *as such* even when the emotional implications of the caste system and related stereotyped attitudes or prejudices are included in the social definition of race." John H. Rohrer and Munro S. Edmonson, eds., *The Eighth Generation Grows Up* (New York: Harper Torchbooks, 1964), p. 77. (Italics in the original.)

On the other hand, Lesser and associates have found that while class subculture markedly influences the *absolute* level of certain mental abilities in children, ethnic subculture determines the *relative* level of development of these abilities. G. S. Lesser, G. Fifer, and D. H. Clark, *Mental Abilities of Children from Different Social-Class and Cultural Groups,* Society for Research in Child Development, Serial No. 102, Vol. 30, No. 4 (Chicago: University of Chicago Press, 1965).

15. Quoted by G. Franklin Edwards, "Community and Class Realities," in Talcott Parsons and Kenneth B. Clark, eds., *The Negro American* (Boston: Houghton Mifflin, 1966), p. 298.

16. Dale L. Hiestand, *Economic Growth and Employment Opportunities for Minorities* (New York: Columbia University Press, 1964), p. 53. See

also Joe L. Russell, "Changing Patterns in Employment of Nonwhite Workers," *Monthly Labor Review*, 89 (May 1966): 503–509.

17. The figures are from Harold L. Sheppard, *Effects of Family Planning on Poverty in the United States* (Kalamazoo, Mich.: W. E. Upjohn Institute for Employment Research, October 1967), p. 4.

18. A. B. Hollingshead, *Elmtown's Youth* (New York: Wiley, 1949), pp. 114, 113, 119, 147, 282, 111.

19. Ibid., pp. 110–111.

20. Ibid., pp. 147, 113, 119–120, 116, 117, 331.

21. Thomas R. Brooks, "New York's Finest," *Commentary*, August 1965, p. 31.

22. Gary T. Marx, *Protest and Prejudice* (New York: Harper & Row, 1967), p. 176. It goes without saying that many Negroes might take a very different view of mixed neighborhoods *if they could expect to live in them without risking embarrassment or worse.* On the other hand, it cannot be assumed that this is the only or the main reason for preferring Negro neighborhoods.

23. Cf. Karl E. Taeuber, "Residential Segregation," *Scientific American*, 213 (August 1965): 14.

24. Malcolm Muggeridge points out that calling a place like Harlem a "ghetto" is a perfect example of the kind of falsification of words to make them serve political ends that Orwell deplored in his essay "Politics vs. Literature." According to Muggeridge, "By equating Negro slums with a ghetto, on the one hand white racialism — in itself bad enough in all conscience — is associated with the additional horrors of Nazi anti-Semitism. On the other the white bourgeois champion of the Negro can see his wrongs in terms of pogroms and other distant and remote wickednesses, rather than of nearby and present social and economic inequalities." Letter to the editor of the *New York Times Magazine*, May 5, 1968.

25. Lewis G. Watts et al., *The Middle-Income Negro Family Faces Urban Renewal*, Research Center of the Florence Heller Graduate School for Advanced Studies in Social Welfare (Waltham, Mass.: Brandeis University, 1964). Similar findings for New York are reported in Oscar Handlin, *The Newcomers* (Cambridge, Mass.: Harvard University Press, 1959), p. 92 and Appendix.

26. Ibid., p. 69.

27. Herbert J. Gans, *The Urban Villagers* (New York: The Free Press, 1962), p. 20.

28. Ralph Ellison, in "Federal Role in Urban Affairs," Hearings Before the Subcommittee on Executive Reorganization, Committee on Government Operations, August 30, 1966, U.S. Senate, 89th Congress, 2nd Session, Part 5, p. 1155.

29. Clark, *Dark Ghetto*, p. 25.

30. Watts et al., *The Middle-Income Negro Family*, p. 86.

31. *New York Times*, September 16, 1965.

32. Urie Bronfenbrenner, "The Psychological Costs of Quality and Equality in Education," *Child Development*, 38 (1967): 910.

33. Erik H. Erikson has called attention to the danger that a majority

"may, in its sudden zeal to regain its moral position and to face the facts squarely, inadvertently tend to *confirm* the minority's negative image of itself and this in the very act of dwelling exclusively and even self-indulgently on the majority's sins." Parsons and Clark, *The Negro American,* p. 238. (Italics in the original.)

34. Morris Eagle, "The Puerto Ricans in New York City," in Nathan Glazer and Davis McEntire, eds., *Studies in Housing and Minority Groups* (Berkeley: University of California Press, 1960), pp. 166, 164.

CHAPTER 5

"Youth in the Ghetto," the source of the first quotation at the head of the chapter, was published (in multilith) by HARYOU (Harlem Youth Opportunities Unlimited, Inc.) in 1964. The second quotation is from James R. Dumpson and appears in the transcript of a symposium, "The Future by Design," held by the New York City Planning Commission in October 1964 (p. 130).

1. Constance McLaughlin Green, *The Rise of Urban America* (New York: Harper & Row, 1965), p. 179.
2. Nathan Glazer and Daniel Patrick Moynihan, *Beyond the Melting Pot,* (Cambridge, Mass.: M.I.T. Press and Harvard University Press, 1963), p. 39.
3. Paul Goodman, *Growing Up Absurd* (New York: Vintage Books, 1962), p. 32.
4. Donald Bogue and D. P. Dandekar, *Population Trends and Prospects for the Chicago-Northwestern Indiana Consolidated Metropolitan Area, 1960 to 1990* (Chicago, Population Research and Training Center, March 1962), p. 34.
5. Thomas F. Pettigrew, *A Profile of the Negro American* (Princeton, N.J.: Van Nostrand, 1964), p. 172.
6. A. R. Weber, "Labor Market Perspectives of the New City," in Benjamin Chinitz, ed., *City and Suburb* (Englewood Cliffs, N.J.: Prentice-Hall [Spectrum Books], 1964), pp. 68–69.
7. Daniel Bell, "The Bogey of Automation," *New York Review of Books,* August 26, 1965, p. 24.
8. Robert M. Solow, "Technology and Unemployment," *The Public Interest,* 1 (Fall 1965): 18–19. (Italics in the original.)
9. *Monthly Labor Review,* 91 (December 1968): 36.
10. James Tobin, "On Improving the Economic Status of the Negro," in Talcott Parsons and Kennth B. Clark, eds., *The Negro American* (Boston: Houghton Mifflin, 1966), p. 462.
11. Andrew J. Hargrett, "The Education-Unemployment Relation in Chicago as Revealed in the 1960 Census," *The Journal of Negro Education,* 34 (Spring 1965): 125.
12. Dale L. Hiestand, *Economic Growth and Employment Opportunities for Minorities* (New York: Columbia University Press, 1964), pp. 116, 56–57.
13. Cf. Report of the National Commission on Technology, Automation, and Economic Progress, *Technology and the American Economy,* (Washington, D.C.: U.S. Government Printing Office, February 1966), 1: 21–23.

14. U.S. Department of Labor, Bureau of Labor Statistics, *Employment and Earnings and Monthly Report of the Labor Force,* 15 (June 1969):24, table A-10.
15. *Technology and the American Economy,* p. 16.
16. Ibid., p. 23.
17. *Employment and Earnings and Monthly Report of the Labor Force,* p. 23, table A-8; pp. 17–18, table A-3.
18. Parsons and Clark, *The Negro American,* pp. 458–459.
19. Garth L. Mangum, "Government as Employer of Last Resort," in *Toward Freedom From Want* (Madison, Wis.: Industrial Relations Association, 1968), p. 137. For a more optimistic view (based, however, on evidence from a few years before) see Ronald G. Bodkin, *The Wage-Price Productivity Nexus* (Philadelphia: University of Pennsylvania Press, 1966), p. 280.
20. Milton Friedman, "The Role of Monetary Policy," *American Economic Review,* 58 (March 1968): 7–11; reprinted in Friedman, *The Optimum Quantity of Money and Other Essays* (Chicago: Aldine, 1969).
21. The Fair Labor Standards Act of June 25, 1938, also known as the Wages and Hour Act, 52 Stat. 1060 as amended; the Walsh-Healey Public Contracts Act of June 30, 1936, 49 Stat. 2036, as amended, 41 U.S.C., 35–45. The Walsh-Healey Act regulates hours and wages on federal contracts exceeding $10,000. It has not been effective as a minimum-wage law. See Herbert C. Morton, *Public Contracts and Private Wages* (Washington, D.C.: The Brookings Institution, 1965), pp. 125–126.
22. Workers covered by the $1.60 federal minimum must receive time-and-one-half pay after forty hours a week. Certain classes of workers who became subject to the act under 1966 amendments (e.g., those employed by large hotels, motels, or restaurants, or laundries, hospitals, and schools) received $1.15 in 1968, which will be raised by 15 cents a year until they reach $1.60 in 1971. Some farm workers on larger farms must be paid $1.15.
23. Quoted by Robert H. Bremner, *From the Depths: The Discovery of Poverty in the United States* (New York: New York University Press, 1956), p. 239.
24. The earnings of those in the largest categories of low-paying jobs (janitors, attendants in auto service and parking, sales personnel in food and dairy product stores, laborers in wholesale and retail trade) usually exceed the minimum wage of $2,600 for fifty-two weeks of full-time work. Laurie D. Cummings, "The Employed Poor: Their Characteristics and Occupations," *Monthly Labor Review,* 88 (July 1965): 828–835.
25. George J. Stigler, "The Unjoined Debate," *Chicago Today,* Winter 1966, p. 5.

The effect of the minimum wage on the drugstore soda fountain is illustrative. According to *The Wall Street Journal* (February 6, 1968, p. 1) only 30 percent of the 52,000 drugstores in the United States have fountains now, and the number declines yearly. Some druggists cited the minimum wage as the reason for scrapping the fountain: they could not afford to pay soda jerks the minimum. Others said it was cheaper to install self-service ice cream and soft drink machines. Presumably, the minimum wage is one reason why machines are cheaper. Soda-jerking is (or at any rate was) typically a job for the teen-ager.

For the economic theory involved, see George J. Stigler, "The Economics of Minimum Wage Legislation," *American Economic Review,* 36 (June 1946): 358–365. See also Yale Brozen, "The Effect of Statutory Minimum Wage Increases on Teen-Age Unemployment," *The Journal of Law and Economics,* 12 (April 1969): 109–122. For a less technical treatment, see The Free Society Association, Inc., *The Minimum Wage Rate; Who Really Pays? — An Interview with Yale Brozen and Milton Friedman* (Washington, D.C., April 1966).

For discussions of the minimum wage along with other matters discussed in this section, see Philip H. Wicksteed, *The Common Sense of Political Economy* (London: Routledge and Kegan Paul, 1933) — on minimum wages and unions, 2: 693–695, on overpaying public employees, 1: 343. See also Armen A. Alchian and William R. Allen, *University Economics* (Belmont, Calif.: Wadsworth, 1964), ch. 28.

26. Norman J. Samuels, "Plant Adjustments to the $1 Minimum Wage," *Monthly Labor Review,* 81 (October 1958): 1137.

27. The effect of unions on the wages of their members is often rather slight, however. H. Gregg Lewis says that apart from periods of unusually rapid inflation or deflation, "the average relative wage effect . . . was 0.10–0.20 per percentage point difference in extent of unionism." Lewis, "The Effects of Unions on Industrial Wage Differentials," in *Aspects of Labor Economics,* National Bureau of Economic Research (Princeton, N.J.: Princeton University Press, 1962), p. 332. See also his *Unionism and Relative Wages in the United States* (Chicago: University of Chicago Press, 1963).

28. Walter Gellhorn, quoted by Milton Friedman, *Capitalism and Freedom* (Chicago: University of Chicago Press, 1962), p. 142.

29. Proposed by the New York City License Commissioner (*New York Times,* October 9, 1967). Under this proposal, the city, with a federal subsidy, would also train apprentices. Thus, entry into the occupations would be even further limited.

30. *Boston Globe,* March 21, 1965. A study is reported to have shown that although Negro woman toll collectors scored significantly lower on mental ability tests than did their white counterparts, they received identical ratings from their supervisors for their performance on the job. The interpretation placed on this finding was that the tests were discriminatory. Another possibility, however, is that mental ability has little to do with successful toll collecting (*New York Times,* January 21, 1968).

31. *New York Times,* June 21, 1965.

32. *New York Times,* August 11, 1968.

33. Harlem Youth Opportunities Unlimited, Inc., "Youth in the Ghetto" (New York: multilithed, 1964), pp. 16–17.

34. Goodman, *Growing Up Absurd,* p. 204.

35. Between 1960 and 1965, three-fifths of the total new industrial plants (measured in value, as recorded on building permits) were built outside the central cities. Mollie Orshansky, in "Federal Role in Urban Affairs,"

Hearings Before the Subcommittee on Executive Reorganization, Committee on Government Operations, U.S. Senate, 89th Congress, 2nd Session, Part 9, p. 1873. See also Dorothy K. Newman, "The Decentralization of Jobs," *Monthly Labor Review,* 90 (May 1967): 7–13.

36. Victor R. Fuchs, *The Growing Importance of the Service Industries,* National Bureau of Economic Research Occasional Paper 96 (New York: National Bureau of Economic Research, 1965), pp. 13–14.

This trend reverses itself after 1964 if one uses a definition of services that does not include government work and finances, insurance, and real estate. Even by this narrow definition service employment has continued to grow relative to manufacturing in most years. Bureau of Labor Statistics, *Employment and Earnings,* 14 (May 1968): 45, 59.

37. A West Coast personnel officer explained to an interviewer who was asking about job opportunities for "ghetto" youth:

Let's set aside the whole minority problem for a moment and take the white youngster. I maintain that I can take any young man out of the suburban area of America with his nice washed look and his good speech and his white shirt which he wears comfortably and his polished shoes which look as though they belong on his feet and his well-cut hair and send him out as a tenth-grade dropout and get him a job without a bit of trouble. It is a social image — because of the way he speaks, the way he carries himself. It has nothing to do with whether he can read or do arithmetic or anything else. It has to do with the social problem we are dealing with in the slums. . . . It is his manners, his speech, his way of carrying himself, his own self-confidence, the "neat clean-cut look". . . . Can we put the suburban image on our kids in the slums? I think part of the suburban image is how he fills out a form and how he is able to read instructions, and how he answers the telephone, and what he says when he is asked a question and how he responds.

From Hugh Curtis Clark, "The Neighborhood Youth Corps," unpublished senior honors thesis, Harvard University, 1968, p. 52.

38. The Manpower Development Training Program is described and evaluated by Garth L. Mangum in *Contributions and Costs of Manpower Development and Training,* Policy Papers in Human Resources and Industrial Relations No. 5, Institute of Labor and Industrial Relations, University of Michigan and Wayne State University, with the National Manpower Policy Task Force, Washington, D.C., December 1967.

39. Ibid., p. 15.

40. Wilbur R. Thompson, *A Preface to Urban Economics* (Baltimore: The Johns Hopkins Press, 1965), p. 113.

Raymond Vernon, in his study of the New York region, remarks that the informal minimum wage in New York is likely to force the low-wage segments of industry continually to move outward, looking for an environment in which they can survive. *Metropolis 1985* (Cambridge, Mass.: Harvard University Press, 1960), p. 51.

41. John F. Kain and Joseph J. Persky, "Alternatives to the Gilded Ghetto," *The Public Interest,* 14 (Winter 1969): 82.

42. Michael J. Piore, "Public and Private Responsibilities in On-the-Job Training of Disadvantaged Workers," M.I.T. Department of Economics Working Paper No. 23, June 1968. For accounts of efforts by employers to use "unemployables," see Richard D. James (on the Hotpoint experience) and Kenneth C. Field (on the Detroit auto companies experience) in *The Wall Street Journal,* May 21 and August 12, 1968, respectively.

43. During the hard times of 1857, when starvation was a real possibility for the unemployed, the charitable societies of New York published circulars inviting those who would accept work in the country to register. None did. K. H. Claghorn, *Report to the Industrial Commission on Immigration,* 15 (1901): 463.

44. Newman, "The Decentralization of Jobs," p. 10.

45. As a way of inducing employers to do their best to train workers and to upgrade them as fast as possible, Lester C. Thurow has proposed giving them government grants, the amount of the grant depending upon the increase in the employee's earnings over a five-year period. Under this plan an employer would receive $5,000 (the maximum) if the employee's earnings rose from nothing to $4,000 over five years; if, on the other hand, the employee earned $1,500 to begin with and $1,500 after five years, the employer would get no grant. His proposal was made in testimony before the Joint Economic Committee, May 1968.

46. These programs (the Job Corps, the Neighborhood Youth Corps, and Work Experience and Training) are described and evaluated by Sar A. Levitan in *Anti-Poverty Work and Training Efforts: Goals and Reality,* Policy Papers in Human Resources and Industrial Relations No. 3, The Institute of Labor and Industrial Relations, University of Michigan and Wayne State University, with the National Manpower Policy Task Force, Washington, D.C., August 1967. The following paragraphs depend mainly upon this source.

47. A Behavior and Appearance Code promulgated by the director of the Job Corps prohibits alcoholic beverages, hitchhiking, smoking in bed, and gambling, as well as wearing hats in buildings, failing to shave regularly, and, in the case of women, wearing rollers in public places. It says Corps members are expected to be polite, not swear or use dirty words, avoid being loud or rowdy, be neat and clean and properly dressed according to center rules, and keep hair neat and presentable. *New York Times,* March 19, 1967, p. 32.

48. Levitan, *Anti-Poverty Work and Training Efforts,* p. 37. See also his *The Great Society's Poor Law: A New Approach to Poverty* (Baltimore: The Johns Hopkins Press, 1969), ch. 13.

49. In *Toward Freedom From Want,* pp. 153, 156.

50. The evaluation of J.O.B.S. is based on a personal communication to the writer from Peter B. Doeringer of the Harvard Economics Department. Accounts of other more or less similar efforts are given in Doeringer, ed., *Programs to Employ the Disadvantaged* (Englewood Cliffs, N.J.: Prentice-Hall, 1969).

51. Peter B. Doeringer, *Ghetto Labor Markets — Problems and Programs,*

Harvard Institute of Economic Research, Discussion Paper No. 33, June 1968, p. 9.

52. U.S. Department of Labor, *A Sharper Look at Unemployment in U.S. Cities and Slums,* undated, but probably 1967.

CHAPTER 6

1. U.S. Bureau of the Census, "Trends in Social and Economic Conditions in Metropolitan Areas," Series P-23, No. 27, February 7, 1969, pp. 36 and 39. Also, U.S. Bureau of the Census, Consumer Income Series P-60, No. 55, August 5, 1968, p. 4.

2. The dependency ratios (i.e., number of children under twenty-two for every 100 persons in the "prime working ages," twenty-two to sixty-four) for poor persons living in the central cities of standard metropolitan statistical areas (SMSA's) of 250,000 or more population and for poor persons living in the entire country were 168 and 148, respectively, in 1966. By contrast, the dependency ratio of the nonpoor in the central cities was lower than that of the nonpoor in the entire country — 71 as against 79. Harold L. Sheppard, *Effects of Family Planning on Poverty in the United States* (Kalamazoo, Mich.: The W. E. Upjohn Institute for Employment Research. October 1967), pp. 3–4.

3. "Trends in Social and Economic Conditions in Metropolitan Areas," p. 52. To take account of price rises, the poverty line was redefined in the summer of 1969 at $3,553 for a nonfarm family of four.

4. A two-year income average, however, yields nearly as many low-income families as does a one-year average. *Economic Report of the President* (Washington, D.C.: U.S. Government Printing Office, 1965), p. 165.

5. Margaret Reid, testimony in *House Hearings on the Economic Opportunity Act of 1964,* 88th Congress, 2nd Session, Part 3, p. 1429.

6. Rose D. Friedman, *Poverty — Definition and Perspective* (Washington, D.C.: American Enterprise Institute, February 1965), pp. 34–35.

7. Jacob Riis, "Special Needs of the Poor in New York," *The Forum,* December 1892, p. 493.

8. The relative failure of the poor to use the many preventive health facilities available to them in the cities does not arise wholly from financial factors, although it may be aggravated by them, and it does not arise from lack of awareness of the existence of the facilities, according to Daniel Rosenblatt. Instead it may be in some measure "another dimension of the general lack of future orientation that characterizes blue collar workers."

> For example, regular checkups of automobiles to detect incipient defects are not in the general value system of the urban poor. In similar fashion, household objects are often worn out and discarded rather than repaired at an early stage of disintegration. Installment buying is easily accepted without an awareness of the length of payments.
>
> The body can be seen as simply another class of objects to be worn out but not repaired. Thus, teeth are left without dental care; later there is often small interest in dentures, whether free

or not. In any event, false teeth may be little used. Corrective eye examinations, even for those people who wear glasses, are often neglected — regardless of clinic facilities. It is as though the middle class thinks of the body as a machine to be preserved and kept in perfect running order whether through prosthetic devices, rehabilitation, cosmetic surgery, or perpetual treatment, whereas the poor think of the body as having a limited span of utility: to be enjoyed in youth and then, with age and decrepitude, to be suffered and endured stoically.

Daniel Rosenblatt, "Barriers to Medical Care for the Urban Poor," in Arthur B. Shostak and William Gomberg, eds., *New Perspectives on Poverty* (Englewood Cliffs, N.J.: Prentice-Hall, 1965), pp. 72–73.

9. Quoted (with italics added) in Rose Friedman, *Poverty*, p. 30.
10. Quoted by Robert Hunter, *Poverty* (New York: Harper Torchbooks, 1965), pp. 7–8.
11. Rose Friedman, *Poverty*, pp. 9–10. To the extent that ignorance rather than poverty is the cause of bad diets, diets cannot be expected to improve as incomes rise. Leontine Young, in *Wednesday's Children: A Study of Child Neglect and Abuse* (New York: McGraw-Hill, 1964), p. 123, reports: "Many of the mothers lack the most elemental knowledge of nutrition as well as the will to act. One mother insisted she fed her children well. She bought potato chips and Coca-Cola regularly." With a higher income, this mother might buy more potato chips and Coca-Cola.
12. Intercity differences in the quality of health care for the poor are suggested by infant mortality rates. In Chicago in 1964 the infant mortality rate for poverty areas was 38.5, whereas for nonpoverty areas it was 22.2. In Providence, Rhode Island, in 1949–1951, however, it was 25.9 for the lowest socioeconomic areas and 28.2 for the highest. See Edward C. Stockwell, "Infant Mortality and Socio-Economic Status: A Changing Relationship," *Milbank Memorial Fund Quarterly*, Vol. 40 (January 1962); and U.S. Department of Health, Education and Welfare, Human Investment Programs, *Delivery of Health Services for the Poor* (Washington, D.C.: U.S. Government Printing Office, December 1967), Table 6. See also the essay (which appeared too late to be mentioned in the text) by Julius A. Roth, "The Treatment of the Sick," in John Kosa, Aaron Antonovsky, and Irving Kenneth Zola, eds., *Poverty and Health, A Sociological Analysis* (Cambridge, Mass.: Harvard University Press, 1969), ch. VII.
13. *Delivery of Health Services for the Poor,* Tables 2 and 8.
14. U.S. Congress, House Committee on Education and Labor, *Hearings on the Economic Opportunity Act of 1964,* 88th Congress, 2nd Session, Part 3, p. 1326.
15. Herman P. Miller, "The Dimensions of Poverty," in Ben B. Seligman, ed., *Poverty as a Public Issue* (New York: The Free Press, 1965), p. 24.
16. David Caplovitz, *The Poor Pay More* (New York: The Free Press, 1963), pp. 37–41.
17. Victor R. Fuchs, "Redefining Poverty and Redistributing Income," *The Public Interest,* 8 (Summer 1967): 91.

18. Lester C. Thurow finds that between 1947 and 1965, poverty (using the $3,000 line for families and the $1,500 one for unrelated individuals) declined 0.7 percentage points per year (in constant 1965 dollars). If this rate of decline continues, it would take 23 years to eliminate poverty among families and 55 years to eliminate it among unrelated individuals. Lester C. Thurow, *The Economics of Poverty and Discrimination* (Washington, D.C.: The Brookings Institution, 1969).

19. Robert J. Lampman, "How Much Does the American System of Transfers Benefit the Poor?" in Leonard Goodman, ed., *Economic Progress and Social Welfare* (New York: Columbia University Press, 1966), pp. 125–157. See also his "The Low Income Population and Economic Growth," in U.S. Congress, Joint Economic Committee, *Employment, Growth, and Price Levels,* Study Paper No. 12, 1959–1960.

20. The negative income tax proposal was made in Milton Friedman, *Capitalism and Freedom* (Chicago: University of Chicago Press, 1962), ch. 12. See also Christopher Green, *Negative Taxes and the Poverty Problem* (Washington, D.C.: The Brookings Institution, 1967); James Tobin, Joseph A. Pechman, and Peter M. Mieszkowski, "Is a Negative Income Tax Practical?" *The Yale Law Journal,* 77 (November 1967): 1–27; and James C. Vadakin, "A Critique of the Guaranteed Annual Income," *The Public Interest,* 11 (Spring 1968): 53–66.

21. The loss of output in the economy in 1963 attributable to the disincentive effect of the progressive income tax on high incomes (over $10,000) "may have been of the order of one-third of 1 percent." R. Barlow, H. E. Bracer, and J. N. Morgan, *Economic Behavior of the Affluent* (Washington, D.C.: The Brookings Institution, 1966), p. 146.

22. In its report on the Watts riot, the McCone Commission found that a job at the minimum wage paid about $220 a month, against which there were transportation, clothes, and other expenses. The average Aid to Families with Dependent Children (AFDC) family received $177 to $238 a month, with no work-related expenses. *Violence in the City — An End or a Beginning?* A Report by the Governor's Commission on the Los Angeles Riots, December 2, 1965, p. 72.

23. See Simon Rottenberg, "Misplaced Emphases in Wars on Poverty," *Law and Contemporary Problems,* Winter 1966, pp. 68–71.

24. Martin Rein, "Poverty and Income," *American Child,* 48 (Summer 1966): 9.

25. These and related problems are discussed by E. C. Banfield, Nathan Glazer, and David Gordon in articles on welfare in *The Public Interest,* 16 (Summer 1969).

26. Fuchs, "Redefining Poverty," p. 89.

27. Caplovitz, *The Poor Pay More,* p. 48.

28. Hunter, *Poverty,* pp. 322–323.

29. Cf. David Matza, "The Disreputable Poor," in Neil J. Smelser and Seymour Martin Lipset, eds., *Social Structure and Mobility in Economic Development* (Chicago: Aldine, 1966), esp. pp. 310–317.

30. Oscar Lewis, *The Children of Sanchez* (New York: Random House, 1961), p. xxiv. See also his "The Culture of Poverty," *Scientific American,* 215 (October 1966): 19–25. For a critique of the concept see Jack L.

Roach and O. R. Gursslin, "An Evaluation of the Concept 'Culture of Poverty,'" *Social Forces,* 45 (March 1967): 383–392.

Two valuable official publications describing the "culture of poverty" (without necessarily subscribing to Lewis' conceptualization): Catherine S. Chilman, *Growing Up Poor,* U.S. Department of Health, Education and Welfare, Welfare Administration publication No. 13, May 1966; and Lola M. Irelan, ed., *Low-Income Life Styles,* publication No. 14, 1966.

31. From an unpublished paper by Francis Duehay.
32. Cf. L. L. Geismar and Michael A. LaSorte, *Understanding the Multi-Problem Family* (New York: Association Press, 1964), pp. 56–58.
33. Gordon E. Brown, ed., *The Multi-Problem Dilemma* (Metuchen, N.J.: The Scarecrow Press, 1968), p. 8.
34. J. Leslie Dunstan, *A Light to the City* (Boston: Beacon Press, 1966), p. 106.
35. Rev. Lyman Abbott, Introduction to Mrs. Helen Campbell, *Darkness and Daylight; or, Lights and Shadows of New York Life* (Hartford, Conn.: Hartford Publishing Co., 1896), p. 53. The secret of success in dealing with the "outcast class," Rev. Abbott says, is "personal contact with men and women of higher nature," by which he presumably means higher-class culture (p. 49).
36. Roy Lubove, *The Professional Altruist* (Cambridge, Mass.: Harvard University Press, 1965), p. 16.
37. How far supervision can go even with welfare recipients who are not lower class — the blind, for instance — is described by Jacobus TenBroek and Floyd W. Matson in "The Disabled and the Law of Welfare," *California Law Review,* 54 (May 1966): 831:

> It is the agency of welfare, not the recipient, who decides what life goals are to be followed, what ambitions may be entertained, what services are appropriate, what wants are to be recognized, and what funds allocated to each. In short, the recipient is told *what* he wants as well as how much he is wanting. In the velvet glove of public aid is an iron hand: If the recipient does not comply and conform, he may be removed from the rolls or have his budget reduced. The alternatives are obedience or starvation.

38. Winifred Bell, *Aid to Dependent Children* (New York: Columbia University Press 1965), p. 113.

A recent study compares the progress of fifty multi-problem families receiving intensive social casework (the caseworkers had earned the Master of Social Work degree, had previous field experience, and had less than half the usual caseload) with that of a control group of fifty similar families receiving normal public assistance. After thirty-one months "the essential finding was that while the demonstration group attained a slightly better degree of family functioning, its margin of progress over the control group was not significant in the statistical sense." Brown, *The Multi-Problem Dilemma,* p. 7.

39. Quoted in Harvey W. Zorbaugh, *The Gold Coast and the Slum* (Chicago: University of Chicago Press, 1929), p. 262.
40. There is no standard usage for the terms "community development,"

"community organization," and "community mobilization." The meanings
employed here follow Patricia Cayo Sexton, *Spanish Harlem, Anatomy
of Poverty* (New York: Harper & Row, 1965), pp. 140–141.
41. See, for example, various writings by and about Saul Alinsky, especially
the uncritical account of his doings in Charles Silberman, *Crisis in
Black and White* (New York: Random House, 1964), Ch. 10.
42. Peter Marris and Martin Rein, *Dilemmas of Social Reform* (New York:
Atherton Press, 1967), pp. 222–223. See also Daniel Patrick Moynihan,
*Maximum Feasible Misunderstanding: Community Action in the War
on Poverty* (New York: The Free Press, 1969).
43. Thomas Gladwin, *Poverty U.S.A.* (Boston: Little, Brown, 1967), pp.
168–169.
44. *New York Times,* July 24, 1966.
45. Mobilization for Youth, Inc., *A Proposal for the Prevention and Control
of Delinquency by Expanding Opportunities* (New York: 1961), p. 339.
46. Walter B. Miller, "The Impact of a 'Total-Community' Delinquency
Control Project," *Social Problems,* 10 (Fall 1962): 168–191.
    Two studies of experimental programs found that casework had little
or no effect. In the Cambridge-Somerville delinquency prevention experiment, the hypothesis was tested "that the influence of a skilled and directed friendship on the part of a continuously available counselor may
succeed in preventing delinquency in boys." The conclusion reached was
that "the special work of the counselors was no more effective than the
usual forces in the community in preventing boys from committing delinquent acts." Edwin Powers and Helen Witmer, *Prevention of Delinquency, The Cambridge-Somerville Youth Study* (New York: Columbia
University Press, 1951), pp. viii, 337. A follow-up study traced into
adulthood 253 of the (matched) boys and concluded that "whatever
benefits the treated boys received were not reflected in their criminal
rates." Joan and William McCord, *The Annals of the American Academy of Political and Social Science,* 322 (March 1959): 89–96.
    The other experiment dealt with "potentially delinquent" girls and
covered a six-year period. The conclusion was that individual counseling
was ineffective in improving girls' performance in school and on psychological tests, and in reducing truancy, pregnancy, and school dropout rates. H. J. Meyer et al., *Girls at Vocational High* (New York:
Russell Sage Foundation, 1965).
47. Robert A. Berliner, "Alinskism in Theory and Practice," unpublished
senior honors thesis, Harvard University, 1967.
48. *A Proposal,* p. 133.

CHAPTER 7

The "Dear Abby" correspondence appeared in the (McNaught) syndicated
column on July 11, 1966.

1. Harlem Youth Opportunities Unlimited, Inc., "Youth in the Ghetto"
(New York: multilithed, 1964), p. 33.
2. A special program "aimed at promoting community stability, halting the

departure of the middle class and white families by providing additional personnel and services" was begun in the fall of 1965 in 116 schools in "transitional" areas of New York City. The program, which cost almost $7.7 million in 1966, featured small classes, special opportunities for gifted pupils, and remedial and counseling help for "under-achievers." In the fall of 1967 an evaluation by the Center for Urban Education showed that Negro and Puerto Rican enrollment rose at a faster rate after the program was initiated than before; teachers and principals favored continuing the program but did not feel that it would be effective in reducing migration of middle-class families. *New York Times,* October 18, 1967, p. 32.

3. However, using data from the ninth grade participating in the 1960 Project TALENT study, Combs and Cooley found that in 1964 employment rates of male dropouts and controls were almost identical (87 and 89 percent, respectively, had full-time jobs) and the mean yearly salary of the employed dropouts was slightly more than that of the controls ($3,650 as against $3,500). Unfortunately, the authors write, the results of their study were not consistent with their expectation, which was to reveal that the graduate was much better off than the dropout, a finding that "might help dissuade some students from leaving high-school before graduation." Later follow-up studies by Project TALENT, they say, may "show more precisely the disadvantages of dropping out of high school." Janet Combs and William W. Cooley, "Dropouts: In High School and After School," *American Educational Research Journal,* 5 (May 1968): 352, 362.

4. Gary S. Becker, *Human Capital* (New York: National Bureau of Economic Research [Columbia University Press], 1964), p. 128. See also W. Lee Hansen, "Total and Private Rates of Return to Investment in Schooling," *Journal of Political Economy,* 81 (1963): 128–141; and Thomas I. Ribich, *Education and Poverty* (Washington, D.C.: The Brookings Institution, 1968).

5. Becker, *Human Capital,* p. 125. The question of the meaningfulness of the data is raised in W. G. Bowen and T. A. Finegan "Educational Attainment and Labor Force Participation," *American Economic Review,* 56 (May 1966): 567–582.

6. Daniel E. Diamond, "America's Unskilled Workers: Some Problems and Solutions," dittoed paper, New York University, September 29, 1966. This paper has been helpful on many of the points discussed in this section.

7. "The high school drop-out," Denis F. Johnston writes in *Monthly Labor Review,* 88 (May 1965): 527, "may encounter difficulty in finding a job not because the job he seeks requires the training implied in the completion of high school, but because a growing proportion of his fellow job seekers have their high school diplomas in hand."

Participants at a National Manpower Council conference agreed that "modern technology has made it possible to employ persons with little or no specialized training effectively." The conferees said that they were "less concerned with the applicant's course of study than they were with his possession of a high school diploma and a good scholastic record." These they regarded as "an indication of basic intelligence, good motivation, and ability to absorb training." *A Policy for Skilled Manpower* (New York: Columbia University Press, 1954), pp. 259, 100.

8. Denis F. Johnston and Harvey R. Hamel, "Educational Attainment of Workers in March 1965," *Monthly Labor Review,* 89 (March 1966): 256.

9. Arthur L. Stinchcombe, *Rebellion in a High School* (Chicago: Quadrangle Books, 1964), p. 180.

   Most job-related skills are learned on the job. See the *Annual Report of the Council of Economic Advisers,* January 1965, Table 17, p. 129. See also Jacob Mincer, "On-the-Job Training: Costs, Returns, and Some Implications," *Journal of Political Economy,* 70 (Part 2, Supplement [October 1962]): 50–73.

   Apprenticeship is also of small importance in training workers. See Felician F. Foltman, "An Assessment of Apprenticeship," *Monthly Labor Review,* 87 (January 1964): 33.

10. Ruby Jo Reeves Kennedy, quoted in Lewis Anthony Dexter, *The Tyranny of Schooling* (New York: Basic Books, 1964), pp. 114–116 (italics in the original). See also Arthur R. Jensen, "How Much Can We Boost IQ and Scholastic Achievement?" *Harvard Educational Review,* 39 (Winter 1969): 13–16.

11. See the remarks by Howard R. Stanton in Arthur J. Field, ed., *Urbanization and Work in Modernizing Societies* (Detroit: Caribbean Research Institute, Glengary Press, 1966), pp. 9–13.

12. For an important case in point, see the study by Eli Ginsberg and Douglas W. Bray of the Army's prejudice during World War II against illiterates and slow learners. *The Uneducated* (New York: Columbia University Press, 1953), esp. chs. 6 and 7.

13. Cf. R. Wayne Jones, in Field, *Urbanization and Work,* pp. 57–58.

14. See for example, Allison Davis, "Status Systems and the Socialization of the Child," *American Sociological Review,* 6 (June 1941): 352–354. Davis says that the middle-class child is taught that he will be rewarded if he learns, whereas the lower-class one is taught that he will *not* be:

> As the middle-class child grows older, the effective rewards in maintaining learning are increasingly those of status; they are associated with the prestige of middle- or upper-class rank and culture. The class goals in education, occupation, and status are made to appear real, valuable, and certain to him because he actually begins to experience in his school, clique, and family life some of the prestige responses. The lower-class child, however, *learns* by *not* being rewarded in these prestige relationships that the middle-class goals and gains are neither likely nor desirable for one in his position. He discovers by trial-and-error learning that he is not going to be rewarded in terms of these long-range, status goals, if he is a "good little boy," if he avoids the sexual and recreational exploration available to him in his lower-class environment, or if he studies his lessons. In this learning, he is often more realistic than his teacher, if one judges by the actual cultural role which the society affords him.

15. Herbert J. Gans, *The Urban Villagers* (New York: The Free Press, 1962), p. 133.
16. Cf. Basil Bernstein, "Social Class and Linguistic Development: A Theory of Social Learning," in A. H. Halsey et al., eds., *Education, Economy, and Society* (New York: The Free Press, 1961),pp. 306–307.
17. C. Arnold Anderson, "A Skeptical Note on Education and Mobility," in *Education, Economy, and Society*, p. 176.
18. James S. Coleman et al., *Equality of Educational Opportunity*, Office of Education, U.S. Department of Health, Education and Welfare (Washington, D.C.: U.S. Government Printing Office, 1966). For discussion of Coleman's findings and related matters, see the essays from *Harvard Educational Review, Equal Educational Opportunity* (Cambridge, Mass.: Harvard University Press, 1969).
19. Coleman, et al., p. 302.
20. Ibid., p. 307.
21. Ibid., p. 325. Other studies made before and after the Coleman one have reached this general conclusion. According to Project TALENT:

    It would appear that such talent as the poor quality environment permits to emerge may be adequately developed by the schools in our large cities. If true, this is a tribute to the strenuous efforts of our large city school administrations to equalize opportunity in all of their schools regardless of location. Efforts to equalize quality of home and social environment have not been nearly as effective as have efforts to equalize school environment in our cities.

    John C. Flanagan et al., Project TALENT Office, University of Pittsburgh, "A Survey and Follow-up Study of Educational Plans and Decisions in Relation to Aptitude Patterns: Studies of the American High School," Cooperative Research Project No. 226, 1962, ch. 11, p. 6.
    A study of Chicago and Atlanta high schools found that variations in educational outcomes measured in terms of test scores "are almost wholly conditioned by the socioeconomic environment of the neighborhood," especially income class, housing conditions, occupation of parents, and ethnic status. Jesse Burkhead, with T. G. Fox and J. W. Holland, *Input and Output in Large-City High Schools* (Syracuse, N.Y.: Syracuse University Press, 1967), p. 88.
22. Coleman et al., *Equality of Educational Opportunity*, p. 319.
23. Ibid., p. 320.
24. U.S. Commission on Civil Rights, *Racial Isolation in the Public Schools*, (Washington, D.C.: U.S. Government Printing Office, 1967), Vols. 1, 2 (Appendices).
25. Ibid., 1: 84–91.
26. Ibid., 1: 115–140, esp. 138–139.
27. Still another explanation may be that compensatory education programs have not been well designed. According to J. McV. Hunt: ". . . traditional play school has little to offer the children of the poor, but programs which made an effort to inculcate cognitive skills, language skills, and number skills, whether they be taught directly or incorporated into games, show fair success." "Has Compensatory Education Failed?" *Harvard Educational Review*, 39 (Spring 1969): 297.

28. U.S. Commission on Civil Rights, *Racial Isolation,* p. 90. A study done in Baltimore estimated that only .63 years of the educational disadvantage of Negroes at the 12th grade was attributable to segregation, whereas 2.28 years was attributable to other causes. D. Walker, A. L. Stinchcombe, and M. S. Dill, "School Desegregation in Baltimore," Center for the Study of Social Organization of Schools, Johns Hopkins University, August 1967, p. 4.

29. Bernstein, "Social Class and Linguistic Development," pp. 296, 307. Bernstein uses the term "working class" rather than (as earlier) lower class, but he includes in that class "all members of the semi-skilled and unskilled group except the type of family structure indicated as the base line for the middle-class and associative levels."

30. Richard A. Cloward and James A. Jones, "Social Class: Educational Attitudes and Participation," in A. Harry Passow, ed., *Education in Depressed Areas* (New York: Columbia Teachers College, 1963), p. 193.
    The midnineteenth-century high school deliberately inculcated future-orientedness. Michael B. Katz, *The Irony of Early School Reform* (Cambridge, Mass.: Harvard University Press, 1968), p. 121.

31. Bernstein, "Social Class and Linguistic Development," p. 306 (italics in the original).

32. Cloward and Jones, "Social Class," p. 194.

33. Benjamin S. Bloom, *Stability and Change in Human Characteristics,* (New York: Wiley, 1964), pp. 207–208, 127.
    Martin Deutsch suggests that it is at the three- to four-year-old level that the deprived child might most successfully be helped to catch up. "Facilitating Development in the Pre-School Child: Social and Psychological Perspectives," in Fred M. Hechinger, ed., *Pre-School Education Today* (Garden City, N.Y.: Doubleday, 1966), p. 84.

34. Lloyd N. Morrisett, "Preschool Education: Report of a Conference," *Social Science Research Council Items,* Vol. 20 (June 1966).
    A study made between June 1968 and March 1969 by the Westinghouse Learning Corporation and Ohio State University for the Office of Economic Opportunity showed that children who had participated in Head Start programs did not score significantly higher than a control group on five of six tests. On one test (the Metropolitan Reading Test), those who had attended full-year programs and had just begun first grade were superior by a small but statistically significant margin. *New York Times,* April 14, 1969.

35. Study by Max Wolff, Center for Urban Education in New York, Ferkouf Graduate School of Education, Yeshiva University, as reported in *New York Times,* October 23, 1966.

36. Morrisett, "Preschool Education," p. 19.

37. J. M. Tanner, a British educational psychologist, objects to any school-leaving age as such on the grounds that there is great biological variability in the rate at which children mature:

> We need not a production-line like an apple-sorter, with children falling off at age-given points of 16 or 18, some immature and some rotted by boredom and the stultifying effect of a situation

they feel intuitively to be contrived. A network rather should be the model, with many paths through it, offering to the individual child a route more in accordance with his own particular speed of development and his own particular gifts. Such a system could be built if the barriers between school and industrial community were progressively removed, so that one child went to his apprenticeship as another to a new form. In neither case would the progression be dependent on chronological age, but on physical development, emotional needs, manual capabilities and intelligence. One boy might begin to spend a considerable proportion of his time in an engineering shop from age 13 onwards, though always under the ultimate control of the educational authorities. If at 16 he had after all discovered a talent for figures, he could increase the proportion of time in the schoolroom. Another late-maturing though not very intelligent boy might remain in the more protected school environment till 16 or even 17, emerging gradually into the community as science, humanism and common sense alike dictate, and not at the occurrence of an arbitrary birthday. School-leaving age could be abolished, but "education" continued for all up to 18 or 20. The economic system would have to be arranged so that passage from school to industry or vice versa did not penalize the child financially.

J. M. Tanner, *Education and Physical Growth* (London, University of London Press, 1961), p. 124.
38. Stinchcombe, *Rebellion in a High School,* p. 179.
39. Martin Trow, "The Second Transformation of American Secondary Education," in R. Bendix and S. M. Lipset, eds., *Class, Status, and Power: Social Stratification in Comparative Perspective* (New York: The Free Press, 1966), p. 448.
40. Quoted in E. G. West, *Education and the State* (London: The Institute of Economic Affairs, 1965), p. 36.
41. Mobilization for Youth, Inc., *A Proposal for the Prevention and Control of Delinquency by Expanding Opportunities* (New York: 1961), p. 112.
42. Quoted in Harrison Brown, James Bonner, and John Weir, *The Next Hundred Years* (New York: Viking, 1957), pp. 132–133.
43. Fritz Machlup, *The Production and Distribution of Knowledge in the United States* (Princeton, N.J.: Princeton University Press, 1962), p. 128. (Italics in the original.)
44. Flanagan et al., "A Survey and Follow-up Study," ch. 10, p. 36.
45. Trow, "The Second Transformation," p. 448.
46. Of the boys among them, nearly one-fourth were clerical workers, 17 percent sales workers, 20 percent operatives and kindred workers, 10 percent service workers (not including private household), and 10 percent laborers. U.S. Bureau of the Census, *U.S. Census of the Population: 1960, Volume I: Characteristics of the Population,* Part 34, New York (Washington, D.C.: U.S. Government Printing Office, 1963), Table 123, pp. 34–678 to 34–680.
47. In a personal communication.

CHAPTER 8

The quotation from Henry George at the head of the chapter is from *Social Problems* (New York, 1883), p. 12. The second quotation is from the report of the President's Commission on Law Enforcement and Administration of Justice, *The Challenge of Crime in a Free Society* (Washington, D.C.: U.S. Government Printing Office, February 1967), p. 6.

Crime statistics are notoriously unreliable for many reasons, some of which are inherent in the nature of crime. Nevertheless, it is impossible to discuss the subject without making use of them. The reader should be warned, however, that few perfectly safe factual statements are possible. For a good discussion of the limitations of the data, see Marvin E. Wolfgang, "Urban Crime," in James Q. Wilson, ed., *The Metropolitan Enigma* (Cambridge, Mass.: Harvard University Press, 1968), pp. 253–257.

1. A study in a high-delinquency area of Philadelphia showed that boys born there were much more likely to commit delinquencies, and to commit more serious ones, than boys whose parents had migrated from places where presumably housing, schools, health conditions, and the level of living in general were much poorer. Leonard Savitz, "Delinquency and Migration," in M. E. Wolfgang, L. Savitz, and N. Johnston, *The Sociology of Crime and Delinquency* (New York: Wiley, 1962), pp. 203–204.

   A Washington, D.C., delinquency project in existence from 1964 to 1967 succeeded through the use of programmed instruction in producing educational gains of from three to six grade levels in high school dropouts from slum areas with delinquent careers. However, "the rate of delinquent acts was in no measurable way reduced by participation in the project. Those subjects passing the GED [high school equivalency] test were more delinquent than those failing the test." C. Ray Jeffery and Ina A. Jeffery, "Delinquents and Dropouts: An Experimental Program in Behavior Change," Mimeographed, 1968, Graduate School of Public Administration, New York University. The project was supported in part by contract number OE 6-85-355, U.S. Office of Education.

2. To the extent that the analysis here departs from the usual theory of rational decision-making it owes much to the work of Walter B. Miller. See especially his "The Impact of a 'Total-Community' Delinquency Control Project," *Social Problems,* Vol. 10 (Fall 1962) and his "Theft Behavior in City Gangs," in M. W. Klein and B. G. Myerhoff, eds., *Juvenile Gangs in Context* (Englewood Cliffs, N.J.: Prentice-Hall, 1967). Miller's theoretical work will be systematically presented in *City Gangs* (New York: Wiley, forthcoming).

3. The distinctions made in this paragraph are adapted from Lawrence Kohlberg, "The Child as a Moral Philosopher," *Psychology Today,* September 1968, pp. 25–30.

4. Henry Williamson, *Hustler!,* edited by R. Lincoln Keiser (New York: Avon, 1965), pp. 150–151.

5. Carroll divided three hundred Negro adolescents into "middle" and

"lower" class and had them write explanations of why stealing and cheating are wrong. Some of her findings may be summarized as follows:

	PERCENT GIVING REASON	
Reasons	Middle Class	Lower Class
It is wrong to steal because:		
You might get caught	16	54
Your friends won't like you	43	17
You will get a bad name	28	15
It is wrong to cheat because:		
Someone will find it out	31	56
Someone will cheat you back	—	7
Children will not want to play games with you	58	64

Source: Rebecca Evans Carroll, "Relation of Social Environment to the Moral Ideology and the Personal Aspirations of Negro Boys and Girls," The School Review, 53 (January 1945): 32.

6. Joyce Ann Ladner, "Deviance in the Lower Class Adolescent Sub-Culture," Pruitt-Igoe Project Occasional Paper #3, Department of Sociology-Anthropology, Washington University, St. Louis, September 1966, p. 25.
7. Ibid., p. 26.
8. Allison Davis, Social-Class Influences Upon Learning (Cambridge, Mass.: Harvard University Press, 1948), p. 34.
9. Kenneth Keniston, The Uncommitted (New York: Delta, 1965), p. 287.
10. Norman E. Zinberg, "Facts and Fancies about Drug Addiction," The Public Interest, 6 (Winter 1967): 76–77. Dr. Zinberg calls those who "want nothing but the immediate satisfaction of specific, pleasurable desires" oblivion-seekers, but it is hard to see why.

 Far from being an important component of "experience" as understood by the (expressively) future-oriented individual, "pleasure" seems to be in opposition to it. Thus Dr. Timothy Leary withdrew as guru of a drug-using group because he was "dismayed over mere pleasure-seekers" in the movement. Psychedelic drugs, he said, are "too valuable to be used for mere pleasure" and "should be for developing self-knowledge." New York Times, November 29, 1967.
11. Cf. James Q. Wilson, "Violence," in Daniel Bell, ed., Toward the Year 2000: Work in Progress (Boston: Houghton-Mifflin, 1968), pp. 283–284. Durkheim's discussion of the "egoistic" basis of suicide in the upper classes is relevant to the point being made in the text.
12. What follows draws upon the work of Walter B. Miller cited earlier.
13. David Cumming and Elaine Cumming, "The Everyday Life of Delinquent Boys," in Irwin Deutscher and Elizabeth J. Thompson, eds., Among the People: Encounters with the Poor (New York: Basic Books, 1968), p. 152.
14. David Matza, Delinquency and Drift (New York: Wiley, 1964), pp. 89, 189–190.

15. Keniston, *The Uncommitted*, p. 184. See also pp. 398–399.
16. Walter B. Miller, "Violent Crimes in City Gangs," *The Annals of the American Academy of Political and Social Science,* 364 (March 1966): 112.
17. For evidence on one city, see Theodore N. Ferdinand, "The Criminal Patterns of Boston Since 1849," *American Journal of Sociology,* 73 (July 1967): 84–99.
18. Jacqueline Grennan, "The Age of the Person," *Seventeen,* December 1967, p. 168.
19. *New York Times,* March 12, 1969.
20. Eldridge Cleaver, *Soul On Ice* (New York: Delta, 1968), pp. 13–14.
21. Ibid., pp. 4, 14.
22. In 1962 6 percent of arrests for assault with deadly weapons involved a black suspect and a white complainant and 3 percent involved a white suspect and a black complainant. In 1968 the corresponding figures were 27 percent and 3 percent. The findings are based on a random sample in which every fifth assault was selected. The numbers in the sample were 65 in 1962 and 120 in 1968. The data were supplied to the writer by the chief of the Oakland Police Department.
23. The reference here and in the paragraph that follows is to Miller's statement to the New York State Joint Legislative Committee on Crime and to the Advisory Council on Violence, July 31, 1968. More systematic data tending to the same general conclusion will appear in his forthcoming *City Gangs.*
24. Belton M. Fleisher, *The Economics of Delinquency* (Chicago: Quadrangle Books, 1966), p. 117.
   Cutting delinquency by raising family income in high crime areas is evidently not an *economical* operation. Using Fleisher's data, Ribich estimates that it would take an income gain of $300,000 in a high-delinquency area to bring about a $1,300 reduction in police costs. Thomas I. Ribich, *Education and Poverty* (Washington, D.C.: The Brookings Institution, 1968), p. 121.
25. Judge David L. Bazelon, quoted by Elliot Liebow, *Tally's Corner* (Boston: Little, Brown, 1967), p. 43n.
26. James Q. Wilson, "Crime and Law Enforcement," in Kermit Gordon, ed., *Agenda for the Nation* (Washington, D.C.: The Brookings Institution, 1968), p. 187.
27. *New York Times,* January 27, 1969.
28. F. L. Strodtbeck and J. F. Short, Jr., "Aleatory Risks Versus Short-Run Hedonism in Explanation of Gang Action," *Social Problems,* 12 (Fall 1964): 135.
29. Charles R. Tittle, "Crime Rates and Legal Sanctions," *Social Problems,* 16 (Spring 1969): 409–423.
30. Mary Owen Cameron, *The Booster and the Snitch: Department Store Shoplifting* (New York: The Free Press, 1964), p. 17.
31. Space-General Corporation, *Prevention and Control of Crime and Delinquency,* Final Report Prepared for Youth and Adult Corrections Agency, State of California, mimeo, El Monte, California, July 29, 1965, p. 2.
32. The constitutionality of a Connecticut law authorizing the imprisonment

on a state farm of young women "in manifest danger of falling into habits of vice or leading a vicious life" was recently challenged in the Supreme Court. In a *per curiam* decision three lines long, the Court dismissed the appeal "for want of a properly presented federal question." 89 *Supreme Court Reporter* 1767 (May 26, 1969).

With regard to "preventive detention," i.e., detention pending trial of arrested persons who are judged likely to commit more crimes while awaiting trial, Professor Alan M. Dershowitz of the Harvard Law School remarks that the problem with the system is that it would *seem* to work: "The crime rate probably will go down slightly, and perhaps might be traceable to preventive detention, but what we won't know is how many, what proportion of the people confined, would actually not have committed crimes." He said any such plan ought to be preceded by a long test period, in which judges would select those persons they felt should be detained in order to see if, when not detained, they did actually commit more crimes than others. *New York Times,* January 30, 1969.

CHAPTER 9

1. Report of the Task Force on Assessment of the President's Committee on Law Enforcement and Administration of Justice, *Crime and Its Impact — An Assessment* (Washington, D.C.: U.S. Government Printing Office, 1967), p. 121.
2. Ibid., p. 122.
3. Kenneth B. Clark, "The Wonder Is There Have Been So Few Riots," *New York Times Magazine,* September 5, 1965, p. 10.
4. David Matza, *Delinquency and Drift* (New York: Wiley, 1964), pp. 189–190.
5. Fred Powledge in *New York Times,* August 6, 1964.
6. See Richard C. Wade, *The Urban Frontier* (Chicago: University of Chicago Press [Phoenix Books], 1964), p. 90; and Howard O. Sprogle, *The Philadelphia Police, Past and Present* (Philadelphia, 1887), p. 50.
7. Wade, *The Urban Frontier,* p. 92. In Boston one house a month would not have been nearly enough; more than fifty buildings were fired by incendiaries in 1844 (Arthur Wellington Brayley, *A Complete History of the Boston Fire Department* [Boston, 1889], p. 207). In Philadelphia thirty-four boys aged five to fifteen were arrested in three summer months of 1862 for starting fires. (Sprogle, *The Philadelphia Police,* p. 318).
8. Sprogle, *The Philadelphia Police,* pp. 90, 106. See also Eli K. Price, *The History of the Consolidation of the City of Philadelphia* (Philadelphia: Lippincott, 1873), pp. 118–119.
9. Cf. Richard O'Connor, *Hell's Kitchen* (Philadelphia: Lippincott, 1958). See also Herbert Asbury, *The Gangs of New York* (New York: Knopf, 1927).
10. Roger Lane, *Policing the City, Boston 1822–1885* (Cambridge, Mass.: Harvard University Press, 1967), p. 29.
11. *New York Times,* September 16, 1965.

12. Brayley, *Boston Fire Department,* pp. 15, 31.
13. See Mancur Olson, Jr., *The Logic of Collective Action* (Cambridge, Mass.: Harvard University Press, 1965). The theory as applied to small groups is particularly relevant here; it is summarized on pp. 33–36.
14. George W. Walling, *Recollections of a New York Chief of Police* (New York: Caxton Book Concern, 1887), p. 85.
15. Thomas C. Schelling, *The Strategy of Conflict* (Cambridge, Mass.: Harvard University Press, 1960), p. 90.
16. George Rudé, *The Crowd in History* (New York: Wiley, 1964), p. 238.
17. See E. C. Banfield, "Roots of the Draft Riots," *New York Magazine,* July 29, 1968.
18. This section depends heavily upon a chronology compiled by the Legislative Reference Service of the Library of Congress. It appears in the *Congressional Quarterly* Special Report on Urban Problems and Civil Disorder, No. 36, September 8, 1967, pp. 1708–1712.
19. The Harlem and Bedford-Stuyvesant riots are described in Fred C. Shapiro and James W. Sullivan, *Race Riots, New York 1964* (New York: Crowell, 1964).
20. *New York Times,* November 7, 1964.
21. *New York Times,* September 27, 1964.
22. *New York Times,* September 11, 1964.
23. New York City Planning Commission, "The Future by Design," October 14–16, 1964, transcript, p. 55.
24. *New York Times,* October 7, 1964.
25. Gary T. Marx, *Protest and Prejudice* (New York: Harper & Row, 1967), p. 39. See also the survey reported in the special issue of *Fortune,* December 1967.
26. Comparing a sample of Negro males arrested during the Detroit riot of 1967 with a control group chosen from the area most affected by the riot, Luby found that the arrestees had no more grievances than the controls, that both arrestees and controls felt that they had made substantial progress in the past five years, and that both were remarkably optimistic about the future. Eliot D. Luby, M.D., "A Comparison Between Negro Riot Arrestees and a Riot Area Control Sample," Paper presented at the annual meeting of the American Political Science Association, 1968.
27. Jerry Cohen and William S. Murphy, *Burn, Baby, Burn!* (New York: Avon Books, 1966), pp. 62–63.
28. Newspaperman Don Cormier, quoted in *Burn, Baby, Burn!,* p. 71.
29. Governor's Commission on the Los Angeles Riots, *Violence in the City — An End or a Beginning?,* Los Angeles, December 2, 1965, p. 24.
30. Bayard Rustin, "The Watts 'Manifesto' and the McCone Report," *Commentary,* March 1966, p. 30.
31. *New York Times,* July 24, 1967. John Howard, a sociologist who observed the Detroit riot, later wrote that poor whites played a major role in it. He found the Detroit (and also the Newark) riot to be a "lower-class, rather than racial, revolt." William McCord et al., *Life Styles in the Black Ghetto* (New York: Norton, 1969), p. 273.
32. Quoted in *Education News,* October 16, 1967, p. 16. Luby's study (see

note 26) of a sample of Detroit arrestees and a control group also found the arrestees to be younger than the controls, less often married, more often raised in the urban North, more often raised in a family in which the father was not present during the first 11 years, less affiliated with organizations, less conscious of political leadership, and no more unemployed.

33. For the distinction between "accelerating" and "background" causes, the writer is grateful to Bruce Jacobs.
34. *New York Times,* December 7, 1967.
35. *New York Times,* November 7, 1965.
36. J. Anthony Lukas, "Postscript on Detroit: 'Whitey Hasn't Got the Message,' " *New York Times Magazine,* August 27, 1967, p. 44.
37. Matza, *Delinquency and Drift,* p. 184.
38. Ibid., p. 95.

> Modern guides written for those who work with juveniles stress the importance of supporting the child. Whenever supporting the child leads to statements excusing or understanding his behavior, as they occasionally must, the precepts of subcultural delinquency are also supported. . . .
>
> Statements reinforcing the delinquent's conception of irresponsibility are an integral part of an ideology of child welfare shared by social work, psychoanalysis, and criminology. This ideology presents a causal theory of delinquency which, when it attributes fault, directs it to parent, community, society, or even to the victims of crime.

39. Rustin, "The Watts 'Manifesto,' " p. 30. Vice President Humphrey helped to extenuate the rioting when he said in New Orleans that if he lived in a slum tenement with rats and with no place to go swimming, "You'd have more trouble than you have already, because I've got enough spark left in me to lead a mighty good revolt [sic] under those conditions." *New York Times,* July 19, 1966.
40. *New York Times,* November 7, 1965.
41. There is a striking parallel between the rhetorical strategy of the civil rights leaders in the early 1960's and that of James Mill prior to the passage of the Reform Bill of 1832. See Joseph Hamburger, *James Mill and the Art of Revolution* (New Haven: Yale University Press, 1963).
42. *New York Times,* December 16, 1966.
43. *New York Times,* December 7, 1966.
44. In March 1968, the process of explanation and, by implication, justification reached its apogee with the publication of the report of the National Advisory Commission on Civil Disorders (the Kerner Commission), which found that "white racism," poverty, and powerlessness were mainly responsible for the riots. The next month there were riots in several cities following the assassination of the Rev. Martin Luther King, Jr. These riots followed the familiar pattern of looting, burning, and vandalism, and it was apparent that despite all that had been done to give a political character to these events, most rioters were not there

in order to protest. "It wasn't vengeance," a Chicago poverty worker said, "just material gain." *Wall Street Journal,* April 10, 1968. See also *New York Times,* April 12, 1968.
45. Gresham M. Sykes, *The Society of Captives* (Princeton, N.J.: Princeton University Press, 1958), p. 126.
46. Harlem Youth Opportunities Unlimited, Inc., "Youth in the Ghetto" (New York: multilithed, 1964), p. 20.
47. Paul Goodman, "Utopian Thinking," *Commentary,* July 1961, p. 26.
48. Some deaths were undoubtedly accidental. That the rioters deliberately killed so few may be regarded as additional evidence that they were not motivated by hatred for whites. On the other hand, there have been many riots which unquestionably were outbursts of righteous indignation and in which the rioters, although furious, did not kill. See Rudé, *The Crowd in History,* p. 225.
49. *Education News,* October 16, 1967, p. 16.
50. A claim that might be expected but does not seem to have been made is that the rioting has produced some natural leaders of the slum neighborhoods. That such leaders have not been produced (and there is no reason to believe that they have) is perhaps further evidence of the essentially nonpolitical character of the rioting. In any case, it is interesting that, according to Rudé (*The Crowd in History,* p. 251) very few of the leaders who were produced by the preindustrial riots were ever heard from again once the riots were over.

CHAPTER 10

The quotation at the head of the chapter from Newcomb's *Principles of Political Economy* (New York, Harper and Brothers, 1886), p. 533. The one from Mrs. Fields is from *Lend a Hand* (Boston, 1886), Vol. 1, p. 8.

1. There seems to be no literature on mobility out of (or into) the lowest social class, however defined. The literature on social mobility deals mostly with movement between income and occupational classes, especially from blue-collar to white-collar groups. See Raymond W. Mack et al., *Social Mobility, Thirty Years of Research and Theory, An Annotated Bibliography* (Syracuse, N.Y.: Syracuse University Press, 1957).
2. Urban birthrates tend to be low, but least so among the lowest socioeconomic group. Analyzing data from the 1910 Census, Notestein found that unskilled laborers were the only urban class with a reproduction rate well above what was required for its replacement. His finding does not necessarily mean that the *lower class* (presumably even then a minority of all unskilled laborers) was more than reproducing itself, however; perhaps a lower rate of reproduction in this class was masked by an especially high one among unskilled laborers who were *not* lower class. Frank W. Notestein, "The Differential Rate of Increase Among the Social Classes of the American Population," *Social Forces,* 12 (October 1933): 32.
Students of the relation between intelligence and fertility were for some time misled by their failure to note that though the least intelligent

groups produce more children within marriage, they are the least likely
to marry. Bruce K. Eckland, "Genetics and Sociology: A Reconsidera-
tion," *American Sociological Review,* 32 (April 1967): 182. Conceivably,
this may also be the case with the lower class.
3. Theodore Parker, *Works* (London: Trubner and Co., 1864), 7: 111. A
study in Providence, R.I., in 1865 of age-specific mortality by income
class showed that the infant mortality rate among income-taxpayers was
93 per 1,000 live births as against 193 among non-income-taxpayers.
Cited in Odin W. Anderson, "Infant Mortality and Social and Cultural
Factors: Historical Trends and Current Patterns," in E. Gartly Jaco, ed.,
Patients, Physicians, and Illness (New York: The Free Press, 1958), pp.
10–22.
   In 1911–1916 a study in seven cities showed a total infant mortality
rate of 210.9 per 1,000 live births in the lowest income group (father
had no earnings) and only 59.1 in the highest (father's income $1,250
and over). That the high rates had more to do with class culture than
with poverty *per se* is suggested by the fact that the Jews, although
they lived in tenements as overcrowded as any, had extremely low infant mortality rates. Robert M. Woodbury, *Causal Factors in Infant
Mortality: A Statistical Study Based on Investigation in Eight Cities,*
U.S. Children's Bureau Publication No. 142 (Washington, D.C.: U.S.
Government Printing Office, 1925), p. 157.
4. James J. Walsh, "Irish Mortality in New York and Pennsylvania,"
Studies: An Irish Quarterly Review, 10 (December 1921): 632; see also
Austin O'Malley, "Irish Vital Statistics in America," *Studies: An Irish
Quarterly Review* (December 1918): 623–632.
   Presumably, something like this happened in London fifty to seventy
years ago. Leonard Woolf, in *Sowing, An Autobiography of the Years
1880 to 1904* (New York: Harcourt, Brace and Co., 1960) recalls
(pp. 61–64) the amazing disappearance of appalling lower-class slums
in a few years.
5. Albert D. Biderman, in Raymond A. Bauer, ed., *Social Indicators*
(Cambridge, Mass.: M.I.T. Press, 1966), p. 123. See also Eleanor P.
Hunt and Earl E. Huyck, "Mortality of White and Nonwhite Infants in
Major U.S. Cities," *Health, Education, and Welfare Indicators* (Washington, D.C.: U.S. Government Printing Office, January 1966), pp. 23–41.
6. Lee N. Robins et al., "Drinking Behavior of Young Urban Negro
Men," *Quarterly Journal of Studies on Alcohol,* 29 (September 1968):
657–684.
7. *New York Times,* August 15, 1968.
8. On the necessity of changing life style in order to reduce deaths from
infant mortality, see C. V. Willie and W. B. Rothney, "Racial, Ethnic
and Income Factors in the Epidemiology of Neonatal Mortality,"
American Sociological Review, 27 (August 1962): 526.
9. Lawrence Podell, *Families on Welfare in New York City,* Preliminary
Report No. 6, "Fertility, Illegitimacy, and Birth Control," Center for
Social Research, City University of New York, January 31, 1968.
   For evidence on the spread of knowledge about contraceptive techniques among women of low socioeconomic status, see Pascal K. Whelpton, Arthur A. Campbell, and John E. Patterson, *Fertility and Family*

Planning in the United States (Princeton, N.J.: Princeton University Press, 1966), p. 250.

10. Lee Rainwater, *Family Design: Marital Sexuality, Family Size, and Contraception* (Chicago: Aldine, 1965), p. 212.

11. Mary Peberdy, "Fertility Control for Problem Parents: A Five-Year Experiment in Newcastle Upon Tyne," in J. E. Meade and A. S. Parkes, eds., *Biological Aspects of Social Problems* (New York: Plenum, 1965), pp. 191–198.

12. Rainwater, *Family Design*, pp. 231, 248, 239.

13. Ibid., p. 201.

14. Parker, *Works*, p. 43.

15. Kenneth Boulding, "Reflections on Poverty," *Social Welfare Forum, 1961* (New York: Columbia University Press, for the National Conference on Social Work, 1961), p. 51.

16. S. M. Miller, Frank Riessman, and Arthur A. Seagul, "Poverty and Self-Indulgence: A Critique of the Non-Deferred Gratification Pattern," in Louis A. Ferman et al., eds., *Poverty in America: A Book of Readings* (Ann Arbor, Mich.: University of Michigan Press, 1965), p. 301.

17. For example, W. E. B. DuBois, *The Souls of Black Folk* (first published in 1903; paperback edition, New York: Fawcett, 1961), p. 117:

> Their great defect as laborers lies in their lack of incentive to work beyond the mere pleasure of physical exertion. They are careless because they have not found that it pays to be careful; they are improvident because the improvident ones of their acquaintance get on about as well as the provident.

Allison Davis argues along similar lines in "The Motivation of the Underprivileged Worker," in William Foote Whyte, ed., *Industry and Society* (New York: McGraw Hill, 1946).

18. Elliot Liebow, *Tally's Corner* (Boston: Little, Brown, 1967), pp. 63–66.

19. Gary S. Becker maintains that even much impulsive behavior is in some sense rational. "Irrational Behavior and Economic Theory," *Journal of Political Economy*, 70 (February 1962): pp. 1–13.

20. Cited by James S. Coleman in "Seeman's 'Alienation and Social Learning in a Reformatory,'" *American Journal of Sociology*, 70 (July 1964): 78.

21. Ibid.

22. In *Caste and Class in a Southern Town* (New York: Anchor, 1957), esp. ch. 17, John Dollard emphasizes the lower-class Negro's inability to control impulses, a characteristic which he says was more or less deliberately produced by whites under slavery and then under the furnish system in order to make Negroes more dependent and thus easier to control. The furnish system, he says (p. 406), "is a kind of permanent dole which appeals to the pleasure principle and relieves the Negro of responsibility and the necessity of forethought."

For another striking example of how a population was rendered present-oriented by a very different sort of dole, see the account of the Speenhamland Law (" . . . an automaton for demolishing the standards on which any kind of society could be based") in Karl Polanyi, *The*

Great Transformation (first published in 1944; Boston: Beacon Press, 1957), pp. 77–102.

23. Alvin W. Gouldner, "The Secrets of Organizations," in *The Social Welfare Forum,* Proceedings of the National Conference on Social Welfare (New York: Columbia University Press, 1963), p. 175.

24. The usual procedure is to have the subject tell stories; the span of time covered by the action of the story is then taken as a measure of "time orientation." One of the first studies of this sort was L. L. LeShan, "Time Orientation and Social Class," *Journal of Abnormal and Social Psychology,* 47 (July 1952): 589–592. See also David Epley and David R. Hicks, "Foresight and Hindsight in the TAT," *Journal of Projective Techniques,* 27 (March 1963): 51–59.

25. Jane Addams, "An Effort Toward Social Democracy," *The Forum,* 15 (October 1892): 228.

26. In *Families of the Slums* (New York: Basic Books, 1967), Salvador Minuchin and his colleagues report on the effort of a team of specialists to test a technique of therapy on twelve "hard core" delinquent-producing families, with a control group of ten families that were similar except for not having delinquent children. After a series of thirty one-and-one-half-hour sessions over a period of about eight months in which two therapists and (usually) a caseworker talked to all members of the family except children under the age of six, the researchers concluded that seven of the twelve were clinically improved. The criteria of improvement were not operationally defined and varied from family to family.

On the limitations of psychotherapy as a technique for changing personality, see H. J. Eysenck, "The Effects of Psychotherapy: An Evaluation," *Journal of Consulting Psychology,* 16 (October 1952): 319–324.

27. A. B. Hollingshead and F. C. Redlich, *Social Class and Mental Illness* (New York: Wiley, 1958), p. 348. See also J. Myers and L. Schaffer, "Social Stratification and Psychiatric Practice: A Study of an Out-Patient Clinic," *American Sociological Review,* 19 (June 1954): 310.

28. For a critical review of work in this field, and of that of Bernstein in particular, see Denis Lawton, *Social Class, Language, and Education* (New York: Schocken Books, 1968). The writings of Bernstein on which the account in the text is based are the following: "Some Sociological Determinants of Perception," *British Journal of Sociology,* Vol. 9 (1958): "The Role of Speech in the Development and Transmission of Culture," in Gordon J. Klopf and William A. Holman, eds., *Perspectives on Learning* (New York: Mental Health Materials Center, Inc., 1967); and "Social Structure, Language and Learning" in Joan I. Roberts, ed., *School Children in the Urban Slum* (New York: The Free Press, 1967).

29. Bernstein, "Social Structure," p. 145.

30. A passage from Wittgenstein's *Philosophical Investigations* (New York: Macmillan, 1953), p. 174, is suggestive:

> One can imagine an animal angry, frightened, unhappy, happy, startled. But hopeful? And why not?

> A dog believes his master is at the door. But can he also believe his master will come the day after to-morrow? — And *what* can he not do here? — How do I do it? — How am I supposed to answer this?
> Can only those hope who can talk? Only those who have mastered the use of a language. That is to say, the phenomena of hope are modes of this complicated form of life. . . .

31. Josephine Klein has argued that ego-control presupposes the ability to take the consequences of one's actions into account, i.e., foresight, and that "words are needed to create a conception of an orderly universe in which rationally considered action is more likely to be rewarded than impulsive behavior." Quoted in Lawton, *Social Class,* p. 15.

32. For example, it has been found that illiterates tend to have a "present-tense outlook" (Howard E. Freeman and Gene G. Kassebaum, "The Illiterate in American Society: Some General Hypotheses," *Social Forces,* 34 [May 1956]: 375); sufferers from aphasia tend to behave in a present-oriented manner (Alfred R. Lindsmith and Anselm L. Strauss, *Social Psychology* [rev. ed., New York: Holt, Rinehart & Winston, 1956], p. 143); persons who have undergone lobotomy appear indifferent to the future (Paul Fraisse, *The Psychology of Time* [New York: Harper & Row, 1963], p. 172).

33. Bruno Bettelheim, *The Empty Fortress* (New York: The Free Press, 1968), p. 48.

34. Erik H. Erikson, "The Development of Ritualization," in Donald R. Cutler, ed., *The Religious Situation, 1968* (Boston: Beacon Press, 1968), p. 714.

35. Lee Rainwater, *And the Poor Get Children* (Chicago: Quadrangle Books, 1960), pp. 82–83.

36. H. Wortis et al., "Child-Rearing Practices in a Low Socio-Economic Group," in Joan I. Roberts, ed., *School Children in the Urban Slum* (New York: The Free Press, 1967), p. 469.

37. Harold M. Skeels, *Adult Status of Children with Contrasting Early Life Experiences,* Monographs of the Society for Research in Child Development, Vol. 31, No. 3, Serial No. 105 (Chicago: University of Chicago Press, 1966).

38. Zena Smith Blau, "In Defense of the Jewish Mother," *Midstream* February 1967, p. 47.

39. Very little research has been done on the effects of father-separation on the child. Although such research as exists is inconclusive, it is possible that father-separation may create problems for the child with respect to sex-role identification and superego formation. Leon J. Yarrow, "Separation from Parents During Early Childhood," in M. L. Hoffman and L. W. Hoffman, eds., *Review of Child Development Research* (New York: Russell Sage Foundation, 1964), 1: 117–121.

Some psychologists, too, stress the importance for boys of a father or father-substitute as a "star to steer by." See, for example, Martin Deutsch, *Minority Group and Class Status as Related to Social and Personality Factors in Scholastic Achievement,* Monograph No. 2. Published by the Society for Applied Anthropology, 1960.

40. Yarrow, "Separation," p. 128.
41. Cf. Leontine Young, *Wednesday's Children: A Study of Child Neglect and Abuse* (New York: McGraw-Hill, 1964).
42. Personal communication.
43. K. B. Cheney, "Safeguarding Legal Rights in Providing Protective Service," *Children,* 13 (May–June 1966): 86–92.
44. Cf. Larry B. Silver, M.D., "Child Abuse Syndrome: A Review," *Medical Times Magazine,* 96 (August 1968): 803–820.
45. Arthur R. Jensen, in Martin Deutsch, Irwin Katz, and Arthur R. Jensen, eds., *Social Class, Race, and Psychological Development* (New York: Holt, Rinehart & Winston, 1968), p. 166.
46. Eleanor Pavenstedt, ed., *The Drifters* (Boston: Little, Brown, 1967), p. 199.
47. Ibid., p. 218.
48. Personal communication from James Q. Wilson.
49. Cf. Jack Lessinger, "The Case for Scatteration," *Journal of the American Institute of Planners,* 28 (August 1962): 159–169.
50. Jacobus TenBroek and Floyd W. Matson, "The Disabled and the Law of Welfare," *California Law Review,* 54 (May 1966): 816.
Cloward and Piven complain that "the threatened denial of essential benefits is a powerful sanction to control client behavior." Presumably, the main cause of complaint is the unwarranted identification of "client" with "semi-competent." Richard A. Cloward and Frances Fox Piven, "The Professional Bureaucracies: Benefit Systems as Influence Systems," in Murray Silberman, ed., *The Role of Government in Promoting Social Change* (New York: Columbia University School of Social Work, 1965), p. 54. Reprinted in E. C. Banfield, ed., *Urban Government* (rev. ed., New York: The Free Press, 1968), pp. 666–681.

CHAPTER 11

The quotation at the head of the chapter is from David McClelland, writing in Lucian Pye, ed., *Communications and Political Development* (Princeton, N.J.: Princeton University Press, 1963), p. 152.

1. Leo C. Rosten, *Hollywood, the Movie Colony, the Movie Makers* (New York: Harcourt Brace, 1941), p. 40.
2. Frank H. Knight, *Freedom and Reform* (New York: Harper, 1947), pp. 41–42.
3. Lee Rainwater, "Crucible of Identity: The Negro Lower-Class Family," in Talcott Parsons and Kenneth B. Clark, eds., *The Negro American* (Boston: Houghton Mifflin, 1966), p. 199.
4. *Wall Street Journal,* February 16, 1968, p. 9.
5. The point is developed in E. C. Banfield, "Welfare: A Crisis Without 'Solutions,'" *The Public Interest,* 16 (Summer 1969): 89–101.
6. Governor's Commission on the Los Angeles Riots, *Violence in the City — An End or a Beginning?,* Los Angeles, December 2, 1965, p. 55.
7. Nathan Glazer has argued persuasively that the supposed social benefits from the improvement of housing are mostly myth. See his "Housing

Problems and Housing Policies," *The Public Interest,* No. 7 (Spring 1967): 21–60.

8. See Lee Rainwater and William L. Yancey, *The Moynihan Report and the Politics of Controversy* (Cambridge, Mass.: M.I.T. Press, 1967).

9. See Mancur Olson, Jr., *The Logic of Collective Action* (Cambridge, Mass.: Harvard University Press, 1965).

10. See Anthony Downs, "Why the Government Budget is Too Small in a Democracy," *World Politics,* 12 (July 1960): 541–563.

11. One item on the list — day-care centers for children — is popular. In July 1969 a Gallup Poll found that almost two out of every three adults favored using federal funds to set up day-care centers in communities across the nation.

12. With respect to one of the recommendations, the well-off have an interest that is opposed to that of the poor: in the trade-off between inflation and unemployment (and some economists deny that there is one), the well-off and the poor would in general have different optima.

13. Lionel Trilling, *The Liberal Imagination* (Garden City, N.Y.: Anchor Books, 1953), p. 213.

14. These matters are discussed in E. C. Banfield and James Q. Wilson, *City Politics* (Cambridge, Mass.: Harvard University Press, 1963), esp. chs. 8–10 and pp. 329–346.

15. E. L. Godkin, "The Duty of Educated Men in a Democracy," *The Forum,* 17 (1894): 50.
    Godkin would not be surprised at a British social scientists's finding that the median number of words in a half-hour essay by working-class 15-year-olds is 228, whereas for middle-class children of the same age it is 348. Cited in Denis Lawton, *Social Class, Language, and Education* (New York: Schocken Books, 1968), p. 105.

16. As an example of the new style of politics, consider the interfaith organization of New York City clergymen that threatened that it might support violence if it resulted from a cut in the state welfare budget (a cut that, incidentally, would have left the welfare budget at an all-time high). *New York Times,* April 4, 1969, p. 1.

CHAPTER 12

The quotation at the head of the chapter is from *The Liberal Imagination* (Garden City, N.Y.: Anchor Books, 1953), pp. 214–215.

1. Kenneth Boulding, book review in the *Journal of Business* (January 1963): 121.

2. Gunnar Myrdal, *An American Dilemma* (New York: Harper, 1944), pp. 75–76.

3. Robert K. Merton, *Social Theory and Social Structure* (New York: The Free Press, 1949), p. 181.

4. Harvey Leibenstein, "Allocative Efficiency vs. 'X-Efficiency,'" *American Economic Review,* 56 (June 1966): 392–393.